CARING FOR YOUR ADOLESCENT

Child Care Books from
The American Academy of Pediatrics

Caring For Your Baby and Young Child
Birth to Age 5

Caring For Your School-Age Child
Ages 5 to 12
(FORTHCOMING)

Caring For Your Adolescent
Ages 12 to 21

CARING FOR YOUR ADOLESCENT

Ages 12 to 21

Donald E. Greydanus, M.D., FAAP,
Editor-in-Chief
Professor of Pediatrics and
    Human Development
Michigan State University
Pediatrics Program Director
Kalamazoo Center for Medical Studies

George D. Comerci, M.D., FAAP,
Executive Board Reviewer

Joe M. Sanders, Jr., M.D., FAAP,
Medical Reviewer
Associate Executive Director
American Academy of Pediatrics

Lisa Rae Reisberg, Technical Reviewer
Director, Division of Public Education
American Academy of Pediatrics

Mark T. Grimes, Project Manager
Division of Public Education
American Academy of Pediatrics

Editorial Board:

William A. Daniel, Jr., M.D., FAAP,
Former Director, Division of Adolescent Unit
University of Alabama Medical School

Marianne E. Felice, M.D., FAAP,
Professor of Pediatrics
Vice Chairman, Department of Pediatrics
Director, Division of Adolescent Medicine
University of Maryland Hospital

Iris F. Litt, M.D., FAAP,
Director, Division of Adolescent Medicine
Professor, Department of Pediatrics
Stanford University Medical Center

Robert B. Shearin, M.D., FAAP,
Private Practice, Rockville, Maryland

Victor C. Strasburger, M.D., FAAP,
Director of Adolescent Medicine
Associate Professor, Department of Pediatrics
University of New Mexico School of Medicine

BANTAM BOOKS
NEW YORK • TORONTO • LONDON • SYDNEY • AUCKLAND

NOTE

The information contained in this publication should not be used as a substitute for the medical care and advice of your pediatrician. There may be variations in treatment that your pediatrician may recommend based on the individual facts and circumstances.

CARING FOR YOUR ADOLESCENT:
AGES 12 TO 21
A Bantam book / October 1991

All rights reserved.
Copyright © 1991 by American Academy of Pediatrics
Book design by Richard Oriolo.

No part of this book may be reproduced or transmitted in any form or by any means, electronic or mechanical, including photocopying, recording, or by any information storage and retrieval system, without permission in writing from the publisher.
For information address: Bantam Books.

Library of Congress Cataloging-in-Publication Data
Caring for your adolescent: ages 12 to 21 / American Academy of Pediatrics : Donald E. Greydanus, editor-in-chief.
p. cm.
includes index.
ISBN 0-553-07556-X
1. Parent and teenager—United States. 2. Adolescence.
3. Adolescent psychology. I. Greydanus, Donald E. II. American Academy of Pediatrics.
HQ799, 15. C37 1991
305.23'5—dc20 91-13801
CIP

Published simultaneously in the United States and Canada

Bantam Books are published by Bantam Books, a division of Bantam Doubleday Dell Publishing Group, Inc. Its trademark, consisting of the words "Bantam Books" and the portrayal of a rooster, is Registered in U.S. Patent and Trademark Office and in other countries. Marca Registrada. Bantam Books, 1540 Broadway, New York, New York 10036.

PRINTED IN THE UNITED STATES OF AMERICA

RRH 0

Reviewers and Contributors

Editor-in-Chief
Donald E. Greydanus, M.D.

Editorial Board
William A. Daniel, Jr., M.D.
Marianne E. Felice, M.D.
Iris F. Litt, M.D.
Robert B. Shearin, M.D.
Victor C. Strasburger, M.D.

AAP Executive Board Reviewer
George D. Comerci, M.D.

American Academy of Pediatrics
Executive Director: James E.
    Strain, M.D.
Associate Executive Director: Joe
    M. Sanders, Jr., M.D.
Director, Department of
    Communications: Linda L.
    Martin
Director, Division of Public
    Education: Lisa Rae Reisberg
Project Manager, Division of
    Public Education: Mark T.
    Grimes

Contributors
Richard Bonforte, M.D.
Robert Deisher, M.D.
Patricia Duffner, M.D.

S. Jean Emans, M.D.
Laurence Finberg, M.D.
Norman C. Fost, M.D.
Linda Grant, M.D.
Alfred Healy, M.D.
Margaret Hilgartner, M.D.
H. James Holroyd, M.D.
Sidney Hurwitz, M.D.
Walter Huurman, M.D.
Susan Isbell, Ph.D.
Richard Krugman, M.D.
John Kulig, M.D.
Cheryl Leytham, Ph.D.
E. F. Luckstead, M.D.
Michael Nelson, M.D.
Robert Pantell, M.D.
Larry Patton, M.D.
Stanley Plotkin, M.D.
Albert Pruitt, M.D.
Thomas Riemenschneider, M.D.
S. Kenneth Schonberg, M.D.
Mary-Ann Shafer, M.D.
Martin Ushkow, M.D.
Mark Wolraich, M.D.
John Woodard, M.D.
Joseph Zanga, M.D.
Lonnie Zeltzer, M.D.
Barry Zuckerman, M.D.

Acknowledgments

Writer
Richard Trubo

Secretarial Support
Nancy Ingraffia
Jamie McDowell
Jane Nosek

Special thanks are given for the tireless efforts of the many AAP Council, Committee, Section and Task Force chairpersons and members, who are too numerous to name herein.

This book is dedicated to all the people
who recognize that children are
our greatest inspiration in the present
and our greatest hope for the future.

CONTENTS

viii CONTENTS

FOREWORD

Caring for Your Adolescent: Ages 12 to 21 is the second in a three volume series of child-care books developed by the American Academy of Pediatrics and Feeling Fine Programs. The other books in this series include *Caring for Your Baby and Young Child: Birth to Age 5,* published in Spring 1991, and *Caring for Your School-Age Child: Ages 5 to 12,* forthcoming.

The American Academy of Pediatrics is an organization of 41,000 pediatricians dedicated to the health, safety, and well-being of infants, children, adolescents, and young adults. This book is part of the Academy's ongoing education effort to provide parents with quality information on a broad spectrum of children's health issues.

What distinguishes this book on adolescence from the many others in bookstores and on library shelves is that it has been written and extensively reviewed by members of the American Academy of Pediatrics. A six-member editorial board developed the initial material with the assistance of over thirty contributors and reviewers. The final draft was then reviewed by countless numbers of pediatricians. Because medical information on children's health is constantly changing, every effort has been made to ensure that this book contains the most up-to-date information available.

It is the Academy's hope that this book will become an invaluable resource and reference guide for parents. We believe it is the best source of information on matters of adolescent health and well-being. We are confident readers will find the book extremely valuable, and we encourage readers to use it in concert with the advice and counsel of their own pediatrician, who will provide individual guidance and assistance on issues related to the health of their children.

JAMES E. STRAIN, M.D.
Executive Director

PART I

PARENTING AN ADOLESCENT

CHALLENGES AND REWARDS

*H*ave you ever seriously thought about what your teenager will be like as an adult? If you're like most parents, you've probably done this many times, with your thoughts filled not only with hope but also with some anxieties about what may lie ahead.

Actually, many factors will influence what your adolescent's future may hold. For instance, teenagers are the product of their genetic inheritance, the family and society in which they live, and the care and teaching of their parents. Of course they cannot change the genes they received from their father and mother. They cannot change the world in which they live, either. Their *family,* then, becomes the critical element. And that's where *you* play an important role.

As a parent you can help your youngster cope with growing up, interpret the world for him, warn him of its dangers, provide a good example, and give comfort when needed. No, being a parent isn't easy, but it's one of the most important and potentially rewarding tasks you'll ever undertake. You are your child's first role model and teacher. From his parents he'll learn that he's unique, deeply loved, and worthy of happiness—and these feelings can last a lifetime.

By definition, then, parenting involves the care, teaching, and guidance that eventually enable children to make appropriate decisions for themselves. It is a big job, particularly when adolescents are involved, and there were no courses in school to help you prepare for it. But fortunately the adaptation to this parenting role is a gradual and usually natural process. An adult doesn't suddenly become the parent of a teenager—unless, of course, the youngster is adopted or is a stepchild. In most cases, before ever parenting an adolescent, people have raised a younger child who has grown into this complex but often delightful teenager.

By now you have hopefully resolved any early fantasies you had of being the "perfect" parent. After all, all mothers and fathers make mistakes in rearing children, often wishing a second chance at helping their youngsters grow was available. On the other hand, adolescents make mistakes, too—in most cases, many mistakes. They are immature in their thinking, and they may rebel or believe they're more capable than they really are. And that is where they can get into trouble.

Thus a large part of parenting is knowing that your youngsters will err and that, even so, you should still love and support them, discuss their choices with them, and advise them on how to improve their decisions. Don't be afraid to say no and give reasons for your decisions. And don't expect more from them than they can realistically accomplish.

Of course, as a parent you want to provide the best environment for your teenagers' growth and development. You want to protect them from physical and emotional harm and prepare them to be independent, responsible adults. And, in fact, most parents do a pretty good job, despite their concerns. Best of all, most are proud of what their youngsters become.

Yes, you'll have some difficult times during these adolescent years, but you'll experience many rewards, too. And for most parents these positives far outweigh the negatives. Despite the tough periods, parenting a teenager can be enriching and rewarding.

CHALLENGES AND REWARDS

The changes that occur during adolescence are often confusing to both the teenager and his parents. What's going on? And why is it happening? Although other sections of this book will answer questions like these in detail, we'll begin to explore them in this chapter.

With the onset of puberty (at about ages ten to twelve in girls, twelve to thirteen in boys), rapid physical growth begins. At the same time, an adolescent's thinking processes slowly start to change to those of an adult. Gradually teenagers develop the ability to compare options, make decisions based on reality, and evaluate consequences. In addition, they will observe how older youths act and what behaviors seem acceptable to adults and society. And as a part of their so-called psychosocial development, they will also learn to form significant relationships with others.

These various components of growth can be intimately related to each other—that is, an abnormality in one area can affect growth in another, often temporarily but sometimes permanently. In fact difficulties that initially arose in early childhood can complicate adolescence and eventually adulthood. Everything is tied together.

Even under normal circumstances your child's development in one area can lag behind his growth in others. To explain this better, let's put the issue in some perspective. In general pediatricians classify "early adolescence" as ranging from about ten or eleven years to fourteen years of age in girls and from ages twelve to fifteen in boys; "middle adolescence" refers to the next two years; and "late adolescence" from that point to adulthood. However, while one component of a child's growth may be on track, another aspect may be lagging behind. For example, a girl may reach her full physical maturity at age thirteen, but her thinking processes may not be as developed. She may not yet be able to reason like an adult—and this can cause trouble. You can't expect a very young teenager to act the same as one graduating from high school, no matter what her level of physical maturity.

Sometime during adolescence, however, these factors will all come together. And eventually your teenager will also begin the process of separation from the family. To some parents this can be quite unsettling. But don't despair: it's normal and necessary. An adolescent's putting some distance between herself and her family members doesn't signal her rejection of them. It's just part of the teenager's natural transition to increased independence and heightened responsibility for personal decisions and actions. It is a normal and inevitable step toward adulthood.

Until your teenager fully makes the break from the family, *you* can expect to be a major force in guiding her through many life transitions. For instance, as she approaches adulthood she'll face planning for a job or for higher education, and she can probably use some help in making these decisions.

And then there's the sensitive subject of sex. As part of adolescence, youngsters experience new sexual feelings and urges that are sometimes puzzling, exciting, or troublesome to parents and teenagers alike. All humans must come to grips with their sexuality to achieve happiness, and during adolescence youngsters start coping with these sexual drives, establishing limits and a moral code, and becoming aware of social concepts of maleness and femaleness.

You should be available to answer your teenager's questions—about sexuality or any other matter. But if serious problems should arise—perhaps threatening normal adolescent and eventually even adult functioning—remember that your teenager's pediatrician can help, advising you on whether your teenager's physical, cognitive (thinking), and psychosocial growth are appropriate. And if a problem does exist, the doctor can recommend the best course of action. Early evaluation and, if necessary, treatment are important to prevent any situation from getting out of control.

Challenges

Here is a list of challenges that all parents of teenagers can expect:

1. Prepare for change. Most family members are used to their way of life together, and they often take that for granted. Yes, there may have been crises in the past, but usually they didn't threaten the foundation of the way the family lived. When a child enters puberty, however, things can really begin to change. For some parents their teenager is like a stranger who has come to live with them, and thus a new relationship must be established. To complicate matters, adolescents aren't always the same person from day to day or even hour to hour.

At times these unpredictable changes may start to overwhelm you, but don't give up! Also, don't bear the burden alone as you try to relate to your teenager in a positive manner and work out mutually satisfactory ways of living together. This isn't only your responsibility. All members of the family are affected, and thus all must cooperate in solving any problems and concerns. As part of this process both parents should agree on the essential issues and how to deal with them.

2. Prepare to be tested. Although early and middle adolescents have strong, normal, and necessary urges for independence, one or both parents often disapprove of this sought-after freedom. But even when teenagers become aware that many of their ideas or requests are unacceptable, they have a need to test their parents to determine the limits placed on them.

Many adolescents question parental beliefs about sex, drinking, manners, or money. So prepare for resistance like this to occur. Consider what and why you believe *before* a teenager challenges your opinions, and plan some logical answers in advance.

And what if your adolescent refuses to accept your viewpoint or decision on a particular subject? Tell him firmly that you will not permit the activity in question. The final decision is yours. Keep in mind, however, that he'll continue to test you—and test himself as well—as part of growing up.

While you need to be firm in many areas, there are probably others where you can yield a bit. As your teenager matures, it is wise to allow him increasing control over his life whenever possible. For instance, adolescents frequently challenge their parents' religious beliefs during this time. If that happens in your family, you might consider giving your child some freedom. Even allow him to attend another church if that's what he wants. Eventually he'll probably come back to your moral and value system, even though it may take a while. But if you insist instead on strict adherence to your values from the start, you may drive him away for good.

If you've already established an effective parent–child communication pattern when your teenager was younger, you can resolve most conflicts during adolescence with minimal animosity. Even as you disagree, however, let your love for your teenager shine through. Teenagers shouldn't be abandoned as they test limits. They still need you, probably more than ever.

And what if your adolescent consistently disobeys the home ground rules, comes and goes at will, ignores curfews, or refuses to discuss your concerns? In cases like these you should seek professional counseling to get to the root of the problem and arrive at a solution, hopefully before the problem becomes more difficult to resolve.

3. Prepare for a period of rejection. Even if there are no major clashes in the family, most teenagers reject one or both parents for a time. Adolescents often just need to determine if they can function on their own, without parental guidance. Many times a teenager will temporarily reject one parent and form a closer relationship with the other, usually of the opposite sex. When this happens, there's the possibility of real disruption in the family—often prompting the teenager to bond even closer to the favored parent.

A father, for example, may feel a real psychological boost when an increasingly attractive daughter pays more attention to him. This situation, however, can harm the relationship between husband and wife if he starts to support the daughter in her demands.

If a situation like this occurs in your family, examine the intensity of the rejection aimed at one parent. If your teenager shows increased favoritism toward Dad without significant rejection of Mom—or vice versa—the circumstance is usually temporary; this may be the only way the youngster knows to demonstrate disapproval or to "punish" a parent. On the other hand, if there is outright rejection or rebellion, then he will usually require professional counseling. Through it all, parents need to stay united when dealing with their teenagers.

4. Be flexible. Not all parent–adolescent differences must turn into a major crisis. As a mother or father you need to be flexible and permit your teenager to test, explore, and communicate *within limits.* This concept is something like a rubber band: allow your adolescent to stretch a bit without breaking. Show some tolerance of her striving for independence while retaining control over how far she can go. Remember, *you* are the parent; she is still growing up. Maintain a balance and keep in mind that it's better for an adolescent to learn for herself, within limits, than only to be told what to do.

If you let your youngster do some exploring on her own, she'll probably eventually incorporate many or most of your values into her set of beliefs (see the earlier discussion of religion). Although teenage value systems can be very threatening to parents who may feel their youngster is rejecting everything, research shows that once more maturation takes place the adolescent's value system usually will closely parallel his parents' beliefs. So don't be quite so anxious about things like unconventional hairstyles and unusual clothes.

Even so, bear in mind that children and teenagers do poorly if parents give them *too* much freedom. You need to stay sensibly firm and consistent.

5. Don't take everything seriously. Teenagers are intense. They believe everything in their lives is momentous and urgent. Having had much more life experience than the adolescents in your family, however, you'll probably often recognize that the concerns they consider pressing are really of little relative importance. Even so, don't belittle their opinions. Instead, build your teenagers up as much as possible: you are still the primary source of their self-concept; you provide the validation they need to feel unique and worthy of happiness.

In many instances time has a way of clearing up the "urgent" issues in an adolescent's life, and usually he'll require no major intervention to help resolve them. Discuss possibilities and feelings with your teenager and support her when she's reached a wise decision. Above all, *be patient.*

6. Try to keep your sense of humor. A sense of humor will help you much more than you suspect. Many things happen between parents and teenagers that are funny. If youngsters can see humor in a situation, it may defuse their anger, bring calmness to the situation, and permit better decision making. Never laugh *at* your adolescent but only *with* him. Laughing *at* your teenager can produce embarrassment and possibly an explosive response. This can be a particularly sensitive matter since even a "wrong" *glance* can be the signal that "you're laughing at me." Be careful!

7. Find time to listen . . . REALLY LISTEN! Parents are busy, and so are their children. This is especially true in families in which both parents are working outside the home. As a result you probably often find it difficult to give your teenager undivided attention when he wants you to listen. But both you and your adolescent must be willing to postpone other activities to have serious, candid discussions; if your son or daughter is in a receptive mood and wants to share some concerns and problems, you need to find the time for that to take place.

Fathers in particular often spend much too little time with their youngsters, and when that happens, adolescents frequently interpret this as rejection or lack of interest. To build up closeness and trust between you and your teenagers, set aside some so-called "quality time." Don't let your job and/or volunteer work take you away from them so often that they feel unloved.

If you still have *pre*adolescent children, be sure to make time for them too and then continue that important habit into the teenage years. Go to a baseball game. Take them swimming. Play Scrabble. Try canoeing. Rake the yard together. Take in a sunset. When they're interested in sharing an hour or a day with you, don't waste this golden opportunity. Love means you care enough to spend time. And again, when they want to talk (even if you don't), stop what you're doing and listen.

8. Seek different experiences for your adolescent. Too often our children live in a sheltered world, where they are not exposed to different social environments. Take, for example, a girl growing up in a middle-class family, attending private school, and having friends of comparable social status. She can benefit greatly by participating in programs in which she might spend several weeks helping to paint and refurbish homes and churches in poor neighborhoods, tutoring underprivileged children in reading, visiting the aged, or spending time in a Third World country.

What's the aim of these kinds of experiences? To expose youngsters to other aspects of life and give them a better understanding of the real world and its wondrous diversity. Teenagers of less affluent or poor families also need experiences that widen their horizons and tell them more about the world outside their local surroundings.

9. Examine your own changes. During your child's adolescence, keep two important facts in mind. First, your youngster will rapidly change, and to cope with these changes you'll need to accept, adjust to, and tolerate an individual who's not the same from one moment to another. Second, you need to look at what happens to yourself during this period. Most moms and dads are middle-aged by the time their adolescent leaves high school, and they have concerns not only about their teenager's future but about their own as well.

Some people use the word "middlescence" to describe this time in an adult's life. It's that period from about forty to fifty-five years of age, during which you realize that you aren't as young and energetic as you once were. If you haven't yet achieved relative financial security, you're probably worried about the future, how you'll pay for your child's college education, and what you'll have for your retirement. If your parents are alive, you may be wondering if you'll have the responsibility of caring for them or helping them out financially. Your body is also changing, and menopause in women or the equivalent in men will force you to deal with unexpected feelings from time to time.

As a parent, then, you are going through your own transition, which can affect your relationship with your adolescent. Serious medical and/or emotional problems can reduce your ability to deal effectively with family situations. Remember, though, that your teenager still needs *you*. You must remain the parent; don't allow your youngster to reverse roles with you. Review your personal situation and try to resolve your own problems. Don't be afraid to get professional help to deal with these issues. It will make you a better parent.

10. Don't let your own adolescence influence you too much. When their son or daughter approaches adolescence, many parents think back to their own teenage years and project what may happen to their own youngster. If you were fortunate and had a delightful adolescence, you may assume your own children will be happy, too, and that there will be few family problems. Unfortunately, this isn't necessarily true. In the same way, even if your own teenage years were *un*happy, your teenager may have the opposite experience.

Nevertheless, some psychologists say that when you communicate with your adolescent, there's always a "third person" present: *You as a teenager.* Your own experiences and feelings are there to serve, rightly or wrongly, as examples and to influence your thinking and your communication. While recollections of your own adolescence may provide a valuable perspective, they can also cause unnecessary worry and unfair expectations.

For example, many moms and dads find themselves saying things such as, "When I was your age, I had chores on the farm . . . ," implying, "You lazy slob, you have it so easy." However, your teenager may feel she *doesn't* have it easy, and she may be preoccupied by issues that are really troubling her. Every adolescent is different, and none is an exact copy of a parent. Your youngster really has no way of appreciating *your* childhood experiences! She is living in a different world than yours was. Let her live her own life.

Also, don't repeat the mistakes your own parents made. Some mothers and fathers are too critical of their teenager's sports or academic performance, for instance, in exactly the same way their own parents were of them. That's unfair and potentially damaging to your child.

11. Acquaint yourself with your teenager's environment. Except for what takes place in the home, many parents are isolated from the world in which their children live. Some mothers and fathers would be shocked by the language used at school or within a youngster's peer group. Few parents have seen the movies their adolescent views, and they may have little idea about the violence and sexual themes their teenager sees on television or the information he receives from his friends about alcohol and drugs.

How can you advise your youngsters about these potentially harmful influences if you have no knowledge of what they're being exposed to? As busy as you are, you need to become familiar with the world of your adolescent. Then, with this information in hand, you can make wiser judgments about the influences in her life. As you do, maintain your own values but avoid jumping to hasty conclusions that can alienate your teenager.

12. Think of yourself. Parents should have lives of their own and not live *solely* for their children. Find the time to pursue and enjoy the interests that help you grow. You have a responsibility to yourself—and to your spouse as well. Parenting starts with a good marriage, and if yours is in trouble, get help. If you're not enjoying life in spite of its problems, you're probably giving your teenagers the impression that adulthood and marriage produce only worry and responsibility. Their peers may get similar impressions from their parents. As a result your adolescents may wonder why anyone would want to grow up!

Also, don't spoil your teenagers at your own expense. Many parents give their children everything, leaving the offspring little to anticipate when they're adults. For example, thousands of adolescents have been to Europe, traveled to distant ski resorts during the winter, and received almost all the material possessions they could ever want. At the same time, large numbers of adolescents are sexually active. One could ask, then, what's left to look forward to as an adult.

During this time of life you have the major challenge of seeing yourself as you are, recognizing your strengths and weaknesses, and improving where you can. If you really know yourself, you can better advise your adolescent.

13. When the time comes, be willing to cut the cord and divest yourself of responsibility. As we emphasized earlier, all parents make mistakes when rearing children, and we often believe these unfortunate actions and decisions are the cause of all of our youngsters' problems when they become adults. However, it's wrong for parents to accept the blame for everything bad or undesirable about their children—partly because their offspring can change if they really want to.

Maturing includes taking responsibility for oneself and correcting the effects of any parental errors; it's a cop-out for a child to blame his parents for all his difficulties in life. As the parent you cannot solve all of your youngster's difficulties, and there may well come a time when you tell him, "I did the best I could; if it was wrong, I'm sorry. But you're an adult now. You can change if you wish. So don't blame me the rest of your life for what you are."

Rewards

Every human being seems to be born with the need to belong to a family. In our society, however, all families are not alike. They don't all have two parents. They don't all have brothers and sisters.

No matter what shape a family takes, it still means belonging—in particular, belonging to a group of people related through bloodlines (even an adopted child yearns to know his biological parents). We've heard it said that if the world were being destroyed, the last person alive would be searching for his family.

What are your own rewards in parenthood? In answering that question, many people point to the sheer joy associated with producing children and building a family. And as these children grow into adulthood and eventually bear a child of their own, the parents (who have now become grandparents) often have a feeling of continuity in both the past and the future. They belong. They have the joy of loving children and passing that love from one generation to the next.

There's also the reward of ultimately seeing your children in a new way—as individuals in their own right. It can be fun to watch the physical changes of adolescence, to observe the many uncertainties and decisions affecting teenage relationships, to listen to the opinions expressed at different stages of growth, and to watch the development of this unique person. You're experiencing the transformation of a child into an adult, and it can be exciting!

Adolescents also usually bring a surge of youth and excitement into the family. Most parents enjoy this—although sometimes their responses are inappropriate. For instance, some try to personally adopt their teenager's dress, talk, and actions. Knowingly or unknowingly, they may try to live vicariously through their adolescent, questioning the youngster about dating and other experiences. However, teenagers have a strong need for privacy, and parents should respect this. For the same reason you have no right—except under unusual circumstances—to go through your adolescent's room or read her diary without permission. Some areas of her life are her own.

There's still another reward worth mentioning. Once your teenager reaches adulthood, you can develop a close relationship with her based on mutual respect, friendship, and love, not duty. Unfortunately, though, this type of positive adult relationship often doesn't evolve on its own; it will take some energy and work on everyone's part.

ADOLESCENT RESPONSIBILITY

An adolescent boy told his doctor, "My mother is always yelling at me to be responsible. But I am responsible. I take out the garbage. I've proven myself doing that. So I ought to be able to decide how late I stay out at night and be responsible for coming home. I think *she* has a problem."

To this teenager the two situations—emptying the garbage and staying out late—are of equal significance. But they're not. Adolescents want freedom, but unless they're mature enough for it, they often base their actions on erroneous assumptions and cannot, or do not, consider the consequences. Too often teenagers choose what seems to be good or fun at the moment. They don't have an adult's experience and tend to make more mistakes than an adult does. Thus you should grant greater responsibility to teenagers only when they are capable of effectively dealing with it.

As adolescents grow, you'll find that they want to be responsible for themselves at times and then will reject the offer of responsibility at other times. This swing in mood and desires is typical of early and middle adolescents in particular. By late adolescence these youngsters will have gradually become more responsible for themselves, but even so, they too can make inappropriate decisions. Teenagers can learn from mistakes, however, and it can be valuable for them to suffer the consequences of irresponsible actions.

Therefore, don't shield adolescents from the consequences of their decisions and behaviors. By doing so you may be harming, not helping, them. Let them make early minor mistakes—and let them learn from these errors so they avoid the major ones later on. However, don't ignore what you feel is a *serious* mistake— for example, a teenager who drives while drunk. In this type of situation an adolescent needs some professional help, and your teenager's pediatrician can help or guide you toward the most appropriate health-care professional for that.

Also, keep in mind that not all teenagers are alike. Many accept responsibility well, but others never seem to learn, and they require much more patience and guidance. For some adolescents, as long as Mom or Dad will accept the responsibility and cope with the consequences, they'll make no effort to take charge of their lives.

In general, give as much freedom to teenagers—and expect as much responsibility from them—as you believe is wise. Sometimes you'll be wrong, but do the best you can. Things will eventually turn out all right if your love shows through.

FAMILY CHANGES AND THE RIGHTS OF ADOLESCENTS

Let's compare the functioning of a family to a three-legged stool. For the stool to be useful all three of its legs must support it; if one leg is missing, the stool will have to be propped up. In a similar way the traditional family consists of two parents and the children. If the family is to function well, each of these three components must contribute to the whole. However, when changes in their relationship occur—during adolescence, for example—the entire family structure can unravel. While parents and their *small* children may get along well and establish a foundation for how family members relate to each other, adolescence can change all that. And if the family was already functioning poorly when the child was very young, the teenage years can make things even worse.

Changes in Family Relationships

The stability of your family may become shaky when your young adolescent starts seeking independence, questioning the values of her parents, and becoming more and more influenced by the opinions of peers. The disruptions within the family that result from changes in her thinking and actions may seem as though they'll never end. Fortunately, though, they usually do. In the meantime, however, your teenager's relationship with family members will change—not only with you but also with her siblings, particularly if she tries to assume parent-like authority over them.

In some cases parents *impose* changes in family relationships on the teenager. For example, Mom and Dad might expect her to begin assuming many responsibilities of a parent, providing care for younger brothers and sisters. And that can be a real problem, particularly for an early-maturing adolescent. Most adults might regard this youngster as being older and more capable than she really is. Parents often expect more from her than she can give, and she'll frequently fail in trying to achieve what's demanded of her. By contrast, late-maturing adolescents might have more advanced thinking abilities than adults suspect; thus a small fifteen-year-old boy may be treated as though he were ten or twelve.

As a parent you need to relate to teenagers at their cognitive (thinking) level, not according to their physical appearance. If a youngster has a delayed puberty (i.e., a fourteen-year-old who looks ten), don't deal with him based on his appearance; in the same way, if a twelve-year-old looks seventeen, don't assume he has "extra" maturity.

Now, what behavior can the rest of the family expect from these adolescents? As we've already suggested, teenagers can be counted on to test rules set by their parents; when their behavior is inappropriate, Mom and Dad often must stop it in its tracks. You can also expect some unpredictability in your youngster's actions. For instance, you'll probably encounter short-lived periods of conformity, alternating with pushes for greater independence.

You may feel puzzled by the inconsistencies of an adolescent who sometimes seems to want more freedom than you can allow and at other times appears unwilling to accept any degree of independence offered to her. These shifts in mood and action make your own job all the harder. You'll find it more difficult to be consistent, and you may discover yourself arguing and becoming angry when your teenager's desires and demands change from day to day.

The family can also expect some scheming from the adolescent. Quite often a teenager will ask a parent for permission to do something and, when refused, will try to obtain it from the other parent, who's unaware that the youngster has already made a previous request and been turned down. Or the teenager will quickly determine which parent seems to be in charge of particular aspects of the family's functioning and the best time to ask that parent for approval. Most adolescents try playing parents against one another from time to time. Be aware of this—and stop it as soon as possible. You and your spouse need to communicate with each other to prevent your youngster from manipulating the two of you.

What if your girl or boy becomes openly rebellious? If you're like most parents, you'll usually become upset and try to punish the teenager. Bear in mind that all eyes in the family will be on you. Younger siblings, for instance, are keen observers, and if a teenager is allowed to get away with some previously prohibited actions, the siblings will often adopt the same behaviors sooner or later. On the other hand, if the family views the actions of the teenager as serious, the siblings may become informers in an attempt to escalate the parental punishment.

To be sure, there can be any number of major crises during your child's adolescence, including teenage pregnancy, running away, shoplifting, substance abuse (including drunkenness), and being arrested by the police. When parents learn about events like these, family relationships can be severely disrupted and tested. Most parents cannot believe it at first; but once they're convinced it's true, their initial anger soon turns to sorrow, shame, or resentment. Siblings usually become quiet, often fearing their friends will learn of the family tragedy. When parents really begin to face reality, they may seek professional advice and counsel in coping with the situation. At the same time, they may start supervising their teenager more closely, allowing less freedom than before.

The ultimate outcome of this major disruption can be quite positive: if family members recognize the need to solve the problem and come together to do so, they can form an even closer family bond.

On the other hand, what happens when parents persistently deny or minimize the seriousness of the situation? What if they never really face the issue head-on? Denial may help them cope with the crisis temporarily; but if it continues, only greater harm can occur. Even so, wishing to avoid disgrace or the criticism of others, many parents will completely avoid seeking counseling from professionals (in some families there seems to be a stigma associated with getting help). This attitude is very unfortunate. Everyone in the family could avert considerable pain and sorrow if counseling began early.

The Rights of Adolescents

Let's face it: not all adults should have children. However, many of those who shouldn't do so anyway. As a result some teenagers have problem parents. Children of alcoholic parents, for example, may have many difficulties growing up. Their parents often subject them to physical or emotional abuse. Also, incest occurs more often than generally reported within extended families.

Of course adolescents create many of their own problems, too (although some difficulties—such as incest—are never a teenager's fault). Youngsters often engage in risk-taking behaviors, from drug use to sexual activity. As these young people test themselves and society, they frequently misjudge where to draw the line or how to avoid harm. For example, many young adolescents who engage in sexual activity have little factual information about sex and almost never use contraceptive devices to prevent pregnancy or sexually transmitted diseases (STDs).

These two circumstances—risk-taking behaviors and abuse by adults—are areas in which adolescent legal rights become important. But there are many others, and the legal community is becoming increasingly sensitive to the rights of young people. America's lawmakers are acknowledging that minors do have rights.

Let's examine some of these health-related rights. In most states adolescents have the legal right to obtain—without parental consent—the diagnosis and treatment of suspected sexually transmitted diseases and pregnancy. In passing these laws, legislators recognized that these statutes would encourage teenagers to get immediate attention for these serious problems. STDs are easily spread and can affect others, and yet many young people refuse to discuss their symptoms with their parents. In the same way, teenage pregnancy is associated with complications, especially if the girl doesn't receive prenatal care early.

In many states adolescents of a specified age can also give their own consent for the diagnosis and treatment of illnesses or injuries, although some states require that the young person be self-supporting and not living in the parental home. These laws are particularly relevant for runaway teenagers; each year thousands of them become ill or injured, and it may be impossible to contact their parents for permission to treat them. Many times these teenagers give fictitious names and addresses of their parents. Despite the existence of these laws, however, doctors tend to be sensitive to parental interests and rights too and thus try to obtain parental consent whenever possible.

Here are some other legal rights that have been granted to adolescents:

- **Contraception.** In most states minors can obtain birth control devices on their own.

- **Abortion.** Since a 1976 Supreme Court decision minors in most states have been able to obtain an abortion without parental consent, although more recent decisions have modified this ruling somewhat—for instance, allowing states to limit access only to "mature" minors. (Several states have parental notification statutes of their own.) The courts have also ruled that parents may not force a pregnant minor to have an abortion against her will if she's competent to make that decision. More modifications may occur in the future in this very sensitive and controversial legal arena.

- **Substance abuse.** Without parental consent minors in most states can obtain medical and psychological care for the treatment of alcohol and drug abuse.

- **Rape and sexual abuse.** Some states allow minors access to medical care for sexual abuse or rape, without parental permission.

- **Mental health.** In some states minors over a particular age can commit themselves to a mental hospital, at least long enough for a thorough evaluation.

Keep in mind that these laws vary from state to state. Since it's helpful to understand the rights you and your teenager have when health-related problems arise, check with local attorneys to learn more about the laws in your area.

But the bottom line remains the same: young people (as well as parents) have legal rights. As a parent you need to find out how the law views adolescents—both in general and in your particular state. Some mothers and fathers are surprised to learn about many of the local laws that are in effect. For instance, in some cases a parent has a limited ability to "force" a teenage runaway to return home. Parents may also find it impossible or very difficult to force a teenager into mental health treatment or into an abortion or other action against the youth's wishes. This is a complex area, and we urge you to find out more about it.

THE IMPORTANCE OF LOVE

By definition love is the strong attachment or devotion of one person to another. All of us have experienced love, although there are many types and degrees of this common emotion. Love usually develops instinctively and instantaneously upon the birth or adoption of a child. It's essential for a healthy family life, and it's nurtured by years of care and mutual respect.

Love for your children should be unconditional; to say or imply, "I won't love you unless . . ." is a serious mistake and is never the foundation for healthy, lasting relationships.

Of course love within the family seems to be challenged constantly as a child grows. Your adolescent may frequently behave in ways that are inappropriate, that anger you, or that bring sorrow and even disgrace to other family members. If there's genuine love, however, you can disapprove of your teenager's actions and still love him.

During disagreements you must let your love come through. Children can weather the most difficult experiences if they feel the love of their parents. By contrast, the angriest and most bitter young people are those who feel abandoned by their mother or father. Never do that to your child. You can express love even while taking drastic steps such as admitting your teenager to a substance-abuse residential treatment program or a juvenile detention center. However, if you're having trouble keeping your love alive during family crises, consider getting some professional help. Parenting classes might also be useful. Above all, make a commitment to take the parenting privilege seriously.

One final note: On occasion your adolescent may seem to have stopped loving you. But don't despair. Most often this is only temporary and superficial. His love will eventually resurface.

2

COMMUNICATING WITH YOUR ADOLESCENT

A teenage girl was getting ready to go to a school dance. She suddenly burst into tears and ran into her mother's bedroom. "I can't find my earrings," she said, sobbing. "What am I going to do?"

Her mother appeared to take control of this "crisis" rather quickly. "Don't worry about it, dear," she said. "You can wear my earrings."

The daughter looked at her mom, and anger swept over her face. She turned toward the door, stomped out of the room, and yelled, "You really don't care, do you?"

Clearly this teenager had not heard the same message her mother had tried to convey. Or if she did hear it, she was seeking another kind of response. The mother was trying to help out. But there was an unfortunate breakdown in communication.

Whether they are children or adults, people often don't say what they really mean. Nor do they always hear what's really being said. And this can create all kinds of problems in their lives.

Good communication is essential in every relationship. When parents and teenagers are involved, it's indispensable. The way you communicate determines how you motivate your children, impart your values, and encourage responsibility. By the time your child enters adolescence, you've usually already established how you communicate. And unless you've really worked on your communication skills when your youngster was much younger, communicating during the trying adolescent years can be especially difficult.

Early adolescents in particular are sensitive to how their parents communicate. Psychologist Haim Ginott said, "Help is perceived as indifference, concern as babying, and advice as bossing." No wonder adults find parenting so difficult so often. And no wonder they're often frustrated when they try to communicate with their teenagers.

Of course many adolescents believe that *they* have figured out precisely how to communicate with their parents:

"I know exactly when *not* to tell my mom anything," says one adolescent.

"I can perfectly choose the time and place when my dad is most likely to say yes to whatever I want," explains another.

From the parents' point of view, mothers and fathers gradually learn a lot about their teenager's communication style. For instance, in many cases an adolescent who says very little is probably contemplating something important. Even while seemingly ignoring their parents, adolescents watch, listen, and reach their own (sometimes inaccurate) conclusions about family problems and feelings.

When teenagers aren't being talkative, you might learn almost as much from their body language. Adolescents (and even younger children) send many nonverbal messages during a typical day. Sometimes these physical signals are purposeful—an acceptable form of expression when parents won't tolerate verbal confrontation—but they can also be an unconscious expression of the teenager's feelings.

You too send messages through actions rather than words. However, whether it's coming from parent or child, nonverbal communication can easily be misinterpreted. For example, what does it mean when teenagers leave the room and slam the door? It could be that they're angry. On the other hand, maybe they're terribly sad and on the brink of tears.

Do your best to make sense of the communication going on around you. And without question, take seriously the viewpoints of all your family members. Be aware of your youngsters' needs and opinions and really listen to what they have to say.

As we emphasized earlier, modern families are busy; teenagers and parents always seem to be going somewhere, and there may be few opportunities for the family to be together to talk. How do you solve this problem? Some families set a particular time for everyone to get together and discuss what's on each person's mind (perhaps a general discussion every day during dinner and once a week for a longer discussion); in other families things are less formal, but there's a commitment to deal with problems whenever they occur.

Sometimes the whole family need not be involved in a particular brainstorming session. But at least those members directly concerned with the problem should participate.

MOTIVATION

We all have dreams and high expectations for our children. As parents we want the best for them, usually hoping they'll achieve more than we have.

Quite often, however, parents find themselves asking, "How can I motivate this kid of mine?" In reality, however, that may not be what they're asking at all. If they were more honest, they'd ask, "How can I make my teenager achieve what *I* want for him?"

As you might guess, parents usually can't mold their teenager into what they want, no matter how skillful their communication and parenting skills. The typical adolescent has different priorities from her mother and father, with her interests focused more on what happens *now* than on what will occur in the future.

One girl in the eighth grade said, "My folks are really upset. My grades aren't as good as they were last year. But my social life is terrific. They just don't understand. Why are they always griping about my grades?"

A boy who is a senior in high school said, "My parents are giving me a hard time about what I'm going to study in college. But I don't know what I want to be. And since this is my last year in high school, I want to have fun. I'll think about college when I'm there."

Many parents yearn for a magic wand that could instill motivation in their teenagers. Motivation, however, comes from within. It comes from an inner drive that causes people to act in a particular way, usually with the desire to achieve something, to succeed in a plan of action that will bring about what *they* want. Your teenager needs to be very interested in something to become motivated to learn more about it, to want to succeed, or to be accepted by or admitted to a desired group. Playing the guitar, for example, may seem so essential to your youngster that he'll become highly motivated to practice, to work to obtain money with which to buy a better guitar, and eventually to be selected to join a band that plays at teenage functions.

Again, motivation takes place when the teenager desires something. If you use your most reasoned arguments to try to convince your adolescent to study in school—because the information will be useful in the future or because good grades are necessary to gain admission to college—hitting the books may still not rank high on your teenager's priority list, especially if he's not cognitively mature enough to really understand the future. He himself has to want to study.

How do you get a teenager to want the same things you do? How, for example, do you get your adolescent to study and to strive for success in life? That usually arises from many years of living in a family that expects success. In most cases this kind of motivation has probably been established long before adolescence. Yes, you can influence teenagers and provide direction while recognizing their accomplishments and supporting them during difficult times. However, you cannot *make* them adopt your priorities.

Also, if you're trying to push your teenager toward a particular goal, you need to examine your reasons why. We've all heard about the potentially harmful situation of parents trying to live through their children. For example, a mother may have always wanted to be a ballet star but was unable to realize her dream. Now she demands that her daughter put in hours of practice, constantly telling her how important it is to become a prima ballerina—even though the daughter has little interest in that degree of training. "Tennis mothers" and "baseball fathers" are common, too, and their *real* priority often is not their teenage daughter or son.

So what's the bottom line? Your teenager may not be unmotivated but simply motivated in areas not of your choosing. And that's okay. Parents need to show patience and understanding when their youngster does not live up to their standards. Allow your teenagers to develop their own goals. If you're going to influence them at all, it won't be by talking and then talking some more. It will come primarily from setting an example of leading a productive life. Your own actions will help your teenagers understand the value of doing something well and the rewards for achievement.

WHAT'S RIGHT WITH MY TEENAGER?

"All my parents ever say is 'no' or 'don't.'"

A lot of adolescents feel this way, and in many instances there may be a ring of truth to it. Quite often parents take the positive aspects of their teenager for granted, instead focusing mostly on the negative. Remember that there are many good things about adolescents. Like everyone else, they need recognition and compliments, and they need to know that they are appreciated. When you're pleased with something they've done, tell them.

Early and middle adolescents are still uncertain about themselves, how they appear to others, and what they'll be like as adults. You can boost their self-esteem by telling them how attractive they are, how well they're growing, and that they're becoming more adult in their thinking. Or compliment them on how they handled a difficult social situation or how they came to an appropriate decision. When they do something well, show your parental approval.

By late adolescence most youngsters are more stable. They're beginning to look toward the future, already thinking about leaving home. But despite their maturity, they too need to hear words of admiration and respect. Don't neglect them.

Of course teenagers don't always live up to your standards or deserve praise. Yet more than you might think, they do absorb and incorporate parental values (whether good or bad), although they may alter some of them. As we've already noted, they may experiment with other lifestyles and values for a time, but they usually (though not inevitably) return to the fold. When they do argue about values and ethics, they're often trying to understand their parents' beliefs better and decide whether to adopt them.

There's another critical point worth reemphasizing: if you want your teenager to accept your values, you need to *live* them, not just talk about them. Setting a good example is very important. If you articulate a particular standard but act quite differently, teenagers will get the message—a message that they don't need to be consistent or that values are only relative. Frankly, this is a good way to raise an individual who will have trouble relating to and respecting the rights of others. By setting a *consistent* example, however, you can forcefully communicate your values. And if you see evidence that your adolescent has eventually held on to your standards, congratulate him while explaining the importance of such guidelines for living.

Sibling relationships can be difficult, too, and rivalries among brothers and sisters are quite normal. Now and then you will need to tell your teenagers to stop doing something that infringes on a brother or a sister. However, your adolescents also will relate quite fairly to siblings most of the time. On those occasions, point out how much you appreciate their behavior.

One last reminder: praise works better than criticism. Criticism alone alienates teenagers, interferes with relationships with parents, and promotes poor self-esteem. To influence adolescents, parents need to balance realistic criticism with realistic praise. Take the time to review what's good about your teenager and make sure you communicate that to him.

If you didn't grow up in a home with love, you may need some professional help to deal with your anger about this and about your inability to praise your youngsters freely. Don't pass these negative attitudes on to them. Bring them up in a family that praises them, not tears them down.

3

HOW TO DISCIPLINE EFFECTIVELY

What did discipline mean to you when you were growing up? Did it involve the loss of privileges? Or some extra chores around the house? Or spankings and harsh words?

In Part III of this book we'll discuss the discipline of adolescents in depth. For now, let's examine some of the basic principles.

By definition discipline is the education and training that develops self-control, character, efficiency, and a willingness to accept authority when it's appropriate. In reality, however, it means different things to different people. As a parent you probably think of it as "What do I do to make my teenager mind me?" We can answer that question very succinctly: there are no infallible rules. Every family is different, and effective discipline or rewards in one family may not work in another.

For example, let's take the case of a preschool child who persists in doing something wrong when told not to. In response his mother gives him a couple of swats on his bottom. Another mother, however, might find that a different approach works better—perhaps telling her misbehaving child to go to his room, close the door, and remain there until she permits him to come out. Each parent must find the method that works best in her family.

The rules often change when the child enters adolescence. As we discussed earlier, teenagers go through several stages of development. And as their behaviors change, so might the disciplinary action required to deal with them.

Here is some of what you might expect from your teenager in the years ahead. Early adolescents are striving for freedom, testing limits, and rejecting parental values. These youngsters also tend to be messy, often have poor hygiene, don't complete assigned jobs (especially if Mom or Dad has assigned them), persist in irritating younger siblings (and even parents if they can get away with it), and seem dumbfounded if they're criticized or forced to do something. Much of this behavior is normal for this stage of development. Even so, while you must tolerate their behavior to a certain extent, that doesn't mean they should have the freedom to do whatever they want. Parents must impose limits and standards, and enforce them . . . *within reason.*

By comparison, in middle adolescence teenagers are somewhat more mature. They are becoming used to themselves, they are probably accepted by a preferred group of peers, and thus they direct much of their attention outside the home. As a result peace usually returns to the family and relationships are easier. Even under the best of circumstances, however, there will be periods of regression to behaviors more typical of early adolescence. So be prepared for them. Also, if either a parent or the youngster has any emotional difficulties, this middle period can become a time of extreme turmoil for the entire family.

Then there's late adolescence, in which teenagers are much more in command. They're looking toward the future and are often an asset to family functioning. But they too can make inappropriate decisions or feel uncertain about how to cope with a new situation. Incidentally, as you might expect, a "blurring" or overlapping of these three stages of adolescence may occur; calm and turmoil sometimes come and go in all three stages.

DISCIPLINE IN CHILDHOOD

To some degree disciplinary problems in adolescence actually depend on how you handled misbehavior earlier in your child's life. So let's look for a moment at how parents discipline small children. There are several types of discipline and child rearing. One of these methods includes *overcoercion,* in which parents always force the youngster to do what they want. In this situation, the child has few choices, while the parents (usually the mother) inspect everything and make all the decisions.

When the daughter dresses for school, for example, she's inspected and asked, "Have you got on the right slip? Let me see." And then she's told, "Let me comb your hair. You still don't do it right." By the time the girl leaves the house, Mom has also made certain she has the correct coat or sweater, has the proper lunch money, and has received specific instructions about coming home.

Over the years this child is almost reduced to a robot. The youngster has three choices in coping with the discipline: she can accept it as her fate in life; she can rebel and cause constant trouble; or she can resist and eventually comply.

Most children adopt the last approach. They resist passively until the situation becomes threatening and then accept the inevitable submission to the mother's directives. Teachers often unknowingly make the situation worse by telling the parents that their child could do better, whereupon the mother essentially says, "You push her at school, and I'll push her at home." The child then passively resists *both* teacher and parent.

And what happens when this child becomes a teenager? In adolescence this resistance usually becomes greater or is supplanted by outright rebellion. Years later, when the child becomes an adult and a mother herself, she'll tend to perpetuate this parental behavior to the next generation.

There's also a very different disciplinary style—quite the opposite of overcoercion but just as fraught with problems. In this approach there's *no supervision and almost complete freedom* at a time when the child is unable to cope with making competent decisions. When youngsters grow up in an environment where little concern is shown by a parent, adolescence becomes a time of life in which they often make potentially harmful decisions. Worse yet, these teenagers usually feel unloved, perhaps unwanted, and that the parent doesn't care. As adults they're likely to demand the right to do what they want, and their own parenting skills will suffer because of the model they had as a child.

Then there's the *"prince" or "princess" syndrome,* which sets the child up as a sacred object—and often divides the parents. The father, for instance, may believe that his little girl should have everything she wants, that she's perfect, and he envisions how beautiful she'll become as a young lady. His wife may be more realistic, creating conflict between mother and father.

In a similar way some moms regard their son as a "prince," with the same type of benefits that a princess enjoys. When a boy enters adolescence in this environment, he'll often increase his demands on those around him, becoming manipulative, threatening to withhold his love unless his wishes are met, and finding himself more independent and in conflict with his father. In adulthood he's likely to continue his expectations and demands, which will create problems in his relationship with his wife. As a rule he'll never feel satisfied. And if he has a child, he may fear the competition and resent the youngster.

Still other parents rear their children on the principle of *conditional love,* which we mentioned in the opening chapter. These parents love their child only if he meets their demands. Of course the possibility of losing the love of one's mother or father is a serious threat; youngsters in this position will find themselves always measuring up and trying to meet the goals and objectives set by their parents in an attempt to ensure that they'll be loved.

For these children adolescence only increases their anxiety. After all, teenagers are normally uncertain of themselves and what is expected of them anyway. With the added parental pressures many set rigid goals and deadlines for themselves, subject themselves to severe self-criticism, and drive themselves to succeed. They're constantly trying to measure up to real or perceived expectations of parents and friends. These characteristics will tend to continue into adulthood, often affecting spouse and children as the young adult still strives to achieve what he believes he should.

Other parents use another emotion—*guilt*—as a means of discipline or of forcing a child to conform to their wishes. See if any of these statements sound familiar:

"How could you do this to your mother?"

"When you act that way, everybody will think I'm a poor parent. Why do you do this to me?"

"When you look like you do now, everyone will think I'm a terrible father and can't provide decent clothes for you. I'm ashamed. I think you do this to punish me."

Adolescents usually recognize that guilt is being used as a means of control; in response they'll resist it or perhaps adopt behaviors that bring embarrassment to the parents. Even though teenagers resent these attempts to make them feel guilty, when they become adults themselves, they'll often use the same tactics on a spouse or a child.

Do any of the above examples of discipline and child rearing seem exaggerated to you? They're really not. You'll find the same patterns (occasionally several of them combined) in many families, although sometimes to a less intense degree. These are very real styles of family relationships. And if you recognize them in your own approach to parenting, you need to change.

MAKING DISCIPLINE WORK

No matter how families interact, disagreements between teenagers and parents are inevitable. Fortunately, most of them are settled without major turmoil. In some instances, however, parents must call the teenager to account and discipline him. Adolescents *need consistent discipline from loving parents,* and in fact discipline is one of the best ways of showing your love. Failure to discipline can produce serious rebellion (so-called "acting out" behavior) in adolescence. The sense of being unloved is one of the worst feelings humans can have.

So how do you make discipline work? Most parents develop their disciplinary skills by trial and error. Here's what often happens: As a parent you might instinctively become angry upon learning of a particular misbehavior by your youngster. In response you may make a spur-of-the-moment, unwise statement or decision. For example: "Well, you're grounded for the next three weeks!"

Three weeks? It may have seemed like a wise choice at the time. Upon reflection, however, it may create as many problems as it was intended to manage. For instance, if you don't allow your teenager to go anywhere for almost a month, what trouble does that create for your other children, as well as for you and your spouse? And who will stay home to be sure he complies with the "sentence"?

Here's a better strategy to follow before instituting any punishment: Calm down. Think clearly about the problem. Consider your options. Then come to a workable decision that's fair and consistent. Frankly, this is hard to do in the heat of the moment. However, if you can accomplish it, you'll have fewer regrets about the decisions you make as a disciplinarian.

This style of discipline should begin in early childhood and continue into adolescence. If you get angry and say something that's inappropriate, apologize immediately. Also, particularly during your youngster's teenage years, prepare to negotiate the particular punishment being considered—but still stay in control. This is a delicate but important balance to maintain.

Don't lose sight of the purpose of discipline, either. Discipline is *not* synonymous with punishment but, as noted earlier in this chapter, consists of education and training for self-control and preparation for adulthood. It involves rewards, restrictions, and delaying gratification, all of which must be appropriate for the age of your young child or the developmental level of your adolescent. Give small rewards when young children keep their room tidy, complete an assigned job, or do well in school. Teenagers may receive bigger rewards—such as a new sweater, use of the family car, money for a trip—as a means of recognizing special effort and success.

To repeat, you should begin instituting both rewards and restrictions many years before adolescence to prevent trouble during the teenage years. Once your youngsters reach adolescence, if you allow them to break important rules constantly without being disciplined, you'll only encourage *more* rule violations. And if they gain control of the family, they won't give it up easily.

This book may not provide as many *specific* rules about discipline as you'd like. However, there's a reason for that. Each family is unique in its relationships and values. And thus you need to customize discipline to your family's particular situation. Perhaps parenting classes in your local community or discussions with other parents will give you ideas. Keep learning about parenting—it is a complex but potentially rewarding task!

In general, keep in mind that most adolescents really do want limits. And if an adolescent persistently flaunts the rules of his parents and engages in unacceptable behavior, you need to get help from a professional early—*before* there are any serious effects on the teenager and family ties. This counseling should almost always involve *all* family members, including both parents.

Incidentally, as much as possible Mom and Dad should share the parenting and disciplinary responsibilities. If you and your spouse find that the tasks of parenting divide you rather than bring you together, classes in parenting or marriage—or even formal counseling—can often help.

4

FAMILIES AND
THEIR CHALLENGES

*W*hat is a family? Growing up, most of us had the stereotypical image of a household filled with two parents and probably two or more children of different sexes. This was a truly "traditional family," particularly if the father worked and the mother stayed home.

Now, however, this image might be more the exception than the rule. For instance, there are many single-parent families today. Also, remarriage following a divorce can instantly create the so-called "blended family." Then there's the extended family incorporating close and distant relatives. And sometimes children grow up in alternative families (such as foster families). Each of these types of families has its own strengths, weaknesses, and problems.

SINGLE-PARENT FAMILIES

A single-parent family can be created in several ways. Seventy-five to 80 percent of adolescents who live in single-parent families do so because of divorce. Another 10 to 15 percent find themselves in this family arrangement due to the death of a parent. In the remainder of cases the parent (usually the mother) never married.

Divorce

Statistics vary, but about 50 percent of children in the United States can expect to live for at least seven years in a single-parent family because of divorce or separation. One of seven of these children will experience the effects of at least one additional divorce. Without question divorce is difficult for any child to weather. While some people believe that adolescents can handle this family crisis better than younger children, studies show that this isn't necessarily the case. Many teenagers find a divorce as devastating as a death in the family.

Ideally parents should try to resolve their conflicts with one another through some professional counseling, to prevent a divorce altogether. However, this is not always possible. And when the separation occurs, how bad or how well a teenager reacts depends on several factors—why the divorce came about, the emotional stability of both the parent still in the home and the "expelled" parent, new financial strains caused by the divorce, and how well the extended family and the community provide emotional support. If the other parent lives close by, the new relationship between the parents can have a crucial effect on the children, too.

Remember that children and teenagers are very perceptive. They're quite aware of what goes on in a family, and usually a divorce is not a complete surprise to them. Even so, it can still have a cataclysmic impact, creating new problems for youngsters and forcing them to adapt to a changed environment and a new family structure. During the early stages after a divorce adolescents struggle to find ways of adjusting, which may cause additional difficulties for the parent they're living with. Some adolescents become aggressive and lash out at the mother or father in the home. Others become quiet and isolate themselves from parents and siblings. Many continue to think their parents will remarry and often feel guilty and believe their own actions caused the divorce.

These responses by your teenager and other children in the home require that you try to help them. However, that's hard for some parents to do. In the immediate aftermath of a divorce many moms and dads are preoccupied with their own problems, making it difficult for them to give time and attention to the children.

Even if the mother, for example, sought the divorce, she still might be dealing with feelings of rejection, failure, loneliness, guilt, anger, and financial pressures. Add to that the stress of coping with a new life and greater responsibilities, and she may find all her energy and resources consumed.

That isn't all that may distract Mom. There may be problems with car pools, picking up small children from a day-care center, or supervising an adolescent with free time after school that add to her burdens. Day after day she alone must make decisions, set limits, discipline, deal with the children's problems, take care of clothing, prepare meals, and provide comfort, reassurance of love, and hope for the future. She might direct the time she has left—if there's any—toward her search for a new life for herself. In fact it's very important for her to pursue an adult life apart from her children. It is important for her to draw energy from her job, and her family should provide her with encouragement not to give up.

In years past mothers were almost always awarded custody of the children, but this is no longer true. Quite often the courts now grant joint custody, which can either ease or complicate child–parent relations. Also, fathers are sometimes given sole custody of the children, which for some men can tax their parenting abilities. Men often aren't accustomed to handling the routine tasks related to children, and gaining custody can immediately present them with new stresses.

Absent fathers may feel like they have it easier on a day-to-day basis. However, they aren't immune to the effects of divorce, either. In fact studies show that they're more likely than their ex-spouse to need mental health care. The courts will establish visitation rights (which are really more like responsibilities than rights), and these periods with their teenager can be especially difficult for dads. Unfortunately, many fathers have spent little time with their adolescent children in the past, and suddenly to have a teenager for an entire weekend can be trying for both of them. Many times the father's business can interfere with a scheduled visit—and if he requests that the visit be postponed, the adolescent can interpret that as rejection.

If you're a father who finds himself in this situation, you need to articulate your love and demonstrate your interest in your teenager. You are the parent, and you must constantly show your care and concern.

Unfortunately, the teenager always feels divided loyalties. And adolescents are skilled in playing one parent against the other, giving false reports about what happened during a visit, exaggerating financial needs or parental restrictions, and in general attempting to further animosity between the parents.

Sometimes a teenager will tell one parent how wonderful the other is—even expressing outright favoritism—or will be an angel with one parent and a devil with the other. On occasion teenagers will cause trouble by trying to get the parents together again (although this almost never works). Now and then an adolescent (usually a boy) will attempt to find someone else to replace the absent parent. Be particularly aware of the teenager who manipulates his mom and dad to get everything he wants, letting them compete to be the "best" parent or the one who loves the child "the most." This is bad for everyone in the family.

To complicate matters, there are times when one parent will use the adolescent as a substitute for the ex-spouse. Dad might burden the youngster with his feelings and problems and may even ask for advice. If you notice that you're relating to your teenager this way, get professional help so you can deal more positively with the aftereffects of divorce.

Also, don't use your children as an outlet for your negative feelings about your ex-spouse. Don't put them between the two of you; everyone loses in this unfortunately common scenario. More than anything else, you need to continue actively demonstrating your love for your children, without attacking your former spouse. Remember, the child comes from both parents and needs both of you. Avoid forcing teenagers into the middle of a divorce; they can develop serious emotional problems if this happens. Carefully evaluate how you relate to your children after the divorce—it is vital for all of you.

Amid all the potential problems, don't lose sight of the fact that a divorce isn't always bad for the children or the parents. If the family situation was a harmful one, teenagers may feel great relief when the separation occurs. Yes, they may still feel some anxieties, but the divorce can also be a chance for renewal for both adolescents and parents and an opportunity to correct errors of the past and provide hope for the future.

All teenagers, of course, are not the same, and they may react differently when parents separate. Studies into the effects of divorce are still in their infancy, but here is some of what researchers have learned thus far. First, adolescents in divorced families often fear forming their own relationships involving love. In their minds emotional detachment from others can protect them from further pain.

Teenagers with divorced parents may also have lowered expectations of other persons or even their own future lives, feeling powerless to change things. In one study of early adolescents, teachers believed the level of parental conflict was the most important factor related to a teenager's social competence; the adolescents themselves, however, believed the marital status of their parents had the greatest effect. A clear need for the father was particularly strong in middle and late adolescent boys.

Other research has shown that divorce doesn't necessarily interfere with adolescent development and that teenagers would rather live in a stable one-parent home than in a two-parent home with marked parental conflict. Adolescents were also greatly affected by how parents formed and maintained their *new* adult relationships; for example, a series of live-in boyfriends or girlfriends tends to complicate adolescent adjustment and may often cause risk-taking behavior.

When divorce creates serious problems for parents and/or children, we can't overemphasize the value of professional counseling. *Don't take your troubles to your child;* he can't—and shouldn't have to—deal with them. There are many competent counselors able to help you and your teenager cope with your changing way of life. In addition to individual and family therapy, your youngster might benefit from group sessions with other teenagers from divorced families; there's comfort in knowing others have experienced similar feelings and problems and even in realizing your situation may be better than others. Seek some counseling *before* there's significant deterioration of the parent–child relationship.

Meanwhile, what if you're now on the brink or in the process of a divorce? Short of therapy, how can you ease your teenager through this life transition? Morris Green, a pediatrician who has studied the behavior and emotional needs of children and adolescents, has provided some suggestions for parents in this situation. For example, emphasize to your adolescent that the decision to divorce is yours and/or your spouse's; it was not caused by the children—and it is final.

Tell your teenagers that their needs will be met (if, in fact, that's the case). Make sure your adolescent understands that both parents love him and both will continue to have a close relationship with him—again, if this is true. (If the father will not be available, however, it's often valuable to have a male relative or one respected by the teenager maintain contact with the youngster.)

If possible, avoid moving away from friends, school, and a familiar environment. Also, if you can work it out, the child should consistently receive individual time *with each parent;* don't make excuses for why your children cannot or should not visit the other biological parent. Make a special effort to remember birthdays and holidays and try to attend special events that are important to the teenager. And prepare for many questions and the need to repeat answers on numerous occasions. (If your ex-spouse refuses to follow these guidelines, do the best you can—and get help in dealing with any self-doubts or problems.)

Never-Married Families

Although adult women sometimes have babies out of wedlock, most often never-married families are headed by teenage mothers. Few of these adolescent moms marry before their baby is born; or if they do, many become divorced soon after the birth (teenage marriages rarely remain intact in contemporary society). And with limited education, limited job opportunities, and the real possibility of more children on the way, these young mothers find it increasingly difficult to cope with and support their youngsters. Many end up going on welfare and moving in with their parent(s)—which, ironically, may place them in another family unit without a father.

The offspring in these never-married families can ultimately develop problems during their own adolescence, often as they look to the parent as a role model. Boys in particular may have no father to serve as an example; and both boys and girls are deprived of observing the relationship between a married mother and father. Studies of some of these families have found several generations in which teenage pregnancy was used to "solve" adolescent and family problems—often with negative results.

In general adolescents from a never-married family become independent more quickly than their counterparts in intact families; they're also more likely to absorb the values of peer groups. The single mother is often at a loss as to how to cope with special problems that occur in these families. Again, obtain professional help.

STEPFAMILIES

An average of seven years passes before a divorced woman remarries; divorced men tend to remarry after three years. But there is great variation from person to person. Adolescents also differ in their response to their parent's dating and remarriage, with some encouraging it and others stubbornly resisting the idea.

Children and teenagers are often jealous of the parent's new relationship and frequently become angry that Mom or Dad would "do such a thing." Some teenagers scrutinize each new dating partner as though marriage were imminent. And if they believe that their mother, for instance, really is seriously considering marriage, they'll probably make their feelings known in very strong terms. They may begin severely criticizing the man she's dating and even insult this potential stepfather in his presence. Adolescent girls in particular may have problems with the knowledge that their mother is sexually involved with this new man. In some cases girls try to compete with the mother for the man's attention. Some teenagers become very rebellious (see Part III) in a conscious or unconscious attempt to have the parent(s) focus on them and not on new dating partners.

Through the teenager's eyes remarriage may disrupt the family unit. She may worry that this "stranger" will give directions and make demands. Perhaps most of all, the marriage will shatter any remaining hopes that her biological parents will get back together again.

So just when your teenager is becoming used to life in a single-parent family, remarriage may seem to turn everything upside down. Many times adolescents have difficulty adjusting to a new position in the family—particularly if they perceive it as reducing their importance in the household. Resentful of the stepfather's or stepmother's intrusion, the adolescent may try to convince her parent that this man or woman is unworthy or should leave.

Amid this potential turmoil the new stepfather and stepmother are facing adjustments, too. As a stepparent you'll want to become friends with your spouse's children. Adolescents, however, usually need time to accept a new parental figure and deal with new demands and restrictions. And during this transition time teenagers filled with their own anxieties and needs can make life miserable for everyone else.

To complicate matters further, it's natural for parents to show what's interpreted as favoritism toward their own child, since they're closer to this youngster and know his actions and how he thinks. Their spouse's child, however, is more like a stranger, and they need time to learn his quirks, peculiarities, and special qualities.

Matters can become even more entangled if the newly married couple has one or more children *together,* often making the teenager(s) in the household extremely jealous. More than anything, adolescents may feel ignored and forgotten and, in their frustration, may become very rebellious. Always remember to treat all your children equally.

If you're already living in a "blended family," did you think about issues like these *before* marriage? Or, as often happens, did they get pushed into the background? Ideally the new couple should discuss their plans with a marriage counselor and learn in advance how to deal with likely problems, especially those of teenagers. If you haven't done this preparation and problems have surfaced, seek some professional help now, before life becomes unbearable for both you and your adolescents.

One other point: if you're like most stepparents, you may feel guilty when things don't go well for children in the new family. However, your first duty is really to your spouse; if that relationship is good, then you can find ways to improve interactions with the children. Remember that adolescents can change, and when given support and understanding they'll often become more adaptable and agreeable to the new family structure. Time usually helps smooth the way, too, as members of the family gradually learn to live together. Again, *let your love shine through!*

EXTENDED FAMILIES

In common parlance an extended family unit is usually made up of two sets of grandparents and an assortment of aunts, uncles, cousins, and perhaps other persons. But in today's society not many older people live with their children, and few visit frequently. Other relatives probably live hundreds or thousands of miles away, and they too are seen only occasionally.

Thus the old concept of an extended family has changed. As a result grandparents often find it difficult to form close attachments to their own grandchildren (much less come to love stepgrandchildren).

If you are a grandparent, remember you are a valuable role model for your grandchildren. Before you move away in retirement, think about the importance of retaining a healthy relationship with them. You are an essential link to their past—and they need you. At times some grandparents have even stepped into the parenting role when the real parents have treated their children in a harmful way. Although some researchers have noted a trend for today's parents and grandparents to have more concern for their own lives than their children's or grandchildren's, keep the following point in mind: raising children is a lifelong occupation!

Sometimes, however, grandparents do live close, or one may even live with his or her children and grandchildren. However, this is not always a smooth living arrangement. Yes, grandparents (particularly grandmothers) are traditionally seen as kindly old people who are helpful, wise, and delightful to have around. Unfortunately, that's often a myth. When grandparents come to live with the family, they may be handicapped, senile, mean, and demanding. Alzheimer's disease, terminal cancer, and other problems can occur. In these instances parents often expect the adolescent to help provide care and tolerate any peculiarities. The presence of a grandparent can also put greater financial demands on the household in general.

Adding another person to the family, then, requires some adjustments. Before Grandma or Grandpa ever moves in, you and your family need to do a lot of planning. Then, as problems arise, everyone must deal with them as quickly as possible.

ADOPTION

Adopted children most often come into their new family as infants or very young children. As they grow up, they regard their parents as their biological mother and father. Thus, when they become old enough to be told they're adopted, understandably they have many questions.

During adolescence other problems can develop. Sometimes teenagers emotionally reject their adoptive parents, insisting that their mom and dad have no right to give orders or establish rules. In general this type of conduct is a sign of their increasing independence and uncertainty as to who they are. When such behaviors occur, a family discussion is essential. These are issues that the family can resolve.

We all have a need to belong and to know our roots, and in many cases having kind and loving adoptive parents is not enough. Sooner or later most adopted adolescents want to find out who their biological mother and father were and why these natural parents gave them up for adoption. They may want to make contact with their biological parents, too. Most adoption agencies have policies about this. (In the case of non-agency or foreign adoptions, policies vary widely, and parents should make inquiry with regard to their specific child at the time of the adoption.) In most cases, after talking with the adolescent or young adult, agency personnel will try to contact the natural mother and/or father to determine their willingness to meet the young person. If they're agreeable, the agency may arrange a meeting, often with a social worker present to provide information and professional guidance if needed.

Incidentally, sometimes children are adopted in adolescence, although the number is relatively small. In this case the adoptive parents and the adolescent will probably have to deal with many problems. On the one hand, the new parents will be eager to please, and they'll want love from the teenager. They also may have their own uncertainties about meeting the new demands of parenthood, and they may lack an understanding of normal adolescence.

The adopted teenager may bring some problems of his own into the relationship. Did he live in a series of foster homes, each of which affected him in some way? Or did he live with his natural mother or father? Was he physically abused or sexually molested? Does he have siblings who have been adopted? What values does he have? What is his intellectual ability?

Adoption agencies do their best to "match" children with prospective parents, and they do provide adoptive parents with some pertinent information. A knowledge of the biological parents, for instance, is helpful, since medical and psychological disorders can be passed on genetically. Even so, it's impossible for an agency to know everything about a teenager's past and what he may be feeling. Adoptive parents should realize that a teenager with serious past problems may need professional help to resolve these issues; love alone may not be enough. And if help is necessary, the adoptive parents should not blame themselves but should remember that one's genetic endowment is a very powerful influence on all individuals.

Adopted teenagers also usually know that in most states the law delays finalization of their placement in their new home for one year. So they may feel they're on probation and that if their new parents aren't happy, the agency will take them back. On occasion adolescents will behave in a way to ensure that the adoption will fail, usually because they dislike their new home situation or because they are testing their new circumstances. More often, however, they'll try to fit into the family. In the early weeks and months they may be reticent to express their viewpoints. With time and the development of trust, however, they'll relax and become part of the family. If there are major difficulties, you can usually get help from the adoption agency, which is probably eager to facilitate the formation of a well-functioning family.

By all means, don't let the information in this section discourage you from adopting a teenager. But approach this unique family situation realistically and prepare to deal with problems that could arise. Most children will respond positively to consistent and persistent love over many years.

FOSTER CARE

A child is not placed in foster care unless the circumstances demand it for the youngster's own welfare. Agencies also regard entry into this kind of care as temporary, and they will make efforts to improve the child's own home environment and family relationships so he can return. But when these changes are deemed impossible, they will consider adoption.

Foster parents are an interesting group of people. They care for children and adolescents and often become very attached to them. Because there are limited financial rewards, these individuals usually provide this care primarily because of their love for children or to satisfy an inner need. There may be natural offspring within the household as well as one or more foster children. With experience foster parents usually do an excellent job and provide badly needed care.

When adolescents enter a foster home, they are often cautious about trusting this new family. Whether this is their first or their fifth foster placement, the people will seem strange, and they'll feel uncertain about what's expected of them and who's the dominant adult who rules the family.

If the adolescents are old enough to consider the future, they'll probably begin to ask themselves many questions: "What will become of me? Will I ever return to my own home? Will I be adopted? Will I see my brothers and sisters?" Although each of these questions eventually deserves an answer, both the teenager and the foster parents may have difficulty answering all of them.

Sometimes adolescents leave home voluntarily or a parent throws them out of the house, and they go to live with relatives. Although moving in with an uncle or a grandparent is not typically considered a foster home setting because of legal definitions, it is really a form of foster care.

Some relatives, however, may be reluctant to take in the adolescent; if they finally do, the teenager himself may have difficulty accepting his new living situation and following the ground rules of this new household. At the same time, other children in the family may resent the intrusion. Families need to work out these problems themselves or use the agencies that can help them. Some outside assistance can minimize problems and shorten the adjustment period.

PART II

YOUR TEENAGER'S PHYSICAL GROWTH AND DEVELOPMENT

5

THE SIGNS
OF PUBERTY

*S*o your child is an adolescent! You probably find it hard to believe. After all, don't you still have striking memories of bringing your newborn home from the hospital . . . singing her lullabies . . . walking her to sleep? Doesn't it seem like just a moment ago that you watched her take her first step? When she entered kindergarten? When she read to you for the first time?

Although each of these milestones is a vivid reminder of how your youngster has grown, there is perhaps no more dramatic evidence of her march toward adulthood than her rapid physical development during the teenage years. This is a period in which your child will grow more quickly than at any time since the first year of life. Seemingly overnight, she'll evolve from a child to an adult, growing to your own height and perhaps even taller. Boys will begin sprouting a beard and muscles; girls will develop the features of womanhood. And for most parents it all happens much too quickly.

If you were to look up the word *puberty* in the dictionary, it would be defined as that state of physical development when an individual first becomes able to beget or bear children. However, it is really much more than that. To get a perspective on the dramatic changes that take place during this time, let's compare the physical growth of this period to what has already occurred. After ages two to three years a child grows about two inches and gains five pounds annually. That rate remains quite consistent—until puberty. When a youngster enters adolescence, there's a radical change, and growth becomes much more rapid, often accelerating to twice the pace of early childhood.

Why does this growth spurt begin when it does? We're not exactly sure. However, as you may have already seen in your own family, there can be a wide variation from person to person in the age at which this rapid growth starts and the speed at which it proceeds. These factors are determined by the genetic "programming" that each boy or girl inherits, influenced by how he sees and interprets the world around him.

As important as this physical growth is, it's only one aspect of puberty. Many other kinds of changes take place during adolescence, too. For instance, psychological and social development gradually evolves during this time. Thinking skills mature as well. And as these processes take place, each can influence the others— sometimes hastening but other times slowing down overall progress.

The physical growth, however, is what most grabs our attention. Almost every successive generation in the last century has been taller than the preceding one, and both boys and girls are maturing earlier, too. For instance, girls now experience the beginning of menstruation (menarche) earlier than in the past (on average it occurs at about twelve-and-a-half years of age in the United States). Why have these changes occurred? Improved nutrition, health, and the environment deserve much of the credit, but there are probably other factors as well, some of which researchers may not have identified yet.

No matter how fast or slowly your children have grown to this point, however, you've probably enjoyed watching them move through the stages of life, and adolescence will be no exception. Even so, it's a difficult time for teenagers. And if you doubt that, think back to your own adolescence and how you coped with the rapid alterations in your own body. You probably felt very awkward and self-conscious at times—the same feelings that your adolescent is probably experiencing now.

When a teenage boy's bones suddenly become so large that he doesn't know what to do with them, it can almost be comical—as long as you're not the one going through it. Or when his voice "cracks" as he speaks, others might find it amusing, but it will be annoying and embarrassing to him. In much the same way, as your teenager undergoes changes in his thinking, and as he begins to act and relate to other persons differently, you'll find it fascinating, although your youngster may be struggling to get through it all.

In the rest of this section we'll concentrate on normal physical growth—and the real or perceived problems of growth—of this period of life.

NORMAL GROWTH IN ADOLESCENCE

All teenagers proceed through the same sequence of physical changes. But as we've already noted, the time that physical growth begins, its velocity and magnitude, and the age at which it's completed are extremely variable.

Just think for a moment about the girls and boys in a typical seventh-grade classroom. Most of the girls are bigger than the boys, but there are exceptions. A few girls still look more like children than adolescents. One or two boys are probably very tall, looking like high school students, but many others have only just begun to grow, and a few haven't yet started. So even though they're all the same age, and even though all are probably quite normal, wide variations exist.

What Can You Expect?

Increases in physical size are the most obvious changes during puberty. During the year of greatest growth a boy will gain about four inches in height. By the time his growth spurt is completely over, he'll have experienced a height increase of about eight inches. The growth in girls, although not quite as dramatic, is still significant. The average gain in height for females during their peak year is a bit more than three inches. However, the rate of growth for girls slows significantly after menstruation begins.

Once the peak period of growth is finished, will there be any additional increases in height? In most cases a little more growth will occur. On average both boys and girls eventually gain an additional one-half to one inch in height. By late adolescence teenagers have reached 99 percent of their adult height.

Even if your own teenager is now only on the brink of puberty—if he's perhaps a few months or a year away from this time of life—he's still not totally immune to bodily changes. Both boys and girls add some fat during this prepubertal period, although the rate of fat accumulation decreases during this time. Then, once they eventually begin the growth spurt itself, boys will lose this fat, while in girls it will be rearranged to form what's called a "feminine figure."

Some boys are chubby just before they start to grow taller, but with their rapid increase in height they'll actually look skinny. Then, after the peak of their growth spurt, they'll gain weight and their quantity of muscle will increase. At the time of most accelerated growth, girls put on about eleven pounds and boys thirteen. By the end of puberty the average boy will have gained a total of forty pounds, much of which is muscle; the average girl will gain about twenty-five pounds.

Almost every part of the body participates in this surge of adolescent growth. But the most obvious changes are in the skeletal, muscular, and reproductive systems. Here's the order in which these changes will occur in your own teenager:

Usually the legs lengthen first; then the thigh width becomes greater. After that there's an increase in shoulder width, followed by growth in the trunk length. This lengthening of the trunk and legs is largely responsible for the adolescent's increase in height.

When it comes to changes in the bones, some of the most obvious ones occur in the teenager's face, particularly the lower jaw, which becomes longer. This change in facial appearance will probably startle your adolescent's grandparents, aunts, and uncles, especially those who don't see him very often.

Other major physical transitions are important to keep in mind, too, including an increase in muscle size and strength. Before the onset of puberty little difference exists between the strength of girls and that of boys. However, all that changes very fast during adolescence. Girls apparently stop increasing their strength about the time of their first menstrual period. By contrast, boys continue to add muscle mass and strength for about a year and a half *after* their peak height increase, eventually becoming much stronger than most girls.

There's still more. During adolescence many human organs (such as the heart, liver, kidneys, and digestive tract) become larger. At the same time, the composition and function of many glands become altered, some increasing their activities and others assuming less importance in the overall growth scheme.

In boys the larynx (voice box) becomes larger, usually following a period when bodily growth has been most rapid. A "crack" in your son's voice will usually occur during this time. Finally, once the larynx has enlarged to its full growth, his voice will lower and deepen. At the same time, he'll also begin to grow hair in the armpits (axillae) that's usually a little darker than the hair on his head. Hair will also sprout on his legs and arms, and he'll begin growing a scanty mustache on his upper lip. Girls too develop hair in the armpits and on the extremities, but usually to a lesser extent than boys. This is also the time when the sweat glands change, and teenagers begin to use deodorants.

The Reproductive System

Adults often associate puberty with major sexual changes, including alterations in the reproductive system and the appearance of the characteristics that differentiate the sexes. Frankly, these changes alarm many parents—which is not necessarily the way their teenagers react; in general young people may have some anxiety about their bodily changes, but they're also fascinated with how their bodies are evolving.

Here's a brief overview of some of what adolescents can expect. In girls the vagina becomes larger and its cellular and chemical composition changes. The ovaries become larger, too, although ovulation sometimes doesn't occur until many months after the first menstrual period. In boys the testicles enlarge, and later sperm are produced. These changes are all interrelated, and in many cases one must occur before another can develop.

Although changes like these often take place sequentially, keep in mind that from teenager to teenager they can begin at different times and proceed at different paces. That could create problems for a pediatrician trying to determine where particular teenagers stand in their progress toward physical maturity, since the doctor can't depend on chronological age alone. So when a doctor needs this kind of information, she will turn to one of two available techniques to help her out.

First, the doctor can rely on the most accurate of these methods—namely, taking X rays of the wrists and some other bones that have distinct characteristics at different stages of growth. For example, a fourteen-year-old girl may have a bone age typical of a girl of eleven, indicating that she has progressed slowly toward full maturity. By contrast, a twelve-year-old girl who is very tall may have a "bone age" of fifteen years.

While this information can be useful to doctors, there are several complicating factors they need to bear in mind. For example, X rays take time and can be expensive. Fortunately, your teenager's doctor can use another method to obtain comparable information. Because the secondary sex characteristics (breasts, genitals, pubic hair) mature in sequential stages, a pediatrician can observe their status in a particular patient and then assign a rating that's nearly as accurate as bone-age determinations. In establishing a girl's so-called "sex maturity rating" or SMR, doctors evaluate the pattern and characteristics of pubic hair and the form and contour of the breasts. In boys genital changes and the quantity and pattern of pubic hair determine this ranking. The SMRs consist of a five-point scale, with one indicating prepubertal and five meaning adult status.

With these ratings as a guideline your teenager's doctor can determine when your youngster can expect to go through growth periods, menses, and other transitions—and what may be normal and abnormal.

Using the Sex
Maturity Ratings

When the growth spurt of teenagers begins, most of them have a lot of questions on their minds. "How tall or short will I be? Will I be fat or muscular? Attractive or unattractive?"

Early adolescents in particular become quite preoccupied by themselves, spending a lot of time inspecting their bodies, whether searching for a pimple or wondering if their breasts will become larger. During this period they'll want and demand more privacy. They'll frequently lock the bathroom or bedroom door, taking care not to expose certain bodily parts to parents or siblings. And as one physical change after another takes place, they'll be constantly wondering, "Am I normal?" Adolescents can answer this question for themselves if they have some understanding of sex maturity ratings.

When your son or daughter begins to grow, you or the family's pediatrician may find it useful to discuss SMRs with your youngster. Refer to the charts on page 53 for a description of each SMR category. Make some simple drawings as you talk about the changes that occur in each SMR. Many teenagers will keep these sketches, referring to them in the future as they estimate their own stage of development.

Females. In girls breast buds appear between the ages of eight and thirteen years. If this process has not occurred by about age thirteen, many doctors consider puberty to be delayed; even so, this may not be a sign of an abnormality and, in fact, breast budding will begin later.

As the breasts grow, pubic hair will begin to appear on the inner borders of the labia. Your daughter will experience very rapid growth, shooting up about three inches within several months, more than she probably grew in a full year before puberty. This fast growth typically takes place between SMR 2 and SMR 3 (by contrast, boys experience their biggest growth spurt between SMR 3 and SMR 4).

The first menstrual period occurs in most girls by the time the breasts are at SMR 4 and pubic hair is at SMR 3, although it can begin earlier. When you or your daughter recognizes that her breasts are at SMR 2, you should discuss menstruation and feminine hygiene with her. Explain how to use a pad or tampon. Tell her that she can participate in sports and other activities and let her know you'll answer any related questions she may have.

Your daughter's first periods, incidentally, will almost always be painless, since dysmenorrhea (cramps or painful menses) doesn't usually occur until ovulation takes place, which is typically at least several months after the onset of menstruation. She should be aware that irregular periods are normal at this stage of life but that with time they'll become more regular. If she experiences very heavy or persistent flow during several periods, consult her doctor. (Also see Chapter 32.)

If you've worked hard at developing good lines of communication with your daughter, she should feel free to discuss her sexual concerns with you. Basic sex education should actually have begun earlier in childhood, but when she reaches SMR 2, this is a good time to reinforce the previous discussions about topics such as menstruation and hygiene. By SMR 3 and SMR 4 you can provide some additional information, particularly about sexually transmitted diseases and pregnancy.

While you might encourage your daughter to refrain from sexual intercourse, that may not be enough. Keep in mind that peer groups are sources of intense social pressure, and they often provide a lot of inaccurate information. Make sure your adolescent has the straight facts and feels free to come to you or her doctor for answers to her questions. (See Chapter 14.)

Males. Boys are as concerned as girls about their bodies. Although the appearance of pubic hair is their most obvious first indication of puberty, penile growth and enlargement of the testes actually begin before that. Although doctors differ in their definition of delayed development in boys, most believe that a male falls into this category if his testicles have not begun to enlarge by age thirteen-and-a-half; however, this does not mean that an abnormality is present, and the normal changes may simply occur later.

Now, what can your son expect in terms of height increases? When he is at SMR 3 for pubic hair, he'll begin the year of his most rapid height gains, growing about four inches. As we mentioned earlier, boys add fat before they begin to grow taller, but they'll lose much of it at SMR 2. When this loss occurs—followed by dramatic increases in height—you and your son may become concerned that he appears *too* thin. Don't worry. He'll gain weight after his peak height spurt is over. In the meantime you can expect his appetite to increase significantly through this period of rapid growth. Then, during the interval between SMR 4 and SMR 5, he'll develop more muscles, his strength will increase, and he'll generally "fill out."

Many boys, however, aren't satisfied with the normal muscular development of adolescence. They'll see or hear about friends working out with weights and equipment designed to build up muscles, and they'll want to begin this kind of training themselves—often before their body is ready for it. Despite the temptation to begin lifting weights when they're just starting to grow taller, this is almost always a mistake. From a physical standpoint boys would be much better off waiting until mid–SMR 4—a stage in which they have the additional muscle cells necessary for weight lifting. At that time they can begin appropriate exercises to enlarge and strengthen their muscles.

In addition to weight lifting, a number of sports and activities can tax developing bones, joints, and muscles in early puberty. As a rule such demands should not be put on the growing body before it's capable of handling them. Seek some advice on sports participation from a qualified physician or certified sports trainer before your teenager starts any intensive athletic program.

One other important point about sports is essential to emphasize here. Teenage boys intensively involved in sports programs are often tempted to use anabolic steroids. These are hormones that stimulate muscular development, and they are particularly alluring for football players and bodybuilders. However, amateur and professional sports organizations have strongly condemned and unequivocally banned the use of these substances—and for good reason: anabolic steroids can be very injurious, particularly during periods of growth. Tell your son *not* to use them. (See Chapter 31 for more information.)

Besides increased muscles and the developments we've already discussed, teenage boys will notice other changes in their bodies. For instance, although they've had penile erections for their entire lives—even *before* birth, while still in the womb—these erections will become much more frequent during early or mid-puberty, due to an increase in male sex hormones. *All* boys begin to experience erections when they don't anticipate them and have done nothing to cause them. They also occur frequently during sleep.

The same hormones also stimulate new erotic feelings and heightened sensitivity of the genitals in boys, similar to those of the breasts and genital area in girls. During SMR 3 and SMR 4 dreams start to take on a sexual nature, and almost all boys have nocturnal emissions or "wet dreams," in which semen is released through the penis during sleep. This is quite normal, and with age they'll become less frequent and finally stop.

Then there's the subject of masturbation—a common behavior in adolescence (as well as in earlier years). In fact boys often learn about masturbation (self-stimulation of the genitals) before the onset of puberty from their friends. During the teenage years almost all boys, and many girls, masturbate. Despite all the myths to the contrary, there is no harm in this behavior (See Chapter 14).

While masturbation concerns some parents, even more are anxious about the possibility of their teenager having sexual intercourse. By SMR 3 to SMR 4, your son's testicles will have grown sufficiently to produce at least a few sperm, and he can probably ejaculate. This is a good time to discuss with him why postponing sexual intercourse makes good sense. Also, you need to convey information to him about sexually transmitted diseases and pregnancy—and how to protect against them. If you delay this discussion, it may be too late by the time you eventually get around to it: once your youngster reaches SMR 4, there's a greater likelihood that he'll become sexually active; he'll be a mid-adolescent by then, interested in dating, perhaps capable of driving an automobile, and experiencing much greater freedom than earlier in his teenage years.

To add to your concerns, most risk-taking behaviors begin during early adolescence—and then only increase with age. We will discuss this subject later in the book, but for now, keep in mind that SMR 2 and SMR 3 are the best times to begin discussing harmful behaviors such as the use of tobacco, alcohol, and chemical substances.

How Important Are SMRs? Doctors find these sex maturity ratings extremely useful. They tell the physician that a boy at SMR 2, for example, still has considerable growth potential, while one at SMR 4 does not—no matter what their ages. Through the SMRs the doctor has learned to screen his patients carefully for scoliosis (curvature of the spine) between SMR 2 and SMR 4, although he also may have checked for this condition before the growth spurt. And he knows that oral contraceptives might not be advisable earlier than SMR 3.

In your role as a parent you'll find the SMRs helpful, too, although in a different way from your doctor. As we've already suggested, they'll help you decide the most appropriate time to discuss the growth changes that your teenager is about to go through or is presently experiencing. In many situations they're a much better indicator than age of the most pertinent topics of discussion at any given time.

During these conversations you need to reassure your teenager that the changes she's going through are quite normal. If you keep her informed of what to expect, she'll better prepare for and understand the growth stages she's experiencing. And if she feels comfortable with herself, she'll probably assume greater responsibility for her life and well-being.

One other point needs clarifying. Because adolescents need privacy—especially during the early phases of puberty—you'll probably have little opportunity to observe your teenager in order to establish SMRs. However, you can make some estimates. For example, if your daughter has begun to grow taller and you can see signs of breast development, she's probably at SMR 3 for breast development and SMR 2 for pubic hair—the periods of the most rapid increases in height. If she has had her first menstrual period, her sexual development is late SMR 3 or SMR 4. If your son has started to become taller, he's at SMR 3. If hair has begun to appear on his extremities, in the armpits, or on his upper lip, or his voice "cracks" when he speaks, he's probably in SMR 4. And if he has gained weight—"filled out"—he is approaching SMR 5.

Incidentally, the age at which boys and girls begin to date is not related solely to hormone levels—although sexual urges and the stage of growth are powerful influences. Other factors are very important, too, including school grades (as

Freshman vs. Senior) and the dating customs in the community or in the teenager's own peer group. Sometimes these social factors can pressure an adolescent into dating when he or she is not yet ready; conversely, these influences can interfere with a teenager's desire to date.

However, even though dating and other aspects of social growth are complex and affected by many factors, parents still find the SMRs useful in helping them anticipate what their teenager may be undergoing. With the SMRs as a guide you'll be better able to counsel your youngster—and you'll be a better overall parent in the process.

CLASSIFICATION OF SEX MATURITY
RATINGS IN BOYS

Rating	Pubic Hair	Penis	Testes
1	None	Preadolescent	Preadolescent
2	Scanty, long, slightly pigmented	Slightly enlarged	Enlarged scrotum, pink, less smooth
3	Darker, curls, small amount	Longer	Larger
4	Adult type but less; curly, coarse	Larger, breadth increases	Larger, scrotum is darker
5	Adult pattern; spreads to inner thighs	Adult	Adult

Adapted from Tanner, J. M.: 1962. *Growth at adolescence,* ed. 2. Oxford: Blackwell Scientific Publications.

CLASSIFICATION OF SEX MATURITY
RATINGS IN GIRLS

Rating	Pubic Hair	Breasts
1	Preadolescent	Preadolescent
2	Scanty, slightly pigmented, straight, on inner part of labia	Breast elevated as small mound
3	Darker, starts to curl, increased amount	Breast and areola enlarged, no separation
4	Coarse, curly, more but less than in an adult	Areola and future nipple form a secondary mound
5	Adult feminine triangle; spreads to inner surface of thighs	Mature; nipple projects, and areola part of general breast shape

Adapted from Tanner, J. M.: 1962. *Growth at adolescence,* ed. 2. Oxford: Blackwell Scientific Publications.

6

PHYSICAL DEVELOPMENT: WHAT'S NORMAL? WHAT'S NOT?

*I*n your own childhood, can you remember wondering what you would look like as an adult? It is a natural curiosity, and as we pointed out in the previous chapter, your own teenager is almost certainly asking himself the same question.

When your adolescent begins to grow rapidly and undergoes changes in physical and sexual characteristics, he will need some reassurance that everything happening to him is quite normal. Unless you or his doctor has explained how adolescent growth—and the rapidity with which it occurs—can vary from one person to the next, he may become anxious from time to time about his own bodily changes. After all, he can only compare himself with his peers if you haven't raised the subject with him.

Thanks in large part to television and the movies, today's early adolescents in particular have an idealized body image—a hoped-for look—of how they'd like to turn out when they're older. These young teenagers often hope they'll have a body similar to that of a particular movie star or athlete or perhaps a nose resembling that of a model in a fashion magazine. As adolescence proceeds and their bodies continue to change, teenagers usually develop a more realistic body image, and in fact most are relatively pleased with themselves physically, although they'll still probably strive for some improvement. For example, due to a cultural emphasis on thinness, girls in particular are often unhappy with the fat they develop during their growth spurt; however, most adjust to this change and avoid putting on excess weight—but in a few cases they adopt potentially dangerous fad diets trying to lose it.

Young adolescents often look to their parents—or their older siblings or relatives—in hopes of gathering clues as to what they themselves will eventually look like. Depending on their point of view, they may perceive this "research" as a source of reassurance or as an ill omen for the future. In any case this entire exercise may be a futile gesture. After all, even though children often resemble their parents, there can be great physical differences within families, thanks to long lines of inheritance.

Even so, any difference that adolescents see between themselves and their parents can become quite significant to them. If they pose any questions about family features and inheritance, take them seriously, even though these inquiries may seem trivial to you.

There can be other "crises" in teenagers' lives as well—sometimes arising when youngsters develop earlier or later than their peers. For example, some early adolescent girls who start pubertal development before their friends are shy about undressing at school or camp, embarrassed to expose their breasts. On the other hand, other girls consider their early breast enlargement to be a sign of superiority. Different teenagers will react in different ways.

There are other facts about breast development worth discussing with your daughter. Let her know, for instance, that it's not unusual for one breast to be larger than the other, especially during the period of early growth. If this asymmetry is significant, however, consult a physician; there are times that marked differences in the two breasts can cause serious psychological harm, and you and your daughter may decide to deal with this problem as soon as possible. Surgery can correct serious asymmetry when a teenage girl is physically mature, although many girls are content with padding if there are only minor differences in breast size.

Other variations involving the breasts can occur, too. For example, about 2 percent of the population has an extra nipple which may first become noticeable at this time. This is usually harmless, although it is sometimes surgically removed for cosmetic reasons.

As with her breast development, your daughter can view the timing of her first menstrual period as a sign of normal adolescent growth or as an indication that something might be wrong. For instance, when a girl is the only one in her group who has not had a period, she may feel excluded, convinced that something is wrong with her. For many girls their first period will occur at about the same age at which their mother began to menstruate; but again, there can be wide variations. If your daughter has not menstruated by age sixteen or seventeen, or she is more than a year older than the age at which her mother started to menstruate, consult a doctor. Although everything is probably normal, there could be problems needing identification and treatment.

A number of other physiological changes can cause concern among teenage girls and their parents. Several months before menses start, glands within the female genital system often secrete a fluid. This substance can range from clear to white in color and from watery to thick (mucoid) in consistency. The amount of fluid can vary, too, from scant to moderate levels. However, don't worry: this phenomenon (called *physiologic leukorrhea*) is quite normal and can persist for several years.

A teenage girl's anxiety level also usually climbs at the time of her first vaginal examination by a doctor. As a general rule this type of exam is particularly appropriate for investigating gynecological symptoms such as vaginal discharge, abnormal bleeding, persistent absence of menstruation, and severe pain with menstrual periods. A young woman who is sexually active should have this examination each year. (See Chapter 32.)

Many girls, however, find that vaginal examinations are embarrassing or even frightening. For them the skill of the examiner is very important in determining whether their experience is pleasant. Talk with other parents to see which doctor(s) they've found to be gentle and considerate during this procedure.

If your daughter's pediatrician has routinely inspected her external genitalia at each general examination during childhood, she'll probably find the more thorough procedure of a pelvic exam less disturbing. Also, you can prepare and reassure your daughter before this exam by letting her know what will take place.

Explain that her doctor will probably begin by asking her some questions (either directly or on a patient history form) about gynecologically related issues, including the significant events of her puberty (the timing of her first period, breast budding, height spurt) and her dating and sexual intercourse experiences. The doctor also will usually perform a thorough physical exam, including inspection of the breasts.

Tell your daughter that as the pelvic exam begins the doctor should show her, one by one, the instruments he's going to use and explain their function. Then, after visual inspection of her genitals, he'll place a speculum in the vagina so he can carefully inspect both the vagina and the cervix and collect laboratory specimens. Your daughter may need reassurance that this exam does not normally affect an intact hymen; nor can the doctor "tell" if she is not a virgin.

Teenage boys don't routinely have to go through anything quite like a pelvic exam, but that doesn't mean they don't have anxieties of their own related to their physical development. Particularly in early adolescence, many boys worry about themselves and what's happening to their bodies. Let's look at some of the common sources of their distress:

During SMR 3 about 40 percent of boys develop a small lump beneath the nipples, sometimes only on one side. This condition (called *gynecomastia* or *male breast development*) usually disappears in about a year, but in the meantime the lump can be slightly tender, and many boys become concerned about it. Some even wonder, "Am I turning into a girl?" In most instances a little reassurance that the condition will go away is all they need. However, on occasion the breasts become much larger, and other children may unmercifully tease these boys. As a result they may not want to go to camp, and they may even refuse to undress in front of their parents. In some cases this breast enlargement doesn't disappear on its own, and a pediatrician's care is needed. He may recommend elective surgery, which can correct this condition. (See Page 300.)

Incidentally, gynecomastia is quite different from the large breasts that very fat boys have. These overweight teenagers have accumulated fat in the upper chest area, not excess breast tissue. For them surgery is not indicated.

Your son's doctor can also reassure him if he's anxious that his two testicles are not the same size. In most males one testicle (usually the left) normally hangs lower than the other. Also, if your youngster's testicles seem *very* small, his doctor should be consulted to be certain there is no abnormality.

Adolescents can encounter other problems too. When teenagers are overweight—or very tall and skinny—they may be heckled by their peers, perhaps leading them to dislike themselves. Overweight (or short) adolescents sometimes become the class clown, hoping the group will accept them. In other cases they may shun peer groups and become loners. Obese girls in particular need reassurance of their worth and boosts to their self-esteem.

In recent years you may have become frustrated trying to help your teenager lose weight, offering constant support and futilely trying to keep her on one weight-loss program or another. Do your best to encourage her, but also make sure she avoids severe reduction programs and fad diets, particularly during her growth period. (See Chapter 29.)

Some healthy weight-loss plans are available, and your teenager's pediatrician can probably recommend one. However, don't expect automatic success with it.

And even if your teenager repeatedly tries to lose weight on one of these sensible diets—only to gain it back again and again—there's a bright side to this disappointing scenario: sometimes adolescents remember the dietary principles they've learned from a physician or a nutritionist, and they'll eventually lose weight during their young adult life, when their persistence and motivation are greater.

Now, what about an adolescent boy who's tall and very thin? How do you deal with his anxieties? More than anything, reassure him that he'll almost certainly gain weight as he becomes older. Some nutritional counseling can be helpful, too. Also, encourage him to take part in activities in which his height and weight are not a handicap; basketball, for instance, has helped many tall boys overcome their feelings of being different.

There's something else you should communicate to your tall boys: make sure they understand that their muscles will develop and that they will become physically stronger in SMR 4 and SMR 5; until then, they should avoid overexerting themselves. Basketball coaches and eager fathers must remember this as well: don't "burn out" a tall player by expecting too much before his body and his muscles are strong enough to deliver.

Let's finish this chapter with one other common concern of male adolescents—namely, penis size. Not only do most boys frequently think about this, but some parents even bring up the subject with physicians. As for the boys themselves, they may covertly or overtly compare their own penis size with those of their friends. The boys with small penises are often the butt of jokes and remarks from their male peers. Most boys don't realize, however, that the size of another boy's flaccid penis may be a poor indication of how large it is when erect. Also, the sexual functioning of a male is not dependent on his penile size. So tell your son there's no need to be concerned about the size of his penis.

7

WHEN PUBERTY COMES TOO SOON . . . OR TOO LATE

"*I* don't know what I'm going to do," said a six-foot-tall thirteen-year-old boy. "All of my friends are just little kids, and I don't fit in. We can't even play together, because I'm so big. I try to hang around with older guys, but then we get in a car and go places and they want to do things I'm not ready to do. So I don't fit in with them either."

Has your teenager reached puberty long before most of his peers? Or has he shown none of the usual changes of adolescence, while his friends are well along in their own development?

Children of both sexes who fall into either of these developmental extremes are often quite anxious about their growth—or lack of it—and so are their parents. In general early developers are usually happier and more self-confident than their slower-developing peers. But while entering puberty too soon or too late may be nothing more than a reflection of normal genetic programming, it does occasionally indicate a serious organic problem. Whatever the cause, early or late puberty can produce problems that tax the patience and the parenting abilities of mothers and fathers.

PRECOCIOUS
OR EARLY PUBERTY

True "precocious puberty" is very rare. When it does occur, it's almost always due to an abnormality of one or more of the major glands producing the hormones that bring about increased maturity, particularly of the reproductive system. This type of precociousness is usually apparent during very early childhood, and it requires skilled medical diagnosis and treatment.

More often a child will begin puberty much younger than expected, but without any abnormality being present. Girls, for instance, may develop breast buds or have small quantities of pubic hair when they're only seven or eight years old; they might also begin their height spurt as young as nine-and-a-half years of age or start to menstruate when they're ten. Yes, this early maturation occurs infrequently, but it's still not necessarily a sign that anything is wrong.

Since boys develop later than girls, their testicular enlargement and pubic hair can first appear at age ten years, with their height spurt starting about six months later. Even though this is much earlier than average, it's still considered normal. Nevertheless, if your own son or daughter shows signs of puberty at a very young age (usually defined as under eight to eight-and-a-half years in females and under nine-and-a-half to ten years in males), have your family's pediatrician evaluate his or her stage of growth to be certain no real problems exist. Such problems, although uncommon, occur more often in males than females.

The velocity of change in these youngsters can also be dramatic, creating concern among both children and parents. Although most teenagers need several years to complete adolescent growth, some proceed through it in unbelievably short time. When this development occurs extremely rapidly, there can be some potential dangers, primarily related to the youngster's psychological adjustment to his growth patterns.

Early maturers, for instance, know they're different from their peers, particularly if they ever find themselves excluded from group activities. However, their physical characteristics can be a positive influence too: as the tallest and most mature member of the group, they might assume a leadership role, sending their self-esteem soaring. These adolescents in fact are often the "kings" and "queens" of the class because they're bigger, because they can impose their views, and because smaller children frequently admire them. Even so, this superiority doesn't last; the early maturer who is outstanding in sports in the seventh grade, for instance, usually doesn't continue in this "star" status in high school. When his friends catch up with (and sometimes surpass) him, he may find it very difficult to share or relinquish the leadership role he may have assumed.

In the meantime these youngsters usually need a lot of support and understanding in helping them cope with their early puberty, particularly if they feel there's something wrong with them. (This feeling of "being different" is much more common in girls than boys, since boys tend to be proud of being bigger, being stronger, and having more mature sexual characteristics than their male friends.) Adolescents who feel self-conscious will be much better adjusted once they accept the fact that they're really normal and that their friends will eventually reach their stage of development, too—that it's just a matter of time. Until that happens, counseling can sometimes help if the youngster is having adjustment problems.

One other point: when teenagers of both sexes mature very young, they're often vulnerable to sexual abuse by older adolescents or adults. Why are these girls and boys at particularly high risk? In almost all cases they haven't developed the thinking skills and the moral code to protect themselves, and thus they're often easily seduced by friends or relatives. In this situation the danger of pregnancy is very high. As one mother succinctly put it, "Doctor, I think her body got ahead of her mind."

DELAYED PUBERTY

Is your child still waiting for puberty to begin while his friends are well into their own growth spurts? This delayed puberty can occur in both boys and girls, although more boys seem to experience it—and undergo the adjustment difficulties that can accompany it. The further behind their development is, the more stress and anxiety they'll have.

And when do pediatricians consider puberty delayed? Not all doctors agree, but in general the following adolescents fall into this category: a girl whose breast buds have not appeared by age thirteen and a boy whose testicular enlargement has not occurred by age thirteen-and-a-half. Almost always there's nothing abnormal going on with these youngsters, and they'll eventually begin to grow.

Unfortunately, we don't know why there is a delay in a particular adolescent's puberty, but heredity appears to play the most important role. Although certain illnesses can delay the growth spurt, too, they occur only rarely. Even so, consult your family pediatrician if you or your child is worried.

When examining your teenager for possible delayed puberty, the doctor will perform a general examination to eliminate possible organic causes. Usually she will also order some X rays to determine bone age. If the doctor can find no demonstrable cause for the delay—and your adolescent's bone age is less than his chronological age but still appropriate for his height—then everything is probably normal, and more time will usually resolve the concern. However, a doctor also will be able to detect an actual problem if one should exist in a particular case.

Your teenager's pediatrician may want to repeat his evaluation every few months, but in the meantime some reassurance is the best medicine for your youngster. Help him choose activities based on his abilities and *not* on trying to keep up with his more mature peers. Instead of pushing him into football, for example, steer him into swimming, running, art, or music. When he eventually catches up with his peers at a later age, he can compete in other areas too if he has the desire and ability.

Interestingly, when a physician examines fourteen- and fifteen-year-old boys for delayed puberty, he often finds evidence that some very early but subtle changes have, in fact, occurred. For these youngsters, if there's no sign of disease and their bone age is less than their chronological age, the physician may prescribe a series of male sex hormone injections, once a month for about three months. This treatment will speed up pubic hair and genital growth. After the injections the testes will become larger and provide sufficient hormones to ensure continued development.

These injections also often produce dramatic emotional changes in the boys who receive them. Even if a youngster is still short compared to his peers, the presence of more mature pubic hair and genitalia is evidence of his adolescent maleness. That's usually enough to give his ego and self-esteem a real boost. Even so, doctors tend to reserve this treatment only for boys right on the brink of puberty who are at least fourteen years old.

Now, what about girls who experience delayed puberty? They too may feel isolated, although they usually adjust better than boys, perhaps because most girls start the growth spurt sooner than males and a girl with delayed puberty can still fit in with the boys and other small girls at school. Also, adults and most peers don't regard short girls in the same negative way they do short boys.

However, as with boys, a girl with delayed puberty should see her pediatrician to exclude physical conditions or diseases that could affect growth. If her bone age is less than her chronological age, then her doctor may simply reassure her that she'll begin growing soon. He may also remind her that the delayed onset of menstruation is usually not serious; in general she has no need to worry.

STATURE PROBLEMS: WHAT CAN BE DONE?

As much as a teenage boy would like to grow to be six feet tall, it's generally out of his (or anyone else's) control. Because stature is almost always regulated by heredity, short parents usually have short children, and tall parents usually produce tall children. That's just the way genetics work. When one spouse is tall and the other is short, they may have children of varying sizes—and if their son is shorter than their daughter, he'll probably be quite unhappy until he adjusts to this reality.

Some genetic conditions—sickle-cell disease, for example, which is a hereditary blood illness—can affect a child's height, particularly in males. Severe nutritional deprivation and certain illnesses (uncontrolled diabetes mellitus, inflammatory bowel disease, Turner's syndrome, chronic infections) can also contribute to short stature, but these conditions are unusual. Again, more than anything else, heredity determines how tall each of us will be. Helping your children accept themselves for what they are is very important.

Is there a treatment for true growth disorders? Sometimes. For many years doctors have administered growth hormone to treat children whose pituitary gland is impaired, holding back their growth. In fact this hormone has recently become more widely available with new technology that can produce the substance in the laboratory, eliminating the need to obtain it from the glands of humans. As a result many parents are beginning to ask if doctors can also use it to promote additional growth in a normal, healthy child. For example can a healthy, five-foot six-inch boy take the hormone and grow to be five feet ten inches tall?

At present almost no physician is recommending this type of therapy. Researchers don't yet know the long-term results of such treatment. Studies are continuing, but we haven't enough evidence thus far to say conclusively that using growth hormone in normal children is safe and effective.

Ironically, for every short child who wishes to be taller there's often a tall one who wants to be shorter. Particularly in the past, very tall girls were often unhappy with their stature, and their parents became even more concerned. Today, however, tall girls are more readily accepted, and in fact they're often admired and envied. The popularity of women's sports (such as basketball and volleyball) has helped in this regard.

Even so, doctors still sometimes try to limit height increases, most often in young, extremely tall girls. This therapy usually consists of injections of certain types of hormones. However, because the major growth spurt in girls has already occurred by the time menstruation begins, efforts to decrease their predicted growth must be made early, well before menarche. Doctors use this therapy less often than in the past, but if you're interested in finding out more about it, contact a pediatric endocrinologist.

Whether your teenagers are tall or short, you need to build up their self-confidence and help them accept themselves. Point to examples of successful tall or short adults who can be an inspiration to them. And even if they don't like their height, remind them of their other admirable qualities that they can appreciate.

ADJUSTING TO CHANGE

As difficult as adolescent growth can sometimes be, all teenagers somehow endure the experience, hopefully with a minimum of psychological scars. Let's review some of what we've discussed in this part of the book and what you can expect during your child's teenage years.

Early adolescents (eleven to fourteen years of age) are going through the main changes of puberty. These teenagers begin their growth spurt with an idealized body image and a vision of what they hope they'll become. They are beginning to separate themselves from their parents and want to be accepted by peers. Most wonder if the changes in their bodies are normal, since they fear being rejected if they're perceived as different by others.

Middle adolescents (about fifteen to seventeen years of age) are usually past the peak of physical growth. As they develop the ability to think abstractly, plan, compare, and appreciate the future, they tend to accept a realistic body image of themselves. This self-perception gives them stability, and although there may be parts of their body they're unhappy with, they're often able to adjust to them and direct their interests away from themselves toward the outer world. However, if they've experienced delayed puberty or major problems with stature, they may have persistent body image problems, and their psychosocial development may be impaired.

By late adolescence (seventeen to twenty years of age) these youngsters have made additional adjustments. They've accumulated some life experiences and are recognizing the need to prepare for the responsibilities of adulthood. Without doubt the future is assuming greater importance in their lives. For most of these teenagers physical growth is no longer a priority, and they've come to know who they are.

As a parent your task is to help your children pass through adolescence with a minimum of psychological and physical trauma. You need to help ensure that they have the best opportunity to grow physically, cognitively, and psychosocially.

Many children are born with or develop minor or major handicaps in their lives, creating a series of detours in their developmental progress toward adulthood.

Some seriously handicapped adolescents—because of either birth defects or accidents—find it difficult and almost impossible to become independent and self-reliant or to accept their bodies. However, as one teenager said, "Each of us is given only one body. Sometimes it may seem like the wrong body, but it's the only one we have. And we can do a lot with it if we choose to."

Every adolescent—able-bodied or handicapped, short or tall—must learn to care for her body, to work hard at maintaining good health, and to appreciate herself as she is. As a parent you can encourage your teenager to do just that.

PART III

YOUR TEENAGER'S PSYCHOLOGICAL GROWTH AND DEVELOPMENT

8

A DIFFICULT AND
EXCITING TIME

*T*he teenage years are a complex, challenging time—not only for the youngsters themselves but for the rest of the family too. Like it or not, your son or daughter is going through an enormous—but still normal—transition process. Your adolescent is leaving childhood behind and becoming an adult. He is moving from a period of dependence to one of greater autonomy and self-reliance.

At times this life passage will seem to proceed with little difficulty and in fact will often be enjoyable for both you and your youngster. Inevitably, however, there will also be some very turbulent periods of indecision and anxiety, conflict and rebellion. Without a doubt, this can be the most difficult time in a child's life, which makes it an arduous time for parents as well.

In Chapter 1 of this book we discussed many of the changes you can expect in your teenager and in your family during this period and how to cope with them effectively. In this section we'll look at some of these issues in more depth. If you're like most parents, you'll probably welcome all the guidance that's available, not only to help you ease your child through this time but also so you can deal better with your own stresses.

First, keep in mind that each teenager is different. Just as children vary in their rate of physical development, there is some variation in their psychological growth as well. Even so, most teenagers do proceed through some normal developmental stages.

Usually in early adolescence, for example, cognitive capabilities expand and thinking eventually becomes more adultlike. Teenagers begin to analyze the world around them and start to compare and contrast their values with others they hear from friends, at school, and through the media. As a result they may raise questions about your beliefs, become critical of the household rules you've instituted, and challenge your authority from time to time. It's all very normal and part of the maturing process. However, keep in mind that while they're rebelling, it's your responsibility to set some appropriate limits.

Just when you're getting used to coping with these kinds of behaviors, middle adolescence arrives—with quite different challenges. During this period your teenager is more likely to ignore than to defy you. He'll probably become much more reliant on his peers than ever before and spend more time away from home. He also may begin testing the waters in a number of areas—perhaps experimenting with sexuality for the first time, seeing what alcohol and drugs are all about, and trying out new styles of dress. This might be a very frightening period for you.

Finally, in late adolescence, some semblance of sanity may seem to return to the family. Not only do teenagers become more tolerant of Mom and Dad during this time, but they actually return to many of their parents' values and views. They also may start thinking more seriously about their future in terms of careers and lasting relationships. It's a stabilizing time on the brink of adulthood!

Does the knowledge that the difficult periods of adolescence are quite normal and will eventually pass make these times any easier? Probably not much. As you may have already begun to discover, it's just not always easy to cope when teenagers assert their independence and individuality, even though you know it's a necessary step toward adulthood. After all, not too many years ago this was the child who idolized you, who depended on you for comfort and security, who believed you could do no wrong. But then almost overnight he did an about-face. He suddenly saw you as just an ordinary person, a fallible human being. And he may have started telling himself, "Yes, I love my mom—but I also sometimes hate my mom."

During much of your child's adolescence you can expect him to often instinctively say yes whenever you say no. At times he may want nothing more than for you to "leave me alone" (except, of course, when it comes to doing his laundry or giving him spending money). He may loathe the mere thought of being seen with you in public and instead rely on his peers for companionship and comfort. In short, many parents say their teenagers drive them absolutely crazy.

In response to this turmoil you may sometimes behave as erratically as your teenager: one moment you may overprotect him; the next you may want nothing to do with him. You'll find yourself on your own emotional roller coaster, with your parental love sometimes challenged by anger, suspicion, frustration, and mistrust.

Through it all, keep in mind that this oppositional behavior is an important step in your child's establishing himself as an independent, self-reliant adult. It doesn't mean that he's a problem child or that you're a poor parent. Instead his questioning and challenging of values will speed along his own moral development. While as a child he equated right and wrong with rewards and punishment, he's now evolving toward an understanding that right and wrong mean adhering to standards. Eventually he'll do what's right, just because it's the right thing to do.

ADJUSTING TO YOUR CHANGING ADOLESCENT

As we've already suggested, living through your child's adolescence is not always easy. Many parents actually find themselves "mourning" the loss of their child as they adjust to the moody, obstinate person who has taken his place; at the same time, they're reminded of their own aging process and mortality. Meanwhile, their teenagers also may be mourning the loss of their own childhood and family relationships of earlier years.

However, it's important to keep the situation in perspective. As difficult as adolescence may be, it's an essential "rite of passage." You went through it, and so did every other adult. Think back to your own teenage years: How did you rebel? What were your clothes like? Did your parents complain about the music you listened to? In short, were your experiences, attitudes, and relationships really that much different from what's taking place with your own adolescent?

Probably not. This is the time when young people must establish an identity of their own, separate themselves from their parents, and create significant relationships outside of their own families. One of your major tasks is to let your teenager do just that: *to let him grow up.* The self-doubts and difficult experiences of this time of life are inevitable. He needs to learn independence. He needs to begin to find out what adulthood is like. So let him start to make some of the decisions that affect his own life.

Yes, as we've already suggested, you'll need to set some limits. However, within those boundaries you must leave some room for him to spread his wings and get a sense of who he is and who he wants to become. He may reject some excellent advice from you along the way—but that's part of growing up. Fortunately, many of the values you instilled in him prior to adolescence will survive, and they'll probably become part of his belief system as he enters adulthood.

In the meantime, as your teenager asserts himself some changes in the family will inevitably occur. However, even during the most stressful times, don't neglect some basic precepts that can keep the family functioning as smoothly as possible. For instance:

- Continue to listen to one another, even when you're on different sides of the fence.

- Don't confuse the *thing* that bothers you with the *person* who has done it. Yes, at times you'll feel annoyed, angry, even hateful toward your teenager's *behavior.* Every parent does. It's quite normal, but it's certainly no sign that you've stopped loving your youngster. In fact it probably means exactly the opposite—that you care and that you're certainly not indifferent to what's going on in his life. But keep your anger focused on his *actions,* not on him as a human being.

- Avoid constant criticism, no matter how much your teenager's behavior or appearance annoys you. Let the insignificant incidents slide by. As for the bigger issues, let him know that although you disagree, you respect his right to hold a different opinion. And look for times in which you can honestly pay him a compliment.

- Take an interest in what he's doing. When disagreements arise, try to find a compromise that both sides can accept; at worst, you should agree to disagree, at least acknowledging where each of you stands—and why.

- Don't preach and don't nag. Try to keep your dialogue at rational, conversational levels. And be careful about saying things like, "When I was your age . . ."; you probably had more in common with your teenager than you'd care to admit.

As desperately as teenagers may try to "keep their act together," they won't always be able to do so. This is a confusing time for them, with values and goals being defined and redefined. It's also a period in which extreme mood swings are quite normal—not only due to hormonal changes but also in response to the anxieties so common during this time of life. This is a stage when they will make mistakes—but hopefully they will learn from them.

Also, as a parent, be prepared to become your youngster's favorite target of blame—the one who's responsible for all his difficulties, the one who's keeping him from growing up, from having fun, from fitting in with the rest of the kids. And if you are divorced and your child has limited contact with his other parent, you may bear the brunt of his anger toward *both* you and your ex-spouse.

Don't take most of this criticism to heart, however. *And don't give up on your teenager.* So often the parents of adolescents decide, "Nothing I say seems to sink in; I've lost control of my kid." But don't despair. You're the adult with more experience; your child is still growing. So keep trying. Teenagers are watching, listening, and learning more than you may think! The reality is that most young people come through adolescence with few lasting scars. After several years of struggle they actually do get back on track.

By late adolescence your teenager will probably feel much more comfortable spending time with you—and time at home. If you've treated him fairly and consistently, if you've given him room to grow, and if you've continued to give him love (even during the difficult times), he'll probably leave adolescence and enter adulthood with family ties intact.

Of course it's natural for parents to worry a lot. There's nothing unusual about that. However, try not to overreact. You've been a guiding force for your child since birth, and even when the strains of adolescence are at their greatest your influence isn't going to end—if you continue to be an active, caring parent. To love someone means that you continue to give him emotional support, whether times are good or bad, positive or negative.

9

CONQUERING COMMUNICATION PROBLEMS

*H*ow well do you communicate with your teenager? If you're like many other parents, you might answer that question by lamenting, "I just can't get through to her." Or perhaps, "Sometimes I feel like we're speaking a different language; she doesn't seem to understand a word I'm saying."

Not surprisingly, many adolescents may feel exactly the same way. In response to a question about how well they communicate with their parents, their answers will often be something like these: "No matter what I say, he doesn't seem to get the picture," or "I can't get my mom to really listen to how I'm feeling," or "I don't even try to talk to my parents anymore."

This estrangement between the generations is really nothing new. In fact it has probably existed since the beginning of time. Communication has never been easy, whether between husband and wife, employer and employee, or parent and child. During the critical teenage years, however, it can become particularly complex for the family.

Face it: adolescents are often hard to live with and even harder to talk to. Sometimes they'll become so argumentative that discussions can deteriorate into little more than a shouting match. Or as one mother said, "If I'm lucky, he'll answer my questions with a grunt. If he's feeling even less communicative, he won't say anything at all."

From the teenager's point of view the situation is just as exasperating. "My mother doesn't want to talk with me; she wants to lecture me," said one teenage boy. "I'm afraid to tell her anything, because when I do she always finds a way to criticize me."

Brimming with frustration, both parent and adolescent often stop even trying to communicate. A mother may quit asking her teenage son what's going on in school. He may stop telling her about his problems. She may no longer inquire about his friends. He may stop telling her where he's going and when he'll be home. Over time the wall between them becomes almost impenetrable.

In your own family, no matter how well—or how poorly—you and your adolescent are presently communicating, it's essential that you try to make things better. Not only can open channels of communication make the teenage years more enjoyable for the entire family, but they will make it easier for you to exert a positive influence on your adolescent's development.

BREAKING DOWN THE BARRIERS

"I don't think my daughter wants to talk to me. She seems quite content not saying much at all."

At times it may seem as though your teenager has no interest in sharing anything about her life. Ask her a question about her boyfriend—"Where are you and Tom going tonight?"—and she's liable to respond as though you were prying into the most personal secrets of her life.

Even so, don't give up. Despite her resistance to share parts of her life with you, teenagers *do* have a need to communicate with their parents. As much as they may deny it, the family that they've grown up with will remain important—and a significant source of support and comfort—throughout adolescence and adulthood. Yes, there may be times when they want to be left alone and certain things that they want to keep private. But that doesn't mean that they no longer need your nurturing and guidance. They want to know that you still care and that you'll be available when they seek help. They also need your acceptance of their inevitable mistakes and errors of judgment, which are part of the human learning process.

With experience you'll learn which subjects your adolescent is willing to talk about and which ones she considers off-limits. Sex is often one of the most difficult topics to broach; in many families teenagers consider it too personal to discuss whether or not they're sexually active. Be willing to honor those wishes—but without giving up on communication altogether. Yes, discussions of the details of her sexual life may be taboo, but you can still communicate about many other things—what's going on at school, drug use among her peers, or the party she wants to go to on the weekend. And remember, your own views on sexuality are well known to her through many years of parent–child communication.

At times your conversations with your teenager need not be more than small talk; but also look for opportunities to discuss feelings, emotions, responsibility, behaviors, and concepts of right and wrong. Keep in mind that, particularly in early adolescence, your child will be much more receptive to conversations about the "here and now" than to those that require "futuristic" thinking. For example, it's hard reasoning with a fourteen-year-old girl who smokes cigarettes, persuading her that if she doesn't quit she may develop lung cancer or emphysema twenty, thirty, or forty years from now. In much the same way, sexually active teenage girls often have difficulty acknowledging that if they don't use contraceptives today, they may give birth to a live human being nine months from now. It's also often futile to tell a teenager, "If you don't study harder and get a good education, you're not going to get the kind of job you want as an adult." Unfortunately, teenagers—particularly in early adolescence—frequently just can't project into the future or see the link between cause and effect.

Now, what about those moments when your teenager absolutely refuses to talk? Don't take it personally. A lot of her reluctance is probably a part of normal adolescent rebelliousness or her natural need for independence. She may be lashing out at all authority figures in her life, and you're the most convenient target. Or she may just wish to have privacy after a stressful day. Just let her know that you'll always be there when she wants to communicate.

IDENTIFYING YOUR OWN ANXIETIES

Not only is this a difficult transition time for your adolescent, but it's also a complicated time for parents. Some mothers and fathers find it difficult acknowledging that their son or daughter is growing up, that he or she isn't the little child who has been so dependent on them for the past dozen years or more. It's hard dealing with the reality of a child maturing and leaving the nest.

There are other stresses as well. Some parents become angry over specific behavior of their adolescent. When teenagers say they have little interest in spending any time with the rest of the family, that can leave parents indignant. The same can happen when teenagers appear to reject parental values, seem to take the material comforts of their life for granted, and constantly ask for more. When parents believe they have made sacrifices and repressed some of their own desires to make a better life for their family, a seemingly ungrateful teenager can leave them exasperated.

On occasion parents even recognize in themselves some jealousy toward their teenager. This is a transition time for you just as it is for your teenager. As we've discussed earlier in the book, the mid-thirties to mid-forties are often a period when adults question their own ability to reach their personal goals and their satisfaction with life. At the same time, they may notice a loss of energy and youthful vigor and their belief in an indefinite future. If you're dissatisfied with your own life, you may be excessively demanding of your teenager, in the hope that she doesn't make the same "mistakes." Or you may find that you're jealous of what your teenager has in appearance, physical stamina, or seemingly limitless opportunities.

It's not unusual to have anxieties like these. However, they unmistakably can interfere with a fruitful parent–child relationship. They can create a "cold war" in the household that makes communication almost impossible.

To avoid troublesome communication, ask yourself the following questions:

- Do your conversations include statements that are critical of your adolescent? When that happens, you place your teenager in a combative posture and decrease the chances that you'll make any real progress by talking. Criticism tends to create anger and resentment in teenagers, as well as instilling doubts about their own self-worth. For that reason, avoid starting the dialogue with a negative statement such as, "I'm sick and tired of the way you're behaving, and it's time we talked about it!" Throughout the conversation, be honest without being overcritical. Make a conscious effort to be positive in your communication with your teenager. And remember to criticize the behavior, not the person.

- Do you give lengthy lectures that leave your adolescent little or no chance to respond? Good communication requires a *dialogue,* and youngsters should feel they've had an opportunity to express their own point of view, even if you can't agree with it. Don't reject what teenagers are saying outright without giving them a fair hearing. Demonstrate concern, but don't preach.

- Do you sometimes shout in the heat of a disagreement with your youngster? Yelling tends to interfere with any serious give-and-take. You need to become aware of improvements needed in your own communication skills. Tone down the decibel level, and you'll probably accomplish much more.

- Do you insist on talking to your teenager only when *you're* ready to do so, not considering what she's involved in at the moment? Reevaluate your timing if you sometimes get responses like, "Dad, this isn't a good time to talk; I'm right in the middle of studying for tomorrow's history test."

If too many of these scenarios sound familiar, you may share some of the responsibility in any breakdown of communication within the family.

MAKING THE MOST OF COMMUNICATION

Are you making a sincere effort to discover what's on your teenager's mind? Are you willing to invest the time to find out what she's thinking?

You can't realistically expect to resolve the difficult issues in your lives quickly. Thus you should set aside enough time to deal with the issues at hand—whether it takes fifteen minutes or two hours. Remove all distractions, including the television and the telephone. Give your adolescent all of your attention.

If you try to cut the conversation short, the message is that it's your teenager whom you're cutting short. Instead, show her that she's a top priority in your life and that the evening news or an important business call can wait (or that you can postpone a volunteer activity too—perhaps dealing with other children and teenagers).

Also, as we've suggested earlier, commit yourself to *really* listening to everything your teenager has on her mind. Don't say you'll listen but then fail to maintain eye contact. Give your teenager your full attention, sit facing her, and don't let other things distract you. She can misinterpret your inattentiveness as a rejection of her. Also, be sensitive not only to her words but to her nonverbal cues and her emotions as well. Keep an open ear, not allowing preconceived notions to interfere with what you're hearing.

Here are some other communication guidelines:

- In your effort to understand your teenager's point of view, ask questions and try to see why she feels the way she does. In return, ask her to be patient as you express your own thoughts.

- Choose your words carefully so you're not misunderstood. Teenagers will search for all possible "loopholes" in your rules; they're not "bad" for doing so, but it does require that you become quite precise in what you tell them. If you want your daughter home from her after-school meeting by five o'clock, you're better off with a specific message such as "Be home by five" than with a more general "Make sure you're home before dark." The former message is much less subject to confusion. Also, have a good reason why you've chosen five o'clock and explain it to her.

- Find as many situations as possible in which you can give praise and approval to your teenager. Make sure she knows that you take pride in her academic and extracurricular achievements, but *most importantly* in her as a human being. Even during their most rebellious moments teenagers usually worry about disappointing their parents or making them angry; all of this is tied to their fear of losing their parents' love. As a result they do much of their natural experimentation secretively so as not to alienate their family members, who have always been there for them.

- Speak to your teenager as an equal, as someone with opinions you value. Don't use condescending language.

- Be sensitive to the tone of voice and the communication style you're using. Are you aggressive, assertive, or passive? What's your body posture? Sometimes these can convey a more powerful message than the words you use.

- Don't pretend you know all the answers. And when you're wrong, admit it. Don't be afraid to apologize if you make a mistake. You won't lose your stature as a parent and an authority figure by doing so; in fact it will probably be enhanced.

- Not only should you set some fair rules and appropriate limits, but be *consistent* in enforcing them. (In the next chapter we'll describe effective ways of doing this.)

Finally, never lose sight of who this teenager is. Yes, sometimes you may feel as though the child you raised has been kidnapped and replaced overnight by an unfamiliar person whose attire, actions, and attitude may be totally foreign to you. In reality, however, this is still your youngster and still someone you love. It may be hard to feel affectionate when she's being testy and ill-tempered. But even during the most difficult times it's important that you preserve the relationship. Tell your teenager that you really care. Make body contact; touch her. Give her a hug if she'll let you. And continue to make the extra effort to keep the communication flowing—even when you feel *she's* not making an effort.

FOR SOME EXTRA HELP . . .

Most families can benefit from some additional help in breaking down communication barriers. An exercise such as the following one can smooth out some of the problem areas. It can help family members become more skillful in saying what each of you wants to say and in understanding what others are really feeling.

To get the most out of this exercise, the entire family should agree to set aside an hour. Use the questions and statements below to get the process started. Each of you should write down your answers and then read them aloud. Your responses should be honest and should serve as a springboard to discussion. Not only will you convey some important information to one another, but the experience can be an enjoyable sharing time for the entire family.

1. Write down five things you like most about your family. Then write down five things you like least.

2. Finish this sentence: "I wish people in this family would pay more attention when I _____."

3. Complete this sentence: "If someone were coming to live with our family for a month, I'd make sure that he or she knew in advance that _____."

Sometimes you'll have a specific area of conflict that needs to be resolved. It will usually start with a complaint by one person ("You're never home!"). In a case like this there are some concrete guidelines to follow that can help you reach a solution with minimal difficulty. Keep these suggestions in mind while *problem-solving:*

- Set up a particular time and place for your session together. Make sure there will be no interruptions and that one person or the other won't have to leave early. A good time: in the evening when no one has appointments.

- Limit the time and keep it to one topic—for example, thirty minutes on the subject of curfew rules.

- Don't try to problem-solve in the heat of anger.

- Make sure that everyone agrees that problem solving is not a power struggle, where someone wins and someone loses.

- As we suggested earlier, always begin with something positive when stating a problem. For example: "You have been very responsible about letting me know where you're going, but I worry when you don't come home on time." Compare that to a negative opening such as, "You were thirty minutes past curfew!" By being positive you'll remind the other person that you care and that you are aware of his responsible behaviors, despite the existence of a problem.

- Be specific. This is very important but often easy to ignore. Being specific means "Three times this week you were out past curfew." That's much better than "You never come home on time."

- Avoid using overgeneralizations such as "always" or "never."

- Express your feelings: "I become upset when you leave your clothes on the floor." Don't guess about what the other person is feeling; let her tell you what she's experiencing.

- When appropriate, admit your part in the problem: "I do take your sister's side in an argument most of the time, and I'll try to be more fair from now on. But I'd like you *not* to hit your sister."

- Try not to focus on past events or bring up other problem behaviors. Again, discuss only one problem at a time.

- Paraphrase back what the other person has said to see if you're really understanding one another. Don't guess what she is feeling—find out!

- *Focus on solutions.*

- Final solutions should be specific and put in writing. Use a notebook to record agreements and the issues that you've resolved. This will prevent conflicting memories of both the session and the resolution.

No matter how much effort families put into improving their communication skills, they sometimes can't break through the stubborn barriers that may have created problems for years. When that's the case, ask your teenager's pediatrician for help. Particularly if there's a specific issue that the family is having trouble with, your doctor may be able to sit down with everyone and get the dialogue moving in a positive direction. Although you may think of a pediatrician as someone who deals only with physical problems, she also can provide guidance and information relative to most other areas of your teenager's life. If necessary, your doctor can also refer your family to appropriate counseling services in your community to improve communication patterns.

10

WHEN YOUR TEENAGER NEEDS DISCIPLINE

*A*t one time or another most teenagers hear that their adolescent years are the best of their lives. Many parents, however, can hardly wait for this period to be over.

After all, it's not always easy living with someone who often treats household rules with contempt, who argues incessantly, and who sometimes seems to take pleasure in procrastination and temper tantrums. If you say yes, your adolescent invariably says no. If you prefer a clean house, he'll keep his room dirty. And when he stays out beyond his curfew, cuts classes, or uses offensive language, you may start counting the days until his adolescence is finally over.

As unwelcome as some of your teenager's behavior may be, keep in mind what we've said earlier: this is a normal transition period in which adolescents are moving from childhood to adulthood, asserting their individuality, and forming an adult identity. Of course there are varying degrees of "normal"; some teenagers rebel in a "quieter" way than others and don't cause their parents much grief. No matter how they go about declaring their independence, however, some form of rebellion is a necessary part of growing up and a normal developmental stage.

Even though parents anticipate some teenage misconduct, many deal with it rather poorly. For example, some mothers and fathers *overreact* to what they perceive as unacceptable behavior by their teenager. They may confront the adolescent about his every "shortcoming," no matter how trivial. If his haircut is a little unusual or his stereo is too loud, if he whiles away an afternoon by staring into space or complains that the family car isn't new enough, that can make some parents furious and prompt new and stricter rules—before they've really evaluated his *total* behavior, comparing it with a few aberrations.

By contrast, other parents react quite differently—but still inappropriately. For them any "failing" by their adolescent is perceived as a weakness in their own parenting skills. If they've always fantasized about raising the "perfect" child, their youngster's misbehavior is "proof" that they've fallen short in some way. Feeling guilty if their adolescent has problems, they may react by overprotecting him, forcing the child into continued dependence on Mom and Dad and postponing the inevitable growing pains of adolescence.

But there are other options available. Ideally you should be constantly searching for a happy medium between rejecting and overprotecting. Your teenager is going through a difficult time of life. It's natural for him to be rebellious. He'll make some mistakes along the way, and so will you. But while you still need to exercise some discipline and control over him, don't lose sight of the fact that eventually you'll have to set him free to face life on his own. Thus, under your watchful eye, he needs some space to get a sense of what adulthood is like and to begin making decisions for himself.

SETTING SOME LIMITS

"Where are you going?"
  "Out."
  "Who are you going with?"
  "Friends."
  "When will you be back?"
  "Later."

Most parents have had conversations like this one with their teenager. Not much information is conveyed, and Mom and Dad feel frustrated when it's over. They haven't found out much about their teenager's activities—what he'll be doing and when to expect him home.

Of course it's not easy to impose rules on your children. Some parents are afraid of hurting their youngster's feelings if they enforce too many restrictions. Many fall victim to their teenager's pleading, "Nobody else's parents impose a midnight curfew."

Limits are necessary, however. Yes, everyone can appreciate how important it is for teenagers to fit in with the rest of the kids and to be able to do much of what their friends are doing. But don't ignore the fact that your teenager is still your legal responsibility until he reaches eighteen—and if he's like most other adolescents, he may not always use the best judgment when it comes to his own well-being. Teenagers often act impulsively, and their "magical thinking" tends to deny that anything bad is going to happen to them.

The responsibility, then, is largely on your shoulders. If you don't feel it's right for your fifteen-year-old to be out past ten o'clock, or if you don't want him spending time with a particular group of friends, you have the right and the responsibility to assert your authority. Select the issues that are important to you and take a stand on them.

Perhaps it's true that your son or daughter has friends with later curfews than you allow. But that doesn't mean that you're wrong—or that they are. Your way of raising your children—as long as it's consistent and loving—is the best way for your family; there are no right or wrong approaches that apply to everyone.

In the process of setting limits, however, don't lose sight of the importance of maintaining mutual respect between the generations. Talk over the areas of disagreement with your youngsters, be attentive to their point of view, and explain (without yelling or preaching) why you feel as strongly as you do. Also make it clear when negotiation is (or isn't) possible on the particular issue at hand; teenagers will become angry if they feel tricked or manipulated into thinking they have more influence over a decision than they really do.

Be sure you've explained your judgments clearly—for example, "I think it is too dangerous for someone your age to be out past ten o'clock without adult supervision. I love you and worry about your safety." Allow your adolescent to vent his frustrations that "you're treating me like a baby." In the end, if you can't reach an acceptable compromise, the final decision is yours. He may not like every rule, but until he's eighteen, making the decision belongs on your shoulders.

When a rule is put in place, make sure your teenager understands clearly *why* you've imposed it. Some parents believe it's unnecessary to give these kinds of explanations ("Do it because I said so—that's why!"). But, in fact, when adolescents understand the reasons behind the rules, they are much more likely to abide by them. This also requires you to carefully think out the rules and have reasons for them!

For some rules—the really important ones—let your adolescent know that you'll allow no flexibility. For example, if you disapprove of his going to parties with a group of kids who you know use drugs, take a stand and don't waver.

Other matters may not be as important, however. Maybe your son wants to wear his hair longer than you'd prefer. Or perhaps your daughter wants to buy a bathing suit that you consider too daring. These are the kinds of issues—the ones that aren't of "life or death" importance—on which you can give a little. These are the negotiable issues and the bargaining chips. These are the ones you can resolve without a major confrontation, by drawing back a little and letting your teenager have his way. Let him know, "You can make the choice on this one" or "Whatever you decide is going to be okay with me." Teenagers must feel that they have power over some decisions—power that will increase as they mature. This is an important part of normal growth, and parents need to relinquish this control gradually so adolescents can develop some independence. Also, when you begin to give teenagers power over the less significant matters, they are more likely to follow the more important rules—the ones dealing with drinking and driving, for instance, or taking drugs.

Throughout this section we've repeatedly emphasized the importance of letting teenagers begin making some decisions for themselves. During adolescence they have to start feeling a sense of autonomy and responsibility. So the more choices they are permitted to make now—beginning with the ones that will have minimal consequences if their judgment is bad—the better prepared they are going to be to make decisions as an adult.

Many parents find it helpful to write a priority list of important rules. Which ones are you willing to fight over? Which ones can you let slide by?

In the process, keep in mind that "showing who's boss" is seldom helpful; in fact it can turn the parent–child relationship into a counterproductive power struggle. Even some of your "hard and fast" rules might be open to compromise now and then. Let's say that you've set your son's curfew at 10:30. Well, an occasional relaxing of this rule—*agreed on in advance*—might be acceptable. The world's not going to come to an end if you bend the limit to 11:30 on a special occasion; and by doing so, you'll give your teenager the sense that you value his opinion and are sensitive to his wishes. And if his car breaks down and he calls, you may also show some flexibility and even offer him a lift.

Most teenagers will take these family ground rules seriously even if they don't like them. *Particularly if parents are conscientiously living by some rules in their own lives,* it's likely that most of the time adolescents will adhere to their own limits, even if they grumble all along the way.

Despite their sometimes rebellious nature, teenagers still value their families more than they're likely to acknowledge. In fact, when teenagers are feeling peer pressure to do something they'd rather not do—perhaps go to a party where alcohol is being consumed—it's often nice to have their parents' rules to use as an excuse. Caught in a difficult situation, they may find it a relief to say, "I'm sorry, but my parents will ground me if I go with you."

Firm rules are actually quite important in your teenager's life. Adolescents with no guidelines often feel lost, unsafe, and unprotected, or they find themselves in painful situations with little awareness of the consequences. Ironically, parents who seek to control their children are often frustrated by other parents who impose few limits, allowing their youngsters to "roam." Such uncontrolled, angry, and basically unloved children become very rebellious and can serve as poor examples to other teenagers. When your own adolescents see peers with so much "freedom," they may complain to you about your "strictness." Nevertheless, be patient, be loving, and set your limits.

WHEN HE BREAKS THE RULES . . .

Discipline. It's one of the responsibilities of parenting that makes many mothers and fathers feel inadequate. It was hard enough punishing children when they were small and the "crisis" was usually nothing more than their refusal to clean their room or to go to sleep by 8:30. But in adolescence the circumstances become much more challenging, with consequences that could affect the rest of your teenager's life.

Even so, no matter what the age of the child, the underlying principle really shouldn't be that different. If you've clearly and carefully imposed limits, and the youngster breaks them, there should be some consequences. If your teenager hasn't already learned this cause-and-effect relationship, adolescence is a good time for her to get the message. From time to time nearly every teenager will stretch a rule to the limit and break it. When that happens, you need to impose penalties, just as you should reward her good conduct. If you let misbehavior slide by, your adolescent will get the message that she can get away with any-thing—and even worse, that you don't really care what she does.

What should the punishment be? The specifics are up to you. In some families it may mean a loss of privileges—perhaps being grounded for a week or forgoing a baseball game the teenager was looking forward to. In other families, the penalty could be some extra chores around the house. However, the punishment chosen should *never* be *physical* in nature. Talk to other parents about the punishment they impose; in fact it's a good idea to set up regular meetings with other mothers and fathers—perhaps through schools, churches, or synagogues—to explore mutual problems and ideas for solutions.

Not only should your teenager know what the consequences are *before* she breaks the rules, but she should have a voice in deciding in advance what that penalty will be. If she helps to create the punishment, she'll clearly know what awaits her if she misbehaves.

In all situations, be consistent when carrying out the punishment. Except under extenuating circumstances—if the car breaks down, for example—your youngster shouldn't be able to talk or negotiate her way out of being penalized for a missed curfew or a similar violation of the rules. Also, when your teenager misbehaves, make sure she understands precisely what she's done wrong. And emphasize that you're unhappy only with her behavior—but that you're not going to let this get in the way of your love for her. You can't approve of her actions, but you continue to love her—unconditionally. Let your love shine through!

Let's reemphasize one important point: physical force *never* has a place in the punishment of a teenager, or any other child for that matter. Adolescents often describe feeling embarrassed and humiliated when their fathers, for example, punish them physically. It's a form of discipline that often backfires on the parent, leaving the teenager more alienated from the family, more prone to rebellion down the road, and less likely to form positive relationships in the present and the future.

Also avoid verbal aggression, demeaning the youngster, overemphasizing a misdeed, or saying things like, "You're bad and a screwup. You'll never amount to anything. You are going to end up a bum."

WHEN YOU LOSE CONTROL . . .

Sometimes teenage behavior reaches a level so antisocial and so self-destructive that parents really lose control of the situation. As we mentioned earlier, adolescents sometimes act impulsively, without giving much thought to what they're doing and what the consequences may be. And that can lead them into real trouble.

For example, some adolescents begin shoplifting or stealing, not because they or their families couldn't afford the items they're pilfering but just because they think they can get away with it. Or they may become involved in vandalism, throwing a rock through a window in the neighborhood or slashing automobile tires randomly. Even worse, adolescents sometimes commit violence.

Still another "acting out" behavior—running away—has become almost epidemic among teenagers. Many complain that life at home is intolerable, perhaps because of an alcoholic or a sexually or physically abusive parent. Others simply perceive running away as a very dramatic act of rebellion. Some girls flee home when they're pregnant, thinking the streets will be easier to deal with than the reaction of their parents. Some leave home for a week, some for years, and some never to return.

Life on the run may have been romanticized in books like *Huckleberry Finn,* but the reality of it rarely turns out that way. Many runaways stay with friends, but usually this is short-lived. They may eventually find themselves living in parks, begging for spare change, becoming prostitutes, or working for drug dealers to support themselves. Some are physically and sexually assaulted by thieves and pimps; others turn to drugs or criminal activities such as forging checks or stealing.

If your teenager does leave home, call your pediatrician immediately for advice. Find out the laws in your community to see what you can do. The local police department and parents of your child's peers (and sometimes the peers themselves) might help, too. When you finally locate your youngster, arrange for professional counseling immediately for both your child and the family. Your youngster ran away for a reason—find out why and institute appropriate preventive measures so it doesn't happen again.

Just how widespread are these problems of running away and delinquency? Consider these unsettling statistics:

- In a typical year about one million teenagers run away from home. They are usually young adolescents (ages eleven through fifteen).

- Before the age of eighteen one of every nine American teenagers (one of every six males) is referred to juvenile court.

- Adolescents under age eighteen commit 40 percent of all serious crimes.

Who are these delinquent teenagers? Many are doing poorly in school. They don't communicate well with their parents, who have often deprived them of attention and love. No one in the family seems to care where these kids are going and with whom they'll be spending time. In this type of situation teenagers respond to their frustrations by lashing out, by being increasingly aggressive and combative. And ironically, their delinquency becomes a way to finally get immediate attention from their parents.

Some teenagers are "naturally" more rebellious and more prone to delinquent behavior than others due to their personality structure; they'll oppose their parents' rules more strongly and for a longer time than other teenagers will. However, every adolescent who "acts out" clearly does so for a reason. She may be experiencing some serious psychological pain. Or she may be feeling neglected and is trying to get attention from a parent—perhaps a divorced father living thousands of miles away, as she wonders why her father divorced *her* after divorcing her mother. Or she could be making an effort to draw attention away from other family issues (such as Dad's alcoholism or Mom's depression). Or it could be a combination of these kinds of factors.

No matter what the reason, when a teenager does get into trouble with the law, an already weakened family unit can become absolutely devastated. Even if the antisocial behavior is short-lived, disappearing once the individual's internal control mechanisms catch up with her, it can leave some permanent scars in the way family members relate to one another.

When a teenager's serious misconduct persists and even worsens, professional counseling is necessary. This is not an indication that you've failed as a parent; more than anything, it shows just how needy your adolescent has become. Your pediatrician can provide a referral; a school counselor might be able to do the same. You also might want to contact one or more of the organizations listed at the end of this chapter.

It's *critical* to find out why a persistently misbehaving teenager acts the way she does and what you must do to correct this problem. An adolescent who won't listen to her parents will usually open up to an experienced, nonjudgmental counselor who takes the time to develop some rapport with her. However, a teenager who won't communicate with a counselor either may be experiencing some serious psychological difficulties and may need some expert and intensive psychological evaluation and treatment.

In addition, the family should become involved in group or family counseling too. The problem is not the adolescent's alone. Everyone in the family can profit from exploring how and why the communication barriers went up and what each family member needs to do now. The counselor may provide some assistance in developing good communication skills too.

Your teenager also might need to learn more acceptable ways of channeling her energy and anger. She may find that exercise can release some of the pent-up anxiety she's experiencing or that a structured relaxation exercise can help.

Counseling, incidentally, isn't just for teenagers who have engaged in delinquent behavior. It can also help families who are constantly in conflict. If your adolescent has experienced a sudden drop in grades, if she's skipping school, sleeping excessively, or demonstrating sudden changes in behavior (especially anger, prolonged unhappiness, crying outbursts, excessive alcohol or drug use), she and the family require professional help.

A variety of professionals are available, including psychologists, family therapists, adolescent medicine specialists, pediatricians, psychiatrists, school counselors, and others. Ask your teenager's pediatrician or another trusted doctor to help you find a qualified person. If the first one you go to doesn't help, discuss the problem with your pediatrician, who will refer you to another one. You need a therapist who can determine what's troubling your teenager and/or your family and how to improve the situation.

Resources

The following organizations can provide you with information and referrals on subjects discussed in this chapter:

JUVENILE DELINQUENCY

National Council on Crime and Delinquency
Continental Plaza
411 Hackensack Ave.
Hackensack, NJ 07601
(201) 488–0400
A source of information on community-based delinquency prevention programs

National Criminal Justice Reference Service
1015 20th St., NW
Washington, DC 20036
(202) 862–2900 or (800) 424–2856
A clearinghouse of juvenile justice information, including federal programs and legislation

Children's Defense Fund
1520 New Hampshire Ave., NW
Washington, DC 20036
(800) 424–9602
Information on juvenile justice as well as many other youth-related issues—education, child care, and health care

RUNAWAYS

National Runaway Switchboard
(800) 621–4000; in Illinois, (800) 972–6004
A contact service for runaways and parents

National Youth Work Alliance
1346 Connecticut Ave., NW
Washington, DC 20036
(202) 785–0764 or (800) 424–6740
Information for services related to runaways and other youth issues

Office of Human Development
Administration for Children, Youth and Families
P.O. Box 1182
Washington, DC 20013
(202) 755–7724
Administers a national runaway program as well as Head Start

Keep in mind that counseling is not a personal attack on your family; it is a positive approach to improving a negative situation. If counseling identifies errors you have made, don't become angry or defensive and reject further counseling; instead, continue to explore the issues, however painful, so improvements in the family will occur. Encourage your teenager and other family members to do the same. A competent, neutral counselor can help all of you see problems from a helpful perspective—one you may not be able to appreciate now.

As difficult as raising a teenager may seem at times, hang in there. Take comfort in knowing that the idiosyncrasies of adolescence are not unique to your own family but are quite universal. For example, there's nothing unusual about a teenager who embraces you one moment, wanting to tell you everything going on in her life, and then pushes you away the next, clamming up and refusing to answer even the most innocuous questions. Through it all, however, your adolescent needs you, even during those times when she seems to be trying to distance herself.

Be patient. Be caring. Continue to show your love. Be available and approachable. In time you could end up much closer to your adolescent than ever before.

11

PROBLEMS WITH
ALCOHOL AND DRUGS

*H*ave you ever wondered where teenagers get the message that alcohol is the trendy drink of the times? Look no further than your television set. Or perhaps no further than yourself.

First, let's consider television. From situation comedies to dramas to thirty-second commercials, drinking is a fact of life on TV, hour after hour. And more often than not, the characters are sipping drinks while surrounded by material and social success. There are also scenes showing people drinking and then driving. Comedians joke good-naturedly about drunks. Alcohol is often portrayed as a reward for a hard day's work. And in dramatic shows characters frequently proclaim, "I sure could use a drink."

And then there's the home environment. Millions of parents consume alcohol on a daily basis. Others abuse prescribed drugs intended to make them feel better or more relaxed. Teenagers, of course, mirror their parents and society in general. So if you come home from work every day and fix yourself a drink or swallow a pill, don't be surprised if your youngster gets the message that either is just fine.

No wonder, then, that alcohol and drugs have become so much a part of the teenage culture. Of course today's adolescents are not the first generation to experiment with alcohol. In the eighties and the nineties, however, the ante has been raised: never has there been such widespread abuse of both alcohol and illegal drugs by adolescents and young adults.

Even so, you may be able to help your teenager get through adolescence with his body and brain intact. To do so, however, you need to know something about both the legal and the illegal substances now available and exactly what your teenager faces at school and with his friends. This is certainly not an easy time in which to grow up. Today's teenagers must make choices their parents—or any other generation—never faced. During their junior high and high school years most adolescents not only are exposed to marijuana, cocaine, and other drugs, but they're often strongly pressured by their peers to try them.

However, there's also some good news to report: a lot of adolescents try drugs and alcohol, but most do not use them regularly. Also, while it's true that the majority of teenagers will have experimented with marijuana, alcohol, and tobacco by the time they leave high school, only a minority will have actually moved on to stronger drugs. For most, use of these substances is a very occasional (but risky) indulgence usually confined to the weekends.

Nevertheless, as you're undoubtedly aware, you can't take this problem lightly. Most users of alcohol and marijuana have tried them *before* the tenth grade. One study found that by age thirteen about 30 percent of the boys and 20 percent of the girls were experimenting with alcohol; that figure climbed to 93 percent of the boys and 73 percent of the girls by age eighteen. In a recent survey of high school students 70 percent had consumed alcohol within the preceding month.

Young people start using drugs and alcohol for a variety of reasons. Some are simply curious; they've heard that drugs get you "high" and make you feel good— or at least feel different—and they're interested in finding out for themselves. They may also think that drugs will relax them, boost their self-confidence, and make them communicate better with the opposite sex.

Others begin using drugs to fit in with a particular group of friends who are already using these substances. The pressure from peers (as well as from the media) to use drugs should not be underestimated.

Some teenagers decide to cross the line into alcohol/drug use as a dramatic way to assert their independence from their parents—particularly if Mom and Dad have strong prohibitions against drug use and have demanded that they stay away from these substances. Other adolescents see drugs as a "rite of passage"— something to be experienced on the way to adulthood. And as we've already pointed out, when parents drink or smoke cigarettes, their children may decide there's nothing wrong with doing the same thing.

If teenagers move from using to abusing alcohol and drugs, these substances are usually being relied on for reasons other than because "it's fun to get high" or because "they make me one of the gang." In most of these cases teenagers are trying to produce some good feelings to block out very real emotional problems. Drugs are a way for them to escape from the stresses of life—their anxiety over school or their pain over their relationship with their parents or peers. If they regularly take drugs before or during school, their grades will inevitably suffer.

Some adolescents never learn, however, that mood-altering drugs provide only a false sense of escape and pleasure. Drugs don't solve problems, nor do they improve relationships. But because they may make a teenager feel as though they do, he'll keep going back for more. And as he becomes preoccupied by drugs, he'll eventually lose control over their use.

Researchers actually have identified three distinct stages in an adolescent's utilization of drugs:

1. A teenager's exposure to drugs usually beings with experimentation. Drugs are a form of recreation during this phase, and peer pressure is often responsible for an adolescent's introduction to these substances, as is drug use by his own parents. Frequently no obvious behavioral change occurs during this period.

2. Next the teenagers progress to a stage in which they actively seek out drugs. They enter a state of psychological dependence, convinced that drugs make them feel better during stressful times. In the process certain behavioral changes, including some of the following ones, become apparent:

- Excessive time spent alone

- A decline in communication with family members, frequent arguing, and an unusual demand for secretiveness

- Changes in the way they dress and groom

- Deteriorating grades at school and a lack of motivation to do well academically

- A change in their choice of friends

- Repeated or unexplained accidents or fights

- Poor sleeping habits, sluggish behavior, and a lack of energy

- Irregular eating patterns

- Bloodshot eyes (particularly with alcohol and marijuana use)

- Frequent "colds" or nosebleeds (especially with cocaine use)

- Running away from home or attempting suicide

- Mood changes, including irritability and depression

- Hyperactivity (most often seen with drugs such as amphetamines and cocaine)

Keep in mind, however, that many of these symptoms occur periodically in normal, non-drug-using adolescents, and none by itself is a foolproof indicator of drug use. However, if you see several together, your suspicions should be raised. It's better to look to see if a problem really exists—only to learn that your fears were unfounded—than to ignore the warning signs and later learn some "bad" news.

3. Finally the adolescent becomes preoccupied with drugs. Since increased use can become expensive, family possessions may start to disappear, sold for drug money. Trouble with the law may occur as well, especially if the teenager starts selling drugs to support his habit. And if he tries to stop using them, he may become moody, depressed, and irritable.

As dismaying as this three-stage scenario is, keep in mind that most young people never progress past the first (experimentation) stage. For those adolescents who move through all three stages of drug use, the entire process can take months to several years. But it's important to detect drug use as early as possible. In general, the earlier you can identify it, the better the treatment results will be.

ALCOHOL:
HOW CONCERNED SHOULD YOU BE?

Some parents almost breathe a sigh of relief when they find out that their teenager is "only" drinking alcohol. "At least he's not taking drugs," they often say. "Beer isn't that bad for him."

Not true. Alcohol can be a very destructive substance. Even so, it's often perceived as the "lesser of two evils" because it's legal—and thus parents may be more tolerant of its use. Quite often health-care professionals see teenagers acutely intoxicated with alcohol in the hospital emergency room—only to have the parents deny its importance, refuse professional evaluation and treatment, and allow the youth to continue abusing alcohol. This kind of lax attitude has contributed to a continuing increase in alcohol use by teenagers, now making it the most commonly used mind-altering substance.

Adolescent drinking begins disturbingly young, often between eleven and thirteen years of age. And when you consider how accessible alcohol is to a curious teenager, that's really not surprising. After all, it's in the cupboards and refrigerators of many, perhaps most, American homes.

No matter when and where the use of alcohol begins, however, it's a substance almost universally experimented with by adolescents. As we've already mentioned, nearly all teenagers have tried it at least once, and many drink just to get drunk. And while it's still a minority who abuse alcohol—particularly among younger teenagers—one study looked exclusively at high school seniors and found that 30 percent of the girls and nearly half of the boys had become "problem drinkers." It wasn't unusual for a young teenager to drink a six-pack of beer or a bottle of wine *every day*. And while some adults consider beer less of a problem than hard liquor, the truth is this: one can of beer contains the same level of alcohol as a 1.5-ounce shot of whiskey!

Alcohol is a depressant of the nervous system. One of its appeals for people of all ages is that a drink or two relaxes them, making them feel more comfortable and self-assured around others. At the same time, researchers have associated drinking with early sexual intercourse in some teenagers—with the resulting increases in unintended pregnancies and sexually transmitted diseases. And once pregnant, a girl who continues to drink—often unaware she is pregnant—exposes her baby to a greater risk of birth defects (a well-known condition called the *fetal alcohol syndrome*).

As if that weren't enough, excessive amounts of alcohol can impair judgment, provoke risky and even violent behavior, and slow down reaction time. An intoxicated teenager (or anyone else) behind the wheel of a car is a lethal weapon; the leading cause of death of Americans ages fifteen to twenty-four, in fact, is alcohol-related automobile accidents. According to one estimate 15 percent of high school seniors drive while intoxicated. Not surprisingly, then, more than 7,000 teenagers and young adults die in alcohol-related car crashes, and another 40,000 are injured.

There are still other problems. By mixing drugs—for instance, consuming alcohol and marijuana together—the senses can be even further distorted and coordination problems made even worse. Also, whether consumed alone or in combination with other drugs, alcohol can interfere with the normal development and growth of young teenagers and cause permanent physical and psychological impairment (by contributing to injury, poor school performance, depression, and so on). Moreover, suicide and homicide—the second and third leading causes of death in this age group—are strongly associated with drug and alcohol use.

So before you go easy on alcohol consumption by teenagers, don't lose sight of the important fact that its negative effects can be devastating. If your adolescent has become a problem drinker, he may need professional help. Although alcoholism is difficult to treat at any age, programs are available that can help get your teenager off alcohol and back on track.

MARIJUANA AND
OTHER ILLEGAL DRUGS

While alcohol is the drug most often abused by the largest number of adolescents, other substances—such as marijuana and cocaine—can be as damaging. In addition to their health hazards, they have another risky component—namely, their illegal status: get caught with marijuana or cocaine, and you'll have to contend with the law. (The same is true, of course, with teenagers who are below the legal age limit for alcohol purchase but choose to drink anyway.)

Marijuana has been widely available in this country for at least a generation. In fact, when you were growing up, marijuana may have been present on your own high school or college campus, although its use was probably not as extensive as it has been in recent years. Although the use of marijuana peaked in 1979, it still is the most widely used illegal drug in the United States. Nearly half of all students will have tried it by the time they graduate from high school.

Even though marijuana isn't new to young people, researchers now know much more about it than they did even a decade ago. In short, it's not the "safe" drug— or the "harmless little giggle"—that it was once presumed to be.

There is now quite persuasive evidence that use—and particularly overuse— of marijuana can have serious health consequences. Everyone has heard about the euphoria, the gaiety, and the mellow feelings that lure so many people to use the drug. The real concern, though, is the short-term memory loss, the violent mood swings, the anxiety, and the depression it can cause. Regular and heavy users often seem to have no interest in leading productive lives and only seek out additional drugs to take (they're called *polydrug abusers*). This "anti-motivational syndrome" is well known in chronic marijuana users.

If your teenager is using marijuana, you also need to be concerned about its potential damage to organs like the lungs. Not only does marijuana smoke contain more cancer-causing chemicals than an equal amount of tobacco smoke, but it also causes immediate irritation of the bronchial passages, reducing the amount of air that the lungs can transport in and out of the body. Recent research suggests that its potential for lung damage can sometimes be greater than cigarettes since marijuana users usually hold the smoke in their lungs longer than cigarette users do.

Marijuana can also cause motor coordination difficulties in the hours after it has been smoked—thus making driving a real hazard. Studies have also associated it with irregular heart rhythms and a disruption of the normal functioning of the endocrine system. Heavy use reduces male sperm production, too, and can interfere with normal release of a ripened egg in a woman's reproductive cycle.

There's another reason why doctors are much more worried about marijuana's health hazards now than in the past. They point to the heightened potency of the modern-day drug, due to much higher levels of its major mood-altering ingredient (called *THC* or delta-9-tetrahydrocannabinol). In the 1980s THC levels were many times greater than was common two decades ago.

Unfortunately, to teenagers themselves smoking marijuana may represent more than just the use of a drug; it can sometimes become an expression of adolescent rebellion. Some teenagers perceive their use of chemicals as "proof" of their maturity. But even though adolescents need to assert their individuality, they must be taught that experimenting with marijuana isn't the way to do it.

There's still another risk associated with marijuana use. Some experts consider it a "gateway" drug—that is, its use can lead to the abuse of other drugs later in adolescence or adulthood. The same is also true with *alcohol* and *cigarettes;* they are usually forerunners to experimentation with other substances.

Teenagers sometimes use many other types of drugs too, but one in particular—*cocaine*—is important to emphasize here. The abuse of cocaine has become the nation's fastest-growing drug problem. In fact, while marijuana use has actually decreased slightly in recent years, cocaine use has, until very recently, been on the rise—doubling among high school students between the years 1975 and 1985.

Many people considered cocaine a "safe" drug when its popularity first soared in the 1970s. Now, however, we know better. In addition to "snorting" the cocaine powder, many teenagers are now smoking a pastelike version (called "crack"), which is stronger and more addictive. And as the strength of the drug has increased, so have the risks. Today any form of cocaine is dangerous.

What's the appeal of cocaine? Like most other drugs, it makes its users feel good, triggering the pleasure centers in the brain. It's actually one of the most potent drugs we know about, causing an intense sense of euphoria that users are unable to forget and constantly pursue. But within half an hour of taking the drug, there's a backlash effect during which individuals experience depression, anxiety, irritability, and fatigue. To counteract these undesirable feelings, they often use more cocaine.

However, there are even more serious health dangers with cocaine. Not only is cocaine probably the most addicting of all drugs, but its users also run the risk of immediate heart failure. For some people even moderate levels of the drug can cause dramatic increases in the heart rate, leading to potentially lethal abnormal rhythms. This sudden death is a danger whether one is a first-time user or an addict. Regular use of cocaine also increases an individual's vulnerability to seizures. Unfortunately, both of these conditions—convulsions and heart problems—occur more frequently among teenage users of cocaine.

To compound the problems, there's no way to evaluate the toxicity of the cocaine being used. The drug sold to teenagers is often altered, and they can never be sure if they're really getting what they think they are. (This is true for all illegal drugs.)

Several other drugs are popular among today's adolescents. Here's a brief description of those most frequently abused:

Hallucinogens. PCP (phencyclidine) and LSD (d-lysergic acid diethylamide) fall into this category. Although not as common today as in previous years, they are still used by some teenagers, producing a marked distortion of reality and sometimes the "bad trips" that teenagers often describe. Negative reactions to the drugs certainly do occur, causing flashbacks, paranoia, declines in blood pressure, breathing problems, and potentially coma and death.

Amphetamines. These stimulants (sometimes called "uppers") can induce a euphoric feeling. Some teenagers also take them to lose weight and reduce fatigue. However, they are associated with a variety of side effects, ranging from hyperactivity and anxiety to insomnia, high blood pressure, and rapid heartbeats. An overdose of these drugs can cause seizures and even death.

Barbiturates. These agents (sometimes called "downers") are nervous-system depressants or sedatives. While inducing sedation, they also can cause lethargy and slurred speech. When abused, they can produce anxiety, delirium, seizures, and even death. Withdrawal from heavy use of barbiturates can be lethal.

Opiates. Heroin is the best known of the drugs in this category. Although it's taken for its euphoric effects, it also has extremely powerful addictive properties—both physical and psychological. As it is administered, it can also cause serious problems such as skin infections, lung disease, and hepatitis. An overdose can be fatal. While many people once considered heroin a drug of the city ghettos, it has moved into middle-class and suburban neighborhoods. Incidentally, cough medicines sometimes contain codeine, a kind of opiate, which is easily obtained and has abuse potential.

Solvents and Inhalants. Some kids sniff paint, gasoline, aerosols, glue, and other substances to get "high." Youngsters often place the agent on a rag and then sniff it, or they put it in a plastic bag and then inhale. Complications can include irregular heartbeats, liver and kidney damage, breathing problems, and death.

HOW TO PREVENT DRUG USE

At one time or another most teenagers will find themselves in a situation where friends are tempting them to try drugs. They'll have to make the decision to use them or not.

Although it's *their* decision, you should make sure they know in advance the dangers of even experimenting with a mood-altering drug. Yes, it may seem to provide a temporary escape from the stresses of adolescence, but in the process it will interfere with the necessary "growing pains" that everyone must experience in becoming a mature and responsible adult. And by causing everything from social withdrawal to decreased motivation, drugs can make the growing-up process even more difficult.

So it's important for you to get involved *before* a drug problem develops. By taking the following steps, you can increase the chances that your teenager will say no when he's offered drugs.

- Talk with him frequently about subjects relevant to an adolescent's life, including drugs and how they play a role in peer acceptance. Give him the facts about the dangers of drugs. Teach him to make independent judgments, no matter what his friends are doing or saying. And let him know how you feel about drugs.

- Remind him there are ways to manage his emotions and feelings *without* turning to drugs. Most of all, let him know you'll always be there to help him with his problems.

- At every opportunity, build his self-esteem, praising his accomplishments and refraining from frequent criticism.

- Encourage him to participate in wholesome and enjoyable activities that could keep him from using drugs out of boredom. Let him discover that he can have a lot of fun—and get "high"—without drugs.

- Let your teenager know that if he uses drugs, you'll take away some of his highly valued privileges, such as use of the family car.

- If your adolescent is of driving age, insist that he *never* drive when he's been drinking, no matter how little alcohol he's consumed. Even one drink can disrupt his driving ability. Some parents institute a "free-call-home" policy;

if a teenager is drinking, he can call home for a ride without fear of consequences that night. His parents will discuss the incident with him the following day.

■ Make sure your teenager knows not only the physical risks of using drugs but also the legal consequences of getting caught taking them.

■ Set a good example by limiting your own use of alcohol and medications. If you take drugs for a medical problem, you need to explain that to your teenager. If you drink at home, keep it at moderate levels and make it clear to your youngster that you're not using alcohol as a way to cope with your problems. Also, never drink under unsafe conditions (such as while driving) and don't make light of excessive alcohol consumption (e.g., if your teenager becomes intoxicated).

HOW TO STOP DRUG USE

What if you discover that your teenager is abusing drugs or alcohol? First of all, it may be hard for you to accept. Even when the signs strongly point in that direction, many mothers and fathers deny it, often for much too long.

However, it's essential that you acknowledge drug abuse immediately. Once teenagers reach the advanced stages of substance abuse—actively seeking and preoccupied by drugs—three out of four never fully and successfully recover. Thus early counseling and/or treatment are vital.

Harsh lectures aren't going to do much good. Instead, try to find out why your adolescent is using drugs. Give him love and support and insist on arranging together for a way to help him cope with his problems more productively. If he is using drugs only occasionally, set up a trial period—perhaps two weeks or a month—in which he'll agree to stay away from drugs and you'll agree to help him find solutions to the life situations he finds distressing. If he's in a more advanced stage of drug abuse, he will strongly deny he has a problem or even that he is involved with illegal substances; but if you see the warning signs discussed earlier, you must find out the underlying cause and get him help.

Be sure to ask your family's pediatrician for guidance. Drug screening (that is, urine tests) are rarely necessary to diagnose drug abuse. But the doctor may suggest a medical exam for your teenager to see if the drug abuse has caused any physical problems. He or she may then refer your youngster to a drug dependency program or a counselor for help.

WHAT ABOUT CIGARETTES?

Although this chapter has dealt mainly with alcohol and other drug abuse thus far, cigarettes are just as much of a concern. According to one recent study 21 percent of high school seniors are daily smokers. In 1979 the U.S. surgeon general estimated there were six million teenage smokers—and another 100,000 children *under age thirteen* who smoked. Girls tend to use cigarettes more often than boys, but the use of smokeless (or chewing) tobacco is on the rise in boys.

Despite this widespread use of cigarettes, your teenager probably already knows everything she needs to know about their risks. In the media and on every cigarette pack the message is clear: smoking causes heart disease, lung cancer, and emphysema. Cigarettes are the most avoidable cause of death in our society. About 350,000 adults die prematurely each year because of cigarettes.

Your adolescent may *not* know, however, that before a chronic and often-fatal disease develops (even during adolescence), a smoker can develop a chronic cough, chest infections, shortness of breath, and wheezing. Preexisting lung diseases such as asthma can worsen. Smoking can also complicate a pregnancy by causing spontaneous abortion, poor growth of the fetus, and even fetal death. The evidence for all this is overwhelming.

Physical addiction to tobacco is another major problem for those who use cigarettes. This addiction is very difficult to conquer. Also, there are the cosmetic drawbacks associated with smoking—yellow stains on the teeth and bad breath. With so much against cigarettes, it's hard to believe that people continue smoking—except that it is addictive.

While cigarettes get most of the attention, don't overlook so-called "smokeless tobacco," which includes both snuff (finely ground tobacco) and chewing (or leaf) tobacco. They are placed in the mouth or nose and are not ignited. An increasing number of young people are using these products even though they cause bad breath and stained teeth. Both also can lead to nicotine addiction and can damage the lining of the throat and mouth. Even worse, their use can cause cancer of the mouth and the throat as well as gum disease. Like cigarettes, they are a serious health hazard.

Of course advertisements in newspapers and magazines and on billboards—with their youthful models often surrounded by attractive members of the opposite sex—can be rather persuasive in convincing teenagers that tobacco use is not only quite acceptable but is a sign of being "cool" and sophisticated. Your own behavior can have an impact as well: if you smoke, you can't realistically expect your teenager not to. In fact adolescents from families who smoke are twice as likely to smoke themselves. So if you want to do your adolescent a favor, now

---

Substance Abuse Resources

The following agencies can provide you with information on adolescent substance abuse:

Alcoholics Anonymous
Box 452
Grand Central Station
New York, NY 10017
Also see telephone directory for
local chapters

Do-It-Now Foundation
Box 5115
Phoenix, AZ 85010

National Clearinghouse/Alcohol
Information
Box 2345
Rockville, MD 20852
(301) 948–4450

National Clearinghouse/Drug
Abuse Information
Parklawn Building, Room 10 A–56
5600 Fishers Lane
Rockville, MD 20852
(301) 443–4273

National Association for the
Prevention of Narcotic Abuse
305 E. 79th St.
New York, NY 10021

National Clearinghouse on
Smoking and Health
Centers for Disease Control
1600 Cliften Rd.
Building 14
Atlanta, GA 30333

---

is a good time for you to stop—and to convince your teenager to do the same.

Don't underestimate your own influence when it comes to cigarettes, drugs, or any other aspect of your teenager's life. You can be a persuasive force—and when it comes to drugs, some teenagers are beginning to listen. One survey has found that about half of all high school seniors now think that smoking makes a teenager look "insecure," not "cool." More than eight out of ten disagreed with the statement that smokers know how to have more fun in life than nonsmokers.

So even though it seems that teenagers are hard to reach, keep trying. As a parent, you can make an important difference in the choices your adolescent makes. If you're persistent, the message just may get through.

If substance abuse is afflicting your family, help is available. Many health-care professionals are experts in this type of care. As well as your family's pediatrician, the organizations above are good resources for information.

12

DEPRESSION AND
SUICIDE

*F*act: The suicide rate among adolescents has grown so rapidly—tripling in the last twenty-five years—that suicide now ranks as the third leading cause of death among adolescents and second among young adults.

Fact: For every completed adolescent suicide, there are more than sixty unsuccessful attempts in this age group. About 400,000 teenagers try to kill themselves each year.

Who are these young people who resort to suicide? Many adolescents who attempt to kill themselves are depressed. They're feeling hurt, rejected, angry, and hopeless.

Of course nearly all adolescents experience depression from time to time, and most don't become suicidal. However, some teenagers do try to kill themselves, and in others depression can interfere with current and future adjustments to life and its many demands. Thus depression is a problem you should never take lightly.

From experience adults know that most feelings of distress or sadness are only temporary; but when a teenager breaks up with a girlfriend, or when he's turned down by the college he had dreamed of going to, he often believes that his pain will never end. Teenagers don't just say that they *feel* hopeless; they say, "I *am* hopeless." And this hopelessness is what sometimes leads them to suicide. Adolescents just don't have the life experiences to realize yet that sadness is only— or should be only—transient.

LEARNING TO
IDENTIFY DEPRESSION

Depression is a gloomy feeling about life. Everyone feels this way from time to time, but when the condition becomes chronic or severe, it can become quite worrisome.

A number of factors can provoke or exacerbate depression. For instance, if your teenager is unaccepted by his peers, if you or your spouse either overprotects or rejects him, if there are economic or interpersonal stresses in the family, if he's affected by severe family turmoil (such as a divorce), if he's having academic difficulties or is chronically ill—he may be particularly vulnerable to depression.

Several studies show that unrest in the family—and in society in general—can be quite disruptive in an adolescent's life. While many single-parent households, for example, are quite stable, the difficulties of divorce, stepparents, or the changing sexual partners of a single parent can be very disturbing to a teenager. Add to that the more global problems of a high crime rate, limited availability of jobs for many, and world political tensions.

Then there are the everyday concerns of adolescents—the loneliness, the lack of a boyfriend or girlfriend, the confusion about life changes—all of which can become exaggerated in their minds. They can start feeling dejected, hopeless, worthless—and depressed.

Even when depressed adolescents are not suicidal, you should take their depression seriously. Their mood can still interfere significantly with normal adolescent development and impair their future adult functioning in marriage, family, and job.

Depressed young people usually have a reduced interest in their normal activities. They may feel fatigued, they may become restless and have trouble concentrating, and their grades at school may suffer. They may withdraw from their family and/or peers. Their appetite may decline, they may develop eating disorders (anorexia or bulimia), and their sleep patterns may change (sleeping more—or perhaps less—than usual). They may use drugs to help relieve their depression. They also may become preoccupied by the "tragedies" in their lives. In short, they'll seem to find little pleasure in day-to-day living.

Depression might also be present in adolescents who "act out" their emotional problems—that is, those who begin abusing alcohol or drugs, run away from home, become violent, or begin "ditching" school. These kinds of individuals may alternatively have temper tantrums, shoplift, or become sexually promiscuous as a symptom of their depression.

Some depressed teenagers also complain of physical disorders whose cause is difficult to pinpoint. For example, they may have headaches, chest or stomach pains, fatigue, or dizziness. In cases like these a pediatrician should check the adolescent to try to determine what may be at the root of these complaints. He or she may suggest a complete physical exam to help make the diagnosis. However, sometimes even a thorough evaluation like this won't turn up any physical reasons for these illnesses.

As frustrating as this situation may be, your teenager probably isn't imagining his aches and pains. They are quite real, but they have a psychological—not a physiological—basis. Quite often adolescent depression may cause physical symptoms, or so-called "psychosomatic" complaints. Thus, in teenagers, the basis of those headaches or abdominal pains may be depression produced by academic problems, difficulties with peers, or preoccupation with the loss of a girlfriend (or a parent).

TREATING DEPRESSION

When teenagers are in a depressed mood, do they need professional help? Not necessarily. Usually the sadness isn't long-lived, and they will "snap out of it" on their own in a few days. If you talk with them, listen intently, and demonstrate your support, the depression may resolve itself.

In this process it will take more than just advising a teenager to "tough it out." One parent told his daughter, "Depression is a weakness; be strong and don't let your emotions affect you." That kind of advice is inappropriate. Your teenager's emotions *are* important; you should take them seriously and spend time helping him sort them out.

As a first step, acknowledge your teenager's problems. Help him break them down into manageable units and then take them one step at a time. Ask him to talk about his anger, frustration, and sadness. Help him deal with stress more successfully by lowering expectations, changing some things in his environment, and reaching out to others. Along the way you should give him loving support through hugs, touches, and caring statements.

Also, encourage him to become involved in physical activity. Some research shows that exercise can help alleviate depression. Swimming, bicycle riding, jogging, dancing, and other forms of exercise all can have a positive effect (See Chapter 31). Often, however, the depressed individual has no energy for such pursuits.

If your teenager's depressed mood persists, how long should you wait before seeking help? It's difficult to generalize; with some teenagers you shouldn't wait more than a few days, but with others a week or more is appropriate. The depth of the depression is important; if your adolescent is suicidal, get help immediately, no matter how long the depression has lasted.

For some guidance, ask your pediatrician. He or she may recommend counseling or psychotherapy and refer you to a trained professional. Quite often, although teenagers will not talk to their parents about their depression and its causes, a health-care professional may get them to open up. Sometimes a doctor will prescribe antidepressant drugs to help a severely depressed adolescent; as the drugs improve the teenager's mood, a therapist may then be able to start exploring the reasons for the depression and how to manage it. These drugs for depressed youth must be used appropriately, and they never replace the need for counseling.

As we've suggested earlier, depression is a complex disorder with many causes. If your teenager is severely depressed, it doesn't mean you're a poor or a bad parent. Also, if there are family members (mother, father, grandparent, etc.) with a family history of depression, your youngster may have inherited the same tendencies. Just as some individuals inherit a susceptibility to high blood pressure or ulcers, one generation can pass depression on to the next. This genetic component can make youngsters very vulnerable to life's stresses.

In any event, don't ignore the signs of depression. Especially when identified early, depression is a treatable illness.

DEALING WITH ANXIETY

Quite often even health professionals have difficulty distinguishing between depression and anxiety in an adolescent. Like depression, anxiety in young people can be a disabling disorder, interfering with school, interpersonal relationships, and nearly every other aspect of their lives. Some individuals also have physical symptoms along with the psychological ones.

Everybody has experienced anxiety from time to time. Sometimes it has a clear cause: examinations, a job interview, the first time behind the wheel of a car, the first attempt at sexual intercourse. Though this type of anxiety can be quite disruptive, it is transitory and disappears in short order.

But the unpleasant feelings associated with anxiety can also have no apparent cause and can become a chronic condition. This anxiety can be associated with a sense of danger or impending doom, even though there is no obvious justification for this feeling. As one pediatrician has said, "Fear is when you look up, see a 450-pound weight about to fall on your head, and feel discomfort. With anxiety, you feel the discomfort but you don't know the cause."

Anxiety (specifically, separation anxiety) sometimes occurs in younger children. But more serous problems with anxiety often begin in late adolescence or early adulthood and can take many forms. A common type is the so-called "panic disorder," often consisting of episodes of panic attacks (intense fearfulness) and physical symptoms such as heart palpitations, excessive sweating or cold, clammy hands, dizziness or light-headedness, trembling, tingling of the skin, muscle tension, flushes or chills, diarrhea, nausea, and a fear of dying. Hyperventilation is another common indication of this and other types of serious anxiety.

These adolescents also might experience agoraphobia—another form of panic disorder characterized by an irrational fear of leaving familiar surroundings such as home. Thus they may be afraid to go to school because of a fear of crowds, feeling much more secure just staying in their room. The mere thought of venturing out into the world can cause many of the same physical symptoms described above. Panic attacks and agoraphobia can even occur together.

No matter what form the anxiety takes, however, these teenagers may have difficulty falling or staying asleep. They may also have trouble concentrating, and they can be quite irritable. Anxiety can manifest itself as chest pain, headaches, or abdominal pain too, and affect teenagers of any age.

No one knows exactly how prevalent anxiety disorders are among adolescents. But as with depression, anxiety can be provoked by factors ranging from the modern stresses on families to the breakup of the family unit. If a teenager's family has been split by divorce, or if there are serious economic pressures in the household, anxiety may be one way in which he will react. If he feels overwhelming pressure to get excellent grades to gain admission to the college that Dad attended, he may be experiencing genuine panic relative to his schoolwork.

Some adolescent anxiety is associated with growing up, leaving home, and separating from mother and father. The challenge of being independent is too much for some teenagers to bear, and they may panic at the mere thought of it.

As with depression, you shouldn't ignore adolescent anxiety. If your teenager appears to have a persistent anxiety disorder, a pediatrician should evaluate him. The doctor should begin by conducting a complete physical exam, since many medical problems can produce states that mimic anxiety disorders. Once the doctor rules out medical disorders, he or she should look closely at what may be causing the anxiety or the panic attacks. What are the stresses in the youngster's life? Are there problems with peers or the family that could be disturbing to him?

Counseling is often very effective for these young people, helping them deal with and ease their anxiety. Also, if there's a way you can change your youngster's environment to help relieve the stress in his life, you should make a strong effort to do just that.

Doctors sometimes prescribe short-term drug therapy as well. Your family's pediatrician might recommend that your youngster take an antianxiety medication or even an antidepressant drug. But your teenager should never take any medication that hasn't been prescribed specifically for him.

PREVENTING SUICIDE

A nineteen-year-old college sophomore put the finishing touches on his term paper and handed it to his roommate with instructions to turn it in for him. He then got into his car and drove to a forest. He stopped the vehicle and hooked up a hose to channel fumes from the exhaust pipe into the car's interior. He died a few minutes later of carbon monoxide poisoning. He left a note asking his family to forgive him and explaining that he just "could not go on."

As the statistics at the beginning of this chapter underscore, you must take seriously the subject of suicide. It seems incongruous that a teenager—who has experienced relatively little of life—would choose to die. But adolescents—sometimes when their depression is not effectively resolved—do occasionally kill themselves. Boys commit suicide more often than girls, but no one is immune. In one recent survey of high school students 60 percent said they had thought about killing themselves. About 9 percent said they had made at least one attempt.

Why has the youth suicide rate risen so dramatically in recent years? First, the tools for suicide are now much too accessible to adolescents (boys often use firearms to kill themselves; girls usually rely on pills). Perhaps more importantly, researchers believe the pressures of modern life are greater than ever before. The competition for good grades and college admission is stiff. There's also more societal violence in the newspapers and on TV.

A lack of parental interest may be another problem. Many children grow up in divorced households; for other youngsters both of their parents work and their families have limited opportunities to spend time together. According to one study 90 percent of suicidal adolescents believed their families did not understand them. (However, this is such a common teenage complaint that other factors are playing a role, too.) Youngsters also reported that when they tried to communicate their feelings of unhappiness or failure to their parents, their mother and father denied or disregarded their point of view.

Particularly if your teenager has been depressed, you must be vigilant for clues signaling that he may be contemplating suicide:

- Has he undergone a radical personality change?

- Is he having conflict with a girlfriend (or, for girls, with a boyfriend)? Or is he having trouble getting along with other peers or with parents, and has he withdrawn from those he used to feel close to?

- Has there been an unexplained decline in the quality of his schoolwork, and has he failed to live up to his own or someone else's standards (regarding school grades, for example)?

- Does he seem constantly bored, and is he having trouble concentrating?

- Is he exhibiting rebellious behavior that's unexplained and severe?

- Is she pregnant and having difficulty coping with this major life disruption?

- Has he run away from home?

- Is he abusing drugs and/or alcohol?

- Is he complaining of psychosomatic disorders (e.g., headaches, stom-achaches, etc.)? (See Page 109.)

- Have there been changes in his eating or sleeping habits?

- Has there been an unusual neglect of his appearance?

- Is he giving away some of his most prized possessions?

- Is he writing notes or poems about death?

- Has he spoken about suicide, even jokingly? Or has he made comments such as, "That's the last straw," "I can't take it anymore," or, "Nobody cares about me"? (Verbal threats of self-destruction precede four out of five suicidal deaths.)

- Has he made a previous suicide attempt?

Do not become complacent if your adolescent isn't visibly depressed. Although signs of obvious depression may be absent, he may nevertheless make plans to kill himself if he has lost hope for the present or the future. In many cases suicidal teenagers have long-standing problems aggravated by adolescence, and they perceive these difficulties as impossible to resolve. In other instances suicide can be a spur-of-the-moment decision, perhaps related to drug use.

If you suspect that your teenager might be thinking about suicide, don't remain silent. You must take suicidal threats and gestures seriously.

Suicide is preventable, but you must intervene immediately. Directly ask your teenager about it. Don't be afraid to say the word *suicide.* Some parents think they're going to encourage their youngster to kill himself by raising the subject; on the contrary, the thought may be already there—and he may feel relieved that someone has heard his cries for help. Tell him you love him. Ask him to talk about his feelings. And to be safe, if he expresses thoughts of suicide, remove all lethal weapons from the home, including guns, pills, kitchen utensils, razors, and ropes.

Remind your teenager that no matter how devastating his problems seem, they can be worked out, and you're willing to help him do just that. Don't wait for things to clear up on their own. Your youngster can be helped to cope better and improve his life—if you seek the help of a counselor immediately. Ask your family's pediatrician or other trusted physician for a referral. In some cases she may recommend that your adolescent be admitted to an inpatient treatment facility.

What if your teenager has already tried to commit suicide but failed? Even if that attempt was clearly not intended to succeed, don't ignore it. Let him know that you've heard his call for help. Sit down with him and make an earnest effort to find out why he tried to kill himself. Listen carefully and don't dismiss his problems as insignificant, even if they seem so to you. Don't react negatively to him out of your own fear and/or anxiety. Seek professional help immediately.

A variety of treatment options are available, including outpatient and hospital-based (and/or residential) treatment programs. A careful assessment is necessary to determine what type of program is best for your teenager. Questions such as these must be answered: What was the cause of the suicide attempt? Is he depressed? What is his underlying personality? How is the family functioning? How much family support and understanding is there?

In summary, find out what is wrong and what you must do to correct and/or improve the situation. Again, ask your adolescent's pediatrician to point you in the right direction to get the proper help. And there is some good news: out of every 100,000 teenagers, 60,000 may have thoughts of killing themselves, but only a very small number, about nine youngsters, will actually do so.

Much more research is needed to better understand adolescent suicide. But recent studies suggest that those teenagers who do commit suicide may be an unusual group, quite different from the much larger number who go no further than thinking about it. One of the biggest challenges for health-care researchers is to determine who these teenagers are and what can be done for them, particularly when they kill themselves with little presuicidal warning.

Finally, remember yourself if a family member attempts suicide. When a suicide attempt does occur in the family, parents usually feel shocked, sad, angry, and guilty. It's important for you to talk about these feelings with someone you can trust, perhaps a professional counselor.

13

Coping With
Death and Dying

*I*n our death-denying culture most people don't deal with death very well. Accepting and adjusting to a death in the family is difficult for adults, but when it comes to helping our children cope, we find it almost an unbearable task. Whether a youngster has lost a parent, a grandparent, or a sibling, few adults have the tools to help ease her through this life crisis.

The temptation, particularly with adolescents, is to assume—or at least hope—that they can handle it on their own. As a result many parents abdicate their responsibility of guiding teenagers through this experience. But it's risky—and unfair to your child—to make the assumption that she can manage this situation without help. In fact most adolescents can't.

Of course the emotional impact on your teenager will vary, depending on her closeness to the individual who has died. If the deceased was a family acquaintance whom she rarely saw, the death might not affect her much at all. But if her sibling or a parent has died, she can be absolutely devastated by the event and in need of as much support as—or even more than—the adults in the family.

A TEENAGER'S
UNDERSTANDING OF DEATH

Under the age of six children have no realistic concept of death. To them it may represent nothing more than a long nap. As youngsters mature, however, they gradually begin to perceive death as an irreversible event; by age nine they start to recognize that life as we know it does end and that eventually everyone does die. By adolescence children probably understand as well as adults what happens when death occurs.

Despite their intellectual understanding of what dying means, teenagers often have a particularly difficult time dealing with it. For many the teenage years are already, under the best of circumstances, a tumultuous time emotionally. Add to that a death in the family, and it can seem overwhelming to an adolescent.

That's where you come in. Inevitably you'll be going through psychological turmoil, too, when a loved one dies. However, don't leave your teenager stranded without someone to talk to. She'll need to describe her thoughts and share her feelings with a person she can trust. So make yourself available when she needs you.

Some teenagers, of course, will find it easier than others to be open and expressive. Because adolescents are so sensitive to how the world views them, they may make an extra effort to keep their emotions hidden. Or they may hide their feelings in an attempt to be strong and care for other family members. When a young person is quiet like this, try to gently draw information out of her. What is she feeling now about the death? What did the deceased person mean to her? How will she remember the individual? Everyone needs to grieve, and if she's denying the death—perhaps to protect herself from the pain of what has happened—this can put added stress on her.

Some of your teenager's emotions may surprise you. You may find, for example, that she feels guilty or responsible for the death. This reaction may be particularly true if she had felt rivalrous toward the deceased or if she believes she could have somehow prevented the death ("If only I had reminded Dad to take his medicine every night"; "I knew Mom had been drinking—why didn't I take the car keys away from her?").

There are other common responses too. Perhaps your teenager feels rage at being abandoned. Or she might feel angry at the deceased for smoking the cigarettes that gave him lung cancer. She might also have some anxiety as she clearly confronts the reality that she too won't live forever.

Dr. Elisabeth Kubler-Ross and other authorities on death and dying have identified several stages of grief through which everyone must pass. Denial is usually the first stage—a refusal to believe that the loved one has really died. This denial then gives way to despair as the teenager confronts her loss and begins to realize the tragedy of the death. Eventually she moves on to an acceptance of the new circumstances, followed by an adaptation to a life without the deceased. (It's also important to note that the divorce of parents can produce similar grieving reactions in adolescents, especially if one parent withdraws and has minimal contact with his or her teenager.)

During your conversations with your teenager, share your own emotions with her. You're probably feeling many of the same things she is, so let her know that. Don't withdraw at a time when she's probably confused by much of what's going on around her. If she doesn't see you openly grieving, she may wonder why you don't seem to miss the family member who has died.

If the deceased is a sibling of your teenager, choose your words carefully as you talk about him. Parents may speak so highly of the dead child that the surviving one may feel she compares unfavorably to the sibling who has passed away. Don't leave your teenager thinking, "I bet Mom wishes I was the one who had died, not Bobby."

Although most of the emotional turmoil surrounding a death will surface in the first month, the grieving process can last from six months up to two years—and in some cases even longer. During this time, and sometimes thereafter (especially on the anniversary of the death), the distress felt by the teenager may surface in a number of ways. She may become more argumentative, directing a lot of her anger at her parent. Her grades in school may suffer. She also may show signs of depression. According to one study the most severely depressed children are often adolescent boys who have lost their fathers.

Some parents are unable to support their adolescent adequately as they themselves try to deal with the loss of a spouse or another family member. If you're having difficulty helping your teenager through the grieving process, ask relatives, close friends, or your teenager's pediatrician for assistance. Everyone in the family needs support during this trying time. The doctor may suggest professional counseling for the entire family. You might also contact your priest, minister, or rabbi for guidance.

Finally, don't kid yourself—or your teenager—that things haven't changed with the death of someone close to you. The entire family will have adjustments to make. However, the transition will be easier if you keep the channels of communication open and be a constant source of support for one another during this difficult period.

PART IV

YOUR TEENAGER'S SEXUAL GROWTH AND DEVELOPMENT

14

COMMUNICATING
ABOUT SEX

*I*n generations past, people called them "the facts of life" or "the birds and the bees." Fidgety parents would often sit their teenagers down and, as well as they could, explain what human sexuality is all about. Most didn't do a very good job. Others didn't try at all.

At first glance you might think that as a parent today you would find it a little easier to discuss sexuality than your mother or grandmother did. After all, sex is no longer the taboo subject it once was. Images of sexuality routinely enter America's living rooms via the television set. Prime-time television shows, movies on cable TV, and rock-and-roll music are often brimming with graphic sexual references, too.

Even so, many kids still go through adolescence with little or no sexual guidance from Mom or Dad. Although there are varied reasons for this, some parents simply assume that in these more permissive times teenagers already know a lot about sex. And with that in mind, they often forgo that uncomfortable heart-to-heart talk with their adolescent. As the argument goes, don't today's kids know everything anyway?

Not quite. Even in this era, when television, billboards, and magazines constantly communicate sexual messages, teenagers aren't as knowledgeable as you might think. Yes, they may "talk a good game," using some of the same provocative language they've heard on TV or in popular songs. They may convey a sense of sophistication through what they say and how they dress. But, in fact, they probably don't really understand much of what they're exposed to.

Consider this finding from a poll conducted in 1986: only 40 percent of adolescents know it's usually true that a girl is most likely to become pregnant about two weeks after her menstrual period begins; 59 percent gave the wrong answer or said they weren't sure. Other studies have uncovered similar types of common misunderstandings.

Our teenagers, then, aren't as enlightened as they may pretend to be—not only on basic facts but also when it comes to more abstract concepts. For instance, how many know the difference between intimacy and sex? Or between love and lust? Or between love and making love? Not enough, to be sure.

Here, then, is the bottom line: things haven't changed very much over the generations. Adolescents of today want and need answers to the same kinds of questions that teenagers have wondered about for many decades: "Am I normal?" "What does sexual intercourse feel like?" "What will he [or she] think of me if I say no?" Not surprisingly, in a survey of student leaders from every state in the nation, 96 percent favored public school sex education; their faculty sponsors agreed, with 94 percent supporting the idea.

Teenagers have always needed the involvement of their parents to help them deal with the complex aspects of their sexuality. However, Mom and Dad may be even more important now than ever before. After all, never have there been so many diverse influences vying for your youngster's attention, and never have teenagers had to make so many choices. And with the risks so high—particularly with the ominous threat of serious and sometimes lethal sexually transmitted diseases (such as AIDS)—adolescents unquestionably need accurate information and guidance.

Of course growing up has never been easy. No one's suggesting that. But imagine being a high school senior today, when perhaps half of your friends are having sex while the other half aren't. Which behavior and what values would you adopt? And how easy would it be to make those decisions? Some guidance from parents certainly could help.

THE OBSTACLES TO
GOOD COMMUNICATION

Think back to what times were like during your own adolescence. Was it just before the so-called "sexual revolution," when the distinctions between "right" and "wrong" behavior seemed better defined, when "good girls" drew a clearer line and boys seemed more "gentlemanly"? If so, you may feel out of sync with today's changing sexual attitudes and lifestyles. Even if your own standards for sexual behavior have changed, they may still seem old-fashioned and irrelevant today. As a result you may feel particularly ill equipped to talk about sex with your teenager.

However, don't be scared away. There's probably no more important job you do as a parent than to help guide your son or daughter through adolescence. Yes, the times certainly are more complex today, with teenage struggles often focusing on issues such as choosing contraceptives and avoiding sexually transmitted diseases rather than on more innocent concerns like skin blemishes and prom dates. With so much at stake parents need to force themselves to get beyond their own anxieties and take the initiative in discussing sexual subjects with their teenagers.

But how many parents take this responsibility seriously enough? Far too few. While parents as well as children acknowledge that they should talk with one another about sexuality, many parents still shy away from doing so, sometimes because they don't feel competent in this role. Other parents seem to believe there's some value in keeping the kids from knowing "too much."

Although four out of five parents concur that they have an obligation to provide sex education for their children, most studies show that no more than 25 percent of American mothers teach their daughters about sex to any degree; even fewer talk about issues such as contraception and abortion. And as poorly as mothers often perform in this regard, fathers generally are even less reliable sex educators. A prevailing attitude seems to be, "My parents didn't tell me anything about it; I don't discuss it, either."

However, that approach obviously won't meet the pressing needs of today's children. While most teenagers say they've never received *any* advice about sex from either parent, the majority still would prefer that their mother and father become a source of sex information. Even when adolescents seem to resist their parents' involvement, they have a very real need for it.

And what are the consequences if you steer clear of discussions about sex? They could be devastating. Some research shows that teenagers (both boys and girls) who receive sex information from someone other than a parent are more likely to have premarital sex, start having intercourse at a younger age, and have more than one sexual partner. But by encouraging communication, by providing accurate information, by listening willingly, and by offering some sensitive support, you can help your adolescent deal with his or her own sexuality in a responsible way.

MAKING COMMUNICATION WORK

So how do you get started communicating about sex? First of all, the formal educational process about sexuality should really have begun years ago, at least to some degree. After all, although we usually don't think of our small children as sexual beings, they are, beginning at the moment of birth. Their attitudes toward male–female relationships and sexuality start to develop early—by watching how Dad treats Mom, by observing how their parents hug one another, by overhearing adult conversations, by watching their parents react to sexually suggestive TV programs. Thus youngsters receive sex education at home all along, even if their parents never *talk* to them about sex.

So ideally, beginning in the first years of your youngster's life, you should open all lines of communication. As he discovers the differences in the bodies of boys and girls, as he begins to wonder where babies come from, as he satisfies his curiosity by "playing doctor" with friends of the same or the opposite sex, you should be available to provide him with information appropriate for his age. No one should reach adolescence without a basic understanding of sexual "plumbing"—that is, a simple explanation of sexual anatomy, including the male and female sex organs and their functions.

Once your child becomes a teenager, the emphasis of your education should shift. After he has a good understanding of the physiological changes that he's going through (See Chapter 5 for a discussion of normal sexual growth processes), the focus should shift to values. You'll want to deal with issues that help your teenager answer questions like these:

- "At what age should I begin dating?"

- "When is it okay to kiss a boy [or a girl]?"

- "How far is too far?"

- "When am I ready to have sexual intercourse?"

- "Won't having sex help me keep my boyfriend [or girlfriend]?"

Your own value system—even if it seems old-fashioned by today's standards—should provide the answers to questions like these. Although public morality is changing, you can still keep your own set of values. True, you must acknowledge that sex is more out in the open today than ever before. But don't feel embarrassed by how your beliefs may be perceived by others or let that interfere with your family's communication. If you choose not to become more liberal in what you think is permissible and what isn't, there's no need for you to change. And many of your values—no matter what they are—will become your teenager's values, but only if you get them out in the open and let him know what they are.

So if you think premarital sex is wrong, communicate that to your teenager. Or if you think premarital sex is okay but only in a loving, committed relationship, tell your son or daughter just that. In the process, don't overlook explaining *why* you feel as you do. It's not enough to tell adolescents to "just say no" to sex, for example; you have to explain the reasons behind your thinking and why saying no is in their own best interests. If they understand the reasoning behind your beliefs, they're much more likely to adopt them as their own.

You also need to listen to what teenagers are saying. Rather than preaching, make your interactions dialogue. Find out what they know about sex and try to answer their questions as clearly and directly as possible.

However, what happens if your teenagers really don't seem to be listening to you? What if you try talking *with* them about sex (or some other subject) but get absolutely no response to anything you're saying? That kind of reaction—that almost catatonic state—is not uncommon among adolescents. Be sure to give them lots of time to react or comment, but even if there's little or no response, take heart: although teenagers may not be reacting, they hear what you're saying. Even those one-way conversations are not futile.

The same is true if your ideas elicit a violent response from your teenager. Yes, he may react by arguing passionately against what you're saying. He may tell you how antiquated your values are. But that's also a sign that he's heard what you've said. Some of it is bound to have an impact. Thus these two-way conversations, even if they get heated at times, will still help your teenager develop a value system that's responsible and self-protective—although it might be different from your own.

Now, what about your own anxiety about sex? Does discussing sex really embarrass you, whether it's with your teenager or anyone else? Well, you're certainly not alone. If you're uncomfortable with this kind of discussion, it's important to confront and deal effectively with those anxieties, or you risk confusing your child and interfering with the relationship you have.

As one mother said, "I was trying to tell my daughter that sex was a healthy, natural part of life. But at the same time, I'm sure she saw how embarrassed I was. So I don't know what message she really got out of our conversation."

How do you overcome those anxieties? One important step is to acknowledge to yourself—and to your teenager—that some nervousness and embarrassment exists, perhaps because of your own background. Then, as you talk about subjects that make you feel uncomfortable, speak slowly, calmly, and coolly. That seems to help many parents. You can also desensitize yourself to these kinds of discussions by talking with other parents and by becoming involved in the parental components of sex education programs in the schools.

Some parents find they can talk comfortably about certain sexual subjects but not others. Masturbation is one of those "taboo" topics that makes many fathers and mothers (and even some doctors) uneasy. However, keep in mind that masturbation is *normal* adolescent behavior, as it was earlier in infancy and childhood. About 90 percent of males and more than half of females masturbate—and despite centuries-old myths to the contrary, it causes no harm, doesn't contribute to physical or mental illness, and is a common expression of sexuality.

Even so, many teenagers and parents believe that masturbation is an *unacceptable* way to release sexual tension. Of course they're wrong. You need to let your adolescents know that they need not feel guilty if they engage in this activity. Tell them simply and straightforwardly that masturbation is a normal behavior. If it has any negative side at all, it's that many adolescents still have feelings of guilt associated with masturbation or become preoccupied by it. Most important, for most teenagers (and adults), it is emotionally unsatisfying and incapable of meeting the need for intimacy provided by sexual intercourse in a loving relationship.

Now, what about your teenager's anxieties during your discussions with him about sexuality? You can make your dialogues more comfortable for your adolescent by not prying into the details of his personal life that he might prefer not to discuss. Everyone, including your adolescent, is entitled to some privacy, and not everything in his life is your business. If that's the attitude you take—respecting the right of privacy of your adolescent—he'll be more likely to keep the channels of communication open.

Many parents find that rather than asking their teenager, "Are you having sex?" it's usually more comfortable to approach those topics—and communicate your values—more indirectly. For example: "Are there kids your age having sex? What do you think about that?" Parents can also talk about what things were like during their own adolescence, which can help open up a dialogue.

At some point, if you have an excellent rapport with your teenager and explain why you want to know, it might be all right to ask, "Would you feel comfortable telling me if you and Susan [Robert] are having sex?" Ask this question, however, only if you're prepared to deal with the answer, including making suggestions about birth control methods. If you're not ready to deal with that right now, you're probably better off with a more general discussion that doesn't confront the adolescent about his own behavior. Open-ended questions often work well, such as, "I don't know if you and Susan [Robert] are having sex, but I want to be sure that should that happen, you discuss birth control with me or another adult who can give you the information you need."

Finally, some parents become anxious because they're convinced that by imparting information about sex they'll actually be encouraging their youngster to experiment with what he's learned. They fear that by talking about sex they'll legitimize it. As one mother said, "My worry is that the unspoken message will be, 'It's okay to go out and have sex.'"

But that's not true. Think back to your own teenage years for a moment. You probably spent a lot of time thinking about sex. All teenagers do. In all likelihood any discussions you had with your parents didn't plant any ideas in your head that you hadn't been having already.

Some (but not all) studies, in fact, show that good communication can actually have a protective effect—that is, when parent and teenager talk openly, irresponsible sexual behavior *decreases*. According to this research it's simply a myth that when children are taught about sex—at home or in the school—they'll be driven to conduct some "personal research" into the subject. In fact the opposite is true: it's misinformation, or a complete lack of information, that gets most teenagers into trouble. Ignorance is not bliss!

IF YOU JUST CAN'T . . .

For some parents, discussing sex with their teenager—or anyone else, for that matter—is simply impossible. Yes, they may recognize the importance of it, but perhaps because of their own upbringing and their inhibitions, they simply can't talk about it.

Does that describe you? If so, all is not lost. True, no one can communicate the family values better than you or your spouse. But if that's just not possible, there are some other options.

First, there are the schools. Polls consistently show that about 85 percent of parents approve of sex education—including teaching about birth control—in the schools. Keep in mind, however, that while your child may receive some sex education in the classroom, the quality of these programs varies considerably from school to school and district to district. In many cases they consist of little more than a lecture or two on basic anatomy by a physical education teacher. And often they don't begin until *after* many students have already become sexually active.

As an alternative, ask your pediatrician for help in providing your teenager with sex-related information. If your spouse is as inhibited as you, perhaps an aunt or an uncle can assume the role of sex educator. Maybe the family minister, priest, or rabbi can help, too.

Still another option is to give a book on human sexuality to yourself and to your teenager. There are several good ones available, including those listed below.

Books on Human Sexuality

What Teenagers Want to Know About Sex: Questions and Answers, by Boston Children's Hospital Staff with Robert P. Masland, Jr. (Little, Brown, 1988)

What We Told Our Kids About Sex, by Betsy and Michael Weisman (Harcourt Brace Jovanovich, 1987)

How to Talk with Your Child About Sexuality: A Parent's Guide, by the Planned Parenthood Federation of America, Inc., Staff (Doubleday, 1986)

Raising a Child Conservatively in a Sexually Permissive World, by Sol and Judith Gordon (Simon & Schuster, 1989)

Talking with Your Child About Sex: Questions and Answers for Children from Birth to Puberty, by Mary S. Calderone and James W. Ramey (Ballantine, 1983)

The Family Book About Sexuality, by Mary S. Calderone and Eric W. Johnson (Harper & Row, 1990)

Sex: The Facts, the Acts and Your Feelings, by Michael Carrera (Crown, 1981)

Learning About Sex: The Contemporary Guide for Young Adults, by Gary F. Kelly (Barron's, 3rd ed., 1986)

There's one other important point to keep in mind about communicating about sex. No matter who provides your teenager with sexual information—whether it's you, your pediatrician, or a book—you can't necessarily expect your child to follow all the advice explicitly. To a large extent your teenager's behavior is out of your control. Adolescents are becoming young adults and will make up their own mind about many of these issues. Even so, it's critical that you let your youngster know how you feel—honestly and straightforwardly—regardless of how much of it he might ignore.

Also, let your teenagers know that whatever course of action they take, or whatever situation they find themselves in, they can always come to you to talk about it. Even if they were to do something that you'd frown on, you'd still keep an open ear. If your daughter were to become pregnant, for example, you may not approve, but you'd want to know about it. The same would apply to your son if his girlfriend became pregnant. You'd want to help—and your teenager would probably need you more than ever.

So by all means, don't reject your youngsters if they don't follow your advice. You may feel hurt if they don't listen to you, but you need to continue communicating with your children.

Face it: if your son or daughter decides to become sexually active, there's not much you can do about it. Yes, you can educate, advise, and inform—but then only hope for the best. The decision itself really belongs to your teenager. He or she will have the final word on when, where, and with whom to become sexually involved. But no matter what choice your adolescent makes, explain that you'll be accessible to listen to problems and answer questions. *Always!*

15

IS TEENAGE SEXUALITY
OUT OF CONTROL?

"*S*ure I'm having sex with my girlfriend. Most of my friends are having sex, too. What's the big deal?"

To a lot of parents having a sexually active teenager *is* a big deal. But as the statement above suggests, sexual intercourse among adolescents is not uncommon. Just consider these statistics:

- Although just 4 percent of twelve-year-olds have experienced sexual intercourse, that number increases progressively throughout the teenage years. By the age of seventeen slightly more than half of all American adolescents have had sex at least once.

- By age nineteen that number has risen even more dramatically, with 80 percent of boys and 70 percent of girls having engaged in sexual activity.

- The average age for a girl to have intercourse for the first time is about sixteen years; that compares with an average of about fifteen-and-a-half years for boys.

- At every age level during adolescence boys are more sexually active than girls.

There's no doubt about it. More teenagers are having sex—and at an earlier age—than a generation ago. And this fact isn't going unnoticed by most adults. When you ask parents what concerns them most as their children approach adolescence, the subject of sexual "promiscuity" almost always arises.

Yet is all this parental anxiety really justified? In many cases, probably not. Promiscuity is an old word, and for most parents it brings to mind multiple sexual partners. But even in today's world it's a term much more applicable to boys than girls. Most females, in fact, are *not* promiscuous. Studies show that over 50 percent of girls who have had sexual intercourse as teenagers have had only one partner; over 80 percent have had three or fewer. Males, on the other hand, tend to have more partners.

Yes, it's true that many teenagers are having their first sexual experiences at younger ages than their parents probably did. However, researchers report that, particularly with girls, the vast majority of this sexual activity takes place in the context of long-term, committed relationships.

Casual sex, then, isn't the norm. Instead many sexually active adolescents are quite selective about whom they're sleeping with. And some are still waiting until marriage or at least until they meet the person they plan to marry. According to one study about 80 percent of girls said they wouldn't have sexual intercourse with a boy whom they didn't love or weren't going to marry.

If they had to do it over again, many adolescents say they'd wait a little longer before having their first sexual experience. For instance, researchers conducted a survey in Baltimore among 3,500 junior and senior high school students attending inner-city schools. In response to a question about the best age for initial intercourse, 83 percent of the sexually experienced boys and girls cited an age older than the one at which they first had sex; 43 percent reported a best age older than their present age.

Your teenager will constantly hear stories from peers about what they're doing with their boyfriends or girlfriends. As a result some adolescents may feel that "everyone is doing it but me." However, to keep things in perspective, he or she also should have some input about sexuality from you. First, remind your adolescent that some teenagers exaggerate their sexual experiences. Also, be sure to talk about your own values regarding premarital sex and related issues. Is sex permissible in the context of a loving relationship? Should it be avoided until a teenager is mature enough to deal responsibly with the contraception issue? Or should it always wait until marriage, no matter how committed the relationship or how mature the teenager becomes? Communicate clearly—and early—where you stand and how you'd like your teenager to behave sexually.

WHO'S CHOOSING TO HAVE SEX?

Not everyone, of course, is waiting for Mr. or Ms. Right to come along before deciding to have sexual intercourse. Researchers have been able to put together a profile of which teenagers are most likely to engage in early and/or promiscuous sex. And the findings really aren't surprising.

First, there are some teenagers who are simply curious about the physical changes they're going through. They can't wait to grow up and try out their "new" bodies.

But there's even a more pressing issue among many of these adolescents—namely, self-esteem. Teenagers who are sexually active—particularly those who begin as young as ages thirteen, fourteen, or fifteen—may have a very shaky image of themselves. Some say that by engaging in sexual intercourse they begin to feel more physically attractive. At the same time, sexual activity can make them feel important in the eyes of their partner.

More significantly, many of these adolescents often report feeling alienated from their home environment. They describe an emotional estrangement between themselves and their parents. They've probably had very little discussion with Mom and Dad about sexual issues—or about anything else for that matter. By being sexually active, however, they've found a way to try to meet their needs for the closeness, intimacy, and affection that may be missing at home.

What's your own family situation like? Does your teenager get a lot of emotional support at home? If she does, she may not feel the need to look for affection elsewhere. But when a fourteen-year-old girl, for instance, feels neglected by her parents, her boyfriend may be her sole source of comfort. Sex with him may become extremely important in her life. And it may also be her way of ultimately getting some attention at home—particularly if she announces one night to Mom that she might be pregnant!

One study of high school students found that teenagers who had started having sex had less parental support and fewer controls imposed by Mom and Dad. They also encountered less parental disapproval of their disruptive behavior than did young people who had never had sexual intercourse.

A separate study reached similar conclusions. It reported that adolescents who had never had sex felt close to both parents (particularly Mom) and perceived their parents as having a close relationship with one another. By contrast, those teenagers who had experienced sexual intercourse did not feel quite as close to their mothers, felt even more distant from their fathers, and expressed uncertainty over whether their parents loved each other.

Research findings also make another important point: your own role as a sex educator may be particularly influential on the choices your adolescent makes. If you are the primary source of your teenager's sexual instruction, she may be more sexually responsible than her friends who have turned elsewhere for information. Among both boys and girls those who gathered their sexual knowledge from friends or the media were more likely to be sexually active and to have begun having intercourse at a younger age.

As a parent you simply can't afford to abandon your responsibility on these matters. If you're not there to influence your teenager, his or her peers will certainly fill that void. After all, even though adolescence is a time for asserting individuality, most teenagers are also eager to conform to whatever "everyone else is doing"—from wearing the "right" brand of jeans to listening to the hottest rock group. And, of course, in some teenage circles sexual activity seems to be one way to earn peer respect and a sense of belonging.

As unsettling as this may seem, keep in mind that peer pressure isn't necessarily always "negative." There are a lot of different peer groups out there who can influence your teenager. Yes, there are the "experienced" kids on every high school campus, but there are also the academics, the athletes, and perhaps a dozen more groups who have other interests besides sex. It's important to know what peer group your own adolescent is being influenced by. And unless you ask whom she's associating with and what their interests are, you won't find out.

If your daughter, for instance, tells you she's thinking about having sex, ask her why. Does she think it will make her more popular with her friends? Does she feel that her virginity has become a "burden"? Does she simply wonder whether sex is really as the other kids describe it?

When a parent has done an effective job of communicating values about sexuality, and when a teenager's self-esteem is strong, he will have a much better chance of resisting inappropriate peer pressure. And part of your job is to make sure your adolescent is capable of doing that. All teenagers should be able to choose their own best time for having sex, free of pressure from friends. And youngsters who have developed a strong sense of self should be able to resist those peer pressures. Some may simply say, "My parents would kill me if they found out." Others may explain, "Look, this is what I believe, this is what my parents have taught me. I'm not interested in having sex yet. I have other plans for my life."

At some point during adolescence most girls in particular feel some pressure to have sex. This most often occurs when younger females are dating older males and the girls find themselves unable to withstand the pressures placed on them. As a parent you need to know that a fourteen-year-old girl who dates an eighteen-year-old boy may be headed for trouble. Perhaps they've dated a few times, she's started to feel attached to him—and then she hears a line like this: "If you love me, you'll have sex with me."

What happens next? A lot depends on whether she feels good about herself. If she does, she should feel strong enough to resist this kind of pressure, perhaps with lines of her own, such as:

"If you really love me, you won't put this kind of pressure on me."

"I don't really love you yet, so I don't have to have sex with you."

Dr. Sol Gordon believes there's an effective retort to just about any sexual advance. For instance:

BOY: "I'll respect you in the morning."
GIRL: "Good, then I'll see you tomorrow."
Or:
BOY: "All talk, no action."
GIRL: "I'll fix that. How about no talk and no action. Good-bye."
Or:
BOY: "I can tell that you want me."
GIRL: "Yes, I want you to leave."

In our culture it's most often the boy who's applying the pressure for sex and the girl who's resisting. However, females can be aggressive too. Tell your son that he should feel free to say no as well.

In fact, no matter what your child's gender, remind him or her that a lot of high school students still say no all the time—about half of them, to be exact. It may take courage to do so, but there's no truth to the statement that "*everyone* is having sex."

Make sure that your adolescent understands that he or she may not be emotionally ready for sexual intercourse. A lot of teenagers also discover that once sex does enter a relationship the relationship changes. Sometimes it becomes stronger; but other times sex becomes a complicating factor, intensifying the relationship before either partner is really ready and ultimately creating so much stress that it pushes them apart.

When is the best time for teenagers to decide if they will or won't say no? They should make those kinds of decisions *before* they find themselves in a situation where they're actually being tested. Too many adolescents (as well as adults) have never thought in advance about how they would handle this kind of predicament—and under the pressure of the moment have made a decision that they've regretted later.

Some teenagers are so sensitive that they worry about hurting someone's feelings when they say no. And maybe they will. But remind your son or daughter that hurt feelings heal with time; an unintended pregnancy and a baby linger on for much longer—for a lifetime and over generations!

There's one other source of sexual pressure that your teenager may be contending with—namely, the television set. The average teenager watches about twenty-four hours of TV a week, and in a given year he sees more than 14,000 sexual references or innuendos on TV. A lot of that sex is casual, without consequences, and outside of committed relationships. On the afternoon soap operas, which many teenage girls watch avidly, 94 percent of all sexual relationships are between unmarried partners. And if Mom or Dad are at work or are otherwise unavailable to help teenagers put what they see in perspective, young people are likely to believe that what they're seeing is the adult norm.

TV is an educational tool, but when it comes to sex it may be communicating some unwelcome messages. In a recent Harris poll nearly two-thirds of American adults believed that watching television encourages adolescents to become sexually active. More than 80 percent said that TV exaggerates the importance of sex in American life. Teenagers themselves rank TV just behind their peers and parents as an influence on their attitudes and behaviors.

YOUR INFLUENCE COUNTS

Parents do count in their teenager's life. Despite all the other influences, you can have an effect, although at times it may seem like an uphill fight.

As much as they may resist it, remind your teenagers what the studies show about teenage sexuality. Let them know about the research showing that some adolescents feel guilt and anxiety about their sexual behavior. Girls in particular often say that their sexual experiences simply aren't satisfying.

You need to get involved to help your own adolescent through these difficult times. And to be most effective and influential, you must fully accept the reality that your teenager is a sexual being. Some parents have a real problem conceptualizing their "child" as having sexual interests and drives. But all teenagers do. And someday they will have sex.

Before that happens, make the effort to impart your values. You need to convey the attitude that sexuality is normal and healthy. At the same time, teenagers need to know how love fits into the picture and when the right time may come for their first sexual experience. In short, be a parent—educate, train, and nurture.

16

CONTRACEPTION AND YOUR TEENAGER

*J*ust how smart are teenagers about sex? As we've suggested in earlier chapters, a lot of them know less than they think they do. Consider, for example, the following myths about contraception—which many teenagers believe to be fact:

- You can't get pregnant if a boy withdraws before ejaculating.

- The pill is too dangerous to use; it causes cancer.

- Girls can't get pregnant unless they have an orgasm.

- If you take a birth-control pill just before sexual intercourse, you can't get pregnant.

- Condoms break a lot, so it doesn't pay to use them.

- Girls can prevent pregnancy by douching after intercourse.

- You can't really get pregnant if you have sex only once in a while.

Sometimes it's hard to reason with adolescents. Most parents know this all too well. But it can become even harder when the subject is sex. For example, teenage girls may tell you how concerned they are about their friend getting pregnant because she's having sex without any birth control. However, if *they* are doing exactly the same thing, pregnancy is the furthest thing from their mind. They'll often simply say, "Oh, no, it can't happen to me. I won't get pregnant."

Ironically, some parents feel quite at ease, convinced that their teenager won't be having sex since "she wouldn't be foolish enough to take a chance of getting pregnant." But unknown to them, their adolescent may not be worried about pregnancy at all. According to one survey two-thirds of sexually active teenagers never use contraception, or they use it only inconsistently. About half believed they could never get pregnant.

Unfortunately, teenagers can—and do—become pregnant. And the statistics are startling. More than one million adolescents become pregnant each year in the U.S. That's more than 2,500 each day! And it includes 30,000 girls under fifteen years of age. Before they leave their teens, four out of ten girls will become pregnant—most of them unintentionally.

What does all this mean? More than anything, if your teenager has made the decision to have sex, he or she *needs* contraception. And that creates a dilemma for many parents. Maybe you don't agree with your adolescent's decision to have sexual intercourse. Perhaps you're outraged by it. Even so, if he or she has chosen this type of sexual activity, birth control is absolutely essential—and without delay: one-half of all premarital teenage pregnancies occur in the first six months after intercourse has begun, and 10 percent occur in the first month.

Don't count on your teenager's taking the initiative when it comes to contraception. Even when adolescents know all the facts about sex and birth control, they may not use that information wisely. One teenager's explanation is common: "The reason I didn't use any birth control methods is that I didn't expect to have sex. It just happened." Young adolescents also do not have good "futuristic" thinking skills and do not clearly equate a sexual encounter with the possible delivery of a baby nine months later.

And what about those teenagers who do plan their sexual encounters in advance? Are they any more careful? Not necessarily. Some just don't feel comfortable going to a doctor and asking for contraceptives. And they may be even more reluctant to ask Mom to go with them, particularly since that will mean explaining to her why they need birth control.

It shouldn't have to be so complicated. One sensible approach to take with your teenager is to say something like, "I'm worried that you're having sex . . . and I don't approve. I don't believe that you're mature enough yet. But even more than that, I don't want you to become pregnant. So if you decide to become sexually involved, let me know. And we'll make sure that you're protected."

Is this a mixed message? Some parents think so. But it's really not. It's very straightforward and lets your teenager know exactly where you stand and what you're willing to do. Bear in mind that if adolescents have decided to become sexually active, you're probably not going to be able to stop them. But you can help them prevent an unwanted pregnancy. Contact your pediatrician about it and have her talk to your teenager if necessary.

WHICH CONTRACEPTIVE IS BEST?

When sexually active teenagers do use contraception, the overwhelming majority prefer just two types: the pill and condoms. No other methods are anywhere near as popular.

Birth Control Pills

If your daughter is regularly sexually active, oral contraceptives are probably her best choice. Consider these positive factors:

- The pill is effective—about 99.7 percent effective, to be exact. That's a higher success rate than any other form of birth control or any combination of methods.

- The pill is safe. Yes, there has been a lot of negative publicity associated with the pill, particularly its alleged links with strokes, heart attacks, and cancer. For that reason concern about it is high. A 1985 Gallup poll found that three out of every four women believed that the use of oral contraceptives carried "substantial risks."

A lot of those anxieties, however, are rooted in misunderstandings. The pill actually *lowers* the risk of some types of cancer (ovarian, endometrial), and its link to others (particularly cervical cancer) is unproven.*

*The incidence of cervical cancer is increasing among young women, and many factors are implicated by researchers, including earlier onset of coitus, more sexual partners, and increased exposure to sexually transmitted diseases (such as herpes and venereal warts). Teenagers on the pill need regular exams, including Pap smears, which can monitor for cancer of the cervix.

As for its purported cardiovascular side effects, most such complications occur in women who are over thirty-five years old and smoke. The medical literature contains only one report of a pill-related death of an adolescent due to a stroke or a heart attack—and that was back in 1968, when the pill was much stronger than it is today. Teenagers are at an even lower risk for pill-related complications than adult females. Adolescence, in fact, is probably the ideal age to be taking the pill from a medical viewpoint.

- The pill is much safer than the consequences of not using birth control—namely, pregnancy, childbirth, and abortion. For instance, oral contraceptives are nearly ten times safer for your teenage daughter than a full-term pregnancy; they're three times safer than a first-trimester abortion.

- In the newer forms of the pill (which are the ones typically prescribed for teenagers), the dosages of hormones are extremely low. In fact the hormonal content in some of the newer pills varies during the twenty-eight-day cycle to closely mimic a young woman's normal hormone levels.

- Compliance is rather simple. Although the pill must be taken every day, this can quickly become a ritual at the same time each morning or evening, as routine as taking a vitamin tablet with orange juice at breakfast.

- With the pill a girl does not have to carry around anything to be available at the time of intercourse. There are no inconvenient vaginal foams to deal with or any other obvious obstacles to compliance.

But remember, the pill does *not* prevent sexually transmitted diseases. So there is no reason a condom cannot be used as well, especially if there are multiple sex partners.

Condoms

Contraception is not an issue just for girls. True, only females can become pregnant. But it's a joint responsibility of both sexual partners to be sure that it doesn't happen.

Condoms, of course, are the most obvious way a boy can fulfill his responsibility for contraception. While not as effective as the pill, they nevertheless have a good track record, particularly when used in combination with contraceptive foam. Condoms are also relatively inexpensive and very accessible (you don't need a prescription to buy them), there are no associated side effects, and they protect against sexually transmitted diseases.

That's the good news. But there are problems too. Some males just don't know how to use condoms properly. For instance, is your son aware that he needs to put the condom on when his erection first occurs, to avoid the possibility of leakage of sperm? After he ejaculates, does he always withdraw before losing his erection, to minimize the chances that the condom will slip off? And does he know that condoms can be damaged if they're stored improperly (in high temperatures or in a wallet for several months)?

Of course some sexually active boys never misuse condoms—because they never use them in the first place, even when they and their sexual partner aren't taking any other birth control precautions. Ask these boys why they're running such a risk, and they all have a reason. Some say condoms cause discomfort or interfere with sensation and their enjoyment of sex. Others complain that condoms take away from the spontaneity of sex. Then there are those who insist that it seems unnatural to wear them.

Unfortunately, most boys have never been taught to be sexually responsible (though they should be!) and have not been taught to consider their partners' needs (though they should!). Parents (especially fathers) *must* communicate the importance of sexual responsibility.

Actually, some evidence indicates that older boys are starting to become more conscientious, reflecting a positive change in attitude about sexual responsibility. And as you might guess, AIDS is one reason for the increased use of condoms. Although condoms have always offered some protection against sexually transmitted diseases—gonorrhea, syphilis, herpes—none of these infections has ever posed as ominous a threat as AIDS, to heterosexuals as well as homosexuals. When Dr. Everett Koop, the former surgeon general warns that next to abstinence, condoms provide the closest thing to safe sex, many (but still not enough) teenagers are starting to get the message. Condoms may not be a 100 percent safeguard against AIDS, but they're the best protection we have right now, short of celibacy. Every teenager needs to know that.

Even when condoms are being used conscientiously, however, sex is not risk-free. The term "safe sex" is really a misnomer. The only truly safe sex for a teenager is no sex (coitus) at all. At a time when AIDS and other sexually transmitted diseases are epidemic, abstention from intercourse makes sense, particularly for an adolescent who isn't sure of the sexual history of the potential partner. When your teenager has sex with someone, it's tantamount to having sex with everyone he or she has ever slept with!

Other Forms of Contraception

Although pediatricians tend to recommend the pill or condoms as the primary contraceptive choice for teenagers, other options are available as well. However, none of them makes as much sense for this age group. For example, while diaphragms are an effective form of birth control, it's often difficult to get younger teenage girls to use one because of the planning it requires and the self-manipulation involved. The girl must insert the diaphragm no more than six hours before intercourse and must leave it in place for six to eight hours after sex; also, she must use a vaginal contraceptive cream or jelly with the diaphragm and, for even greater protection, a condom as well.

Compliance is also a major problem with other types of contraception, including various "rhythm" methods, spermicides, and the vaginal sponge. These methods require careful attention and planning. Moreover, when used by teenagers these methods have a poor record of effectiveness.

Intrauterine devices (IUDs) were once quite popular in the U.S., but they're not readily available today. Manufacturers have withdrawn most of them from the market to avoid a runaway liability problem that had been threatening to bankrupt some manufacturers. Even when they were widely accessible, however, some doctors did not consider them safe for young women who had never had children, since they increased the chances of infertility later in life. They also had a high expulsion rate, an increase in bleeding problems in girls with multiple partners, and an added risk for pelvic inflammatory disease (a severe genital infection associated with chronic abdominal pain and sterility). (See Chapter 32.)

CAN YOUR PEDIATRICIAN HELP?

Some parents find it impossible to discuss birth control with their teenagers or to help them obtain contraceptives. Quite often moms and dads believe that by making condoms or the pill available to their children they'll be encouraging them to have sex. "If I tell her all about birth control, she'll think I'm saying it's just fine to have sex with her boyfriend," said one mother.

But that just isn't the case. Studies show that information about birth control is not a "corrupting" influence. If anything, it increases the chances that teenagers are going to make wise decisions relative to their sexual behavior. There's another important side benefit as well: by discussing the subject frankly, you will make birth control less of a taboo topic for your adolescent, making it easier for her to talk about it with her own sexual partner when the time comes. Teenagers who have had conversations about birth control with their parents are more likely to use contraceptives when they become sexually active.

Adolescents who fall into special categories—such as the mentally retarded—have needs for birth-control information, too. Despite their retardation, they still have sexual desires and may become sexually active. (See Page 214.)

If you don't feel equipped to discuss the subject with your teenager—because of either inhibition or a lack of knowledge—ask your pediatrician for help. Doctors not only can give both you and your adolescent up-to-date information about contraceptive methods mentioned in this section and other methods, but they'll be able to answer your questions about sexually transmitted diseases (STDs). As we've already mentioned, the incidence of many venereal diseases is on the rise— one more reason why the decision to have sexual intercourse is a very serious one. Because it's much easier to prevent STDs than to cure them, the use of condoms should be considered an important means of limiting the transmission of these serious (and even life-threatening) diseases. Also, as a general guideline a doctor should immediately examine any sexually active teenager who is having pain or redness in the genital area—or who is experiencing abnormal bleeding or discharge—to check for a possible STD. (See Chapter 32.)

17

So Your Daughter Is Pregnant (or Your Son Might Become a Father)

"I had been dating this boy for a month or so. He's seventeen, about two years older than me. He kept asking me to have sex with him. I was afraid I'd lose him, so I finally said yes. And now I'm pregnant. I don't know what I'm going to do."

*E*ach year more than a million teenage girls find themselves in the same predicament—pregnant and confronting probably one of the biggest decisions of their lives. Should they have an abortion? Or should they carry the fetus to term? And if they do give birth, should they keep the baby or give it up for adoption?

These are not easy questions, particularly for an unmarried teenage girl. And they're decisions she shouldn't have to reach on her own. Although this book has continuously emphasized the importance of parent–child communication, this dialogue becomes absolutely essential when the family faces an unwanted teenage pregnancy.

Not surprisingly, even the most cohesive family unit can be tested rigorously at a time like this. To begin with, most pregnant girls are terrified to tell their parents about their predicament. As they often say to their girlfriends, "If I tell my dad, he's going to kill me!" The situation can become even more complicated if the teenager has become pregnant through sexual assault—particularly if the abuse was perpetrated by a father, stepfather, or another male member of the family.

But as a parent you need to know if she's pregnant and any extenuating circumstances that contributed to it. When a pregnant teenager decides to face this situation alone, she often makes choices that actually complicate things. She may run away from home. She may search out a secret abortion. Or she might even consider suicide.

Therefore, long before your daughter ever finds herself pregnant, make sure she understands that no matter what the news, you want her to tell you. No matter how bad the circumstances seem, you want to help her get through the crisis. Of course you may be upset, even angry, when you find out. *But let her know that she can come to you, no matter what!*

HOW CAN YOU HELP BEST?

If your daughter tells you she thinks she's pregnant, there's an obvious first step the family should take: get her a pregnancy test. Although you can buy an at-home pregnancy test in a drugstore, it may not be as accurate as one evaluated in a laboratory. We suggest you contact your pediatrician; if he doesn't conduct the test himself, he can suggest where to have it done.

If you find out that your daughter really is pregnant, then there's a major decision to make. Ideally not only should you and your spouse participate in that decision-making process with your daughter, but the father of her child (and his parents) should play a role, too.

True, some boys will refuse to do so, but others may actually welcome the opportunity to take part in the future of their own child, although they may need encouragement to do so. Some may feel too frightened or guilty to let the teenage girl and/or her parents know they'd like to help resolve the problem they helped create. This can be a traumatic time for the prospective father as well as the pregnant girl, and if you're the parent of such a boy, you need to support him emotionally and see him through this crisis. Even so, while boys should be encouraged to share responsibility for the situation, don't pressure your son into an unwanted marriage to "preserve the family's integrity."

Here are the options available when a pregnancy occurs:

Giving Birth

Nearly half a million teenagers give birth to babies every year. That includes several thousand girls under the age of fourteen. But even though this is certainly not an uncommon occurrence, it's not a decision to approach lightly.

First, consider the risks associated with childbirth. For example, teenagers are more likely to experience toxemia (a pregnancy disorder involving high blood pressure), anemia, and delivery complications than adult women. Also, there's a greater likelihood that their babies will be born premature, have a low birth weight, and even be stillborn.

For the most part, although most girls are biologically able to produce a healthy baby, the major culprit (if problems arise) is inadequate medical care. And here's why: even when they suspect they're pregnant, many girls (especially in early adolescence) deny it for weeks before having a pregnancy test; in the process they're also neglecting the need for prenatal care during the important early months of fetal development. Without exception any girl who's going to carry her baby to term should be under the care of an obstetrician beginning in the first weeks of her pregnancy.

But even if your daughter starts receiving excellent medical care early on, there are other factors to consider. For instance, does she realize that carrying and delivering a child will be terribly disruptive to her life? About 80 percent of pregnant teenagers drop out of school—a decision that has lifelong implications. With a premature end to their education many of these girls find themselves in low-paying jobs when they enter the work force. Unquestionably a full-term pregnancy has the potential of creating an economic nightmare for a young woman that often lasts for the rest of her life and even for future generations!

Once aware of implications like these, your daughter still may decide to deliver her baby. In that case another decision must be reached: should she keep the infant or give it up for adoption?

With the rapid changes in societal mores in recent years, there's no longer a terrible stigma associated with an unmarried girl keeping her baby. That can make things easier for your daughter if this is the course she chooses to take, particularly if she has parental support in this decision. However, she can't realistically assume that her future will be problem-free, either.

When a teenager chooses to raise the baby herself—even if she marries the newborn's father and has his support in the decision—she (and her husband) should consider everything that this decision involves. Do the young mother and father really feel they have the maturity to tend to the nonstop needs of a totally dependent infant, no matter what time of the day or night? Are they willing to accept the limitations on their freedom that parenthood entails, including missed parties and dates? Do they realize that much of their adolescence will come to an end with the responsibility of child raising and that some young people in their situation eventually become so resentful of their circumstances that they abuse their child?

Also, make sure your daughter realizes that if she hasn't already dropped out of school during her pregnancy, she'll probably do so once the responsibilities of motherhood confront her—and that most girls in this situation never go back to school. And does she also realize the obstacles her decision could place on her entry into the work force in the future? If she and the baby's father marry, do they know about the high divorce rate in teenage marriages (about 70 percent or higher), particularly when a child is involved? With that in mind, is she prepared for the possibility of raising her youngster alone?

Confronting dilemmas such as these, some young mothers are choosing to give up their baby for adoption. Unfortunately, the number who select this route is still quite small: only 4 percent of teenage mothers do so. Some girls apparently just cringe at the thought of "giving away my baby." But if your daughter is leaning toward adoption, remind her that she's not rejecting her baby; instead she's giving it to a mature, adult couple able and eager to give the infant love and security. Let her know that both she and her baby may be better off if the newborn is placed with an adoptive family. Considering adoption, in fact, may be a real test of her love for the baby.

There are many competent adoption agencies that will provide information without applying pressure one way or the other.

Abortion

Abortion is a controversial and emotional issue that seems even more highly charged when adolescents are involved. The debate between the identified "right to life" advocates and the "pro-choice" proponents has been carried out on the front pages of America's newspapers for years.

While this war of words continues, the teenage abortion rate remains high. About 400,000 adolescent girls have abortions every year. Teenagers have nearly 33 percent of all abortions in the U.S., although they make up only 16 percent of the childbearing population. In the youngest age group (under age fifteen) abortions outnumber deliveries.

If your daughter is contemplating an abortion, perhaps you're worried about the safety of this procedure. Most of that anxiety is unwarranted. A legal abortion performed in the first trimester (the first thirteen weeks of pregnancy) is extremely safe. In fact, for teenagers (ages fifteen to nineteen), delivering a baby is about fourteen times more likely to result in maternal death than an abortion. Purely from a safety point of view, an abortion carries much less risk than childbirth.

Even so, if your daughter does choose to have an abortion, here's a word of caution: she should have the procedure as early in the pregnancy as possible. The longer she waits, the greater the possibility of complications ranging from infections to abnormal bleeding. Later in the pregnancy abortions are somewhat more elaborate and difficult; rather than using suction or a scraping method, doctors may rely on injections of saline solutions or prostaglandins, and the fetus may not be expelled for several hours. Physicians are more likely to perform this procedure in a hospital or a clinic rather than a doctor's office, and they may recommend an overnight stay. Also, because the cervix must be more widely dilated with this procedure, there's a chance of losing subsequent pregnancies, particularly with *multiple* second-trimester abortions.

The message, then, is don't procrastinate. All the options available to a pregnant teenager are somewhat frightening, so it's understandable for girls to put off their decision as long as they can. But they're taking a terrible chance by doing so, because a late abortion is riskier than an early one. Also, prenatal and maternal care is essential if they choose to keep the baby. So look at the options and consider them carefully—but don't postpone making the decision.

GETTING SOME OUTSIDE HELP

As you read earlier in this chapter, deciding the course of a pregnancy is nothing that a teenage girl (and the father of her baby) should have to do on her own. Your daughter must feel she can always come to you, even with unhappy news. All teenagers make mistakes; that's one of the unpleasant facts about adolescence. So before a crisis like this ever arises, you should repeatedly make it clear to her, "You can always tell me what's happening in your life and about any problem you're having. I'll always be here for you."

A decision to have an abortion, for instance, can be one of the most difficult and stressful moments in a teenager's life. She'll need help, and a significant person in her life is critical during this time. And that usually means Mom. When a girl finds herself pregnant, her mother becomes the most important person in her life—someone who can help her make decisions, someone who can provide emotional support.

Interestingly, in most parts of the country your daughter won't need your consent to have an abortion; even in those states that require parental notification, she can circumvent it by going to court to ask for judicial consent. But she *does* need someone to lean on, someone with whom she can share her fears and anxieties. And that's the most important role you can play, whatever the current legal climate.

However, while you should voice your opinion, don't force a decision on your teenager. By all means, whatever your views on abortion, avoid trying to coerce her with statements such as, "If you keep the baby, don't expect me to take care of it" or, "If you have an abortion, it will be like killing your baby."

If you and your daughter feel you need some additional support in dealing with the options she faces, don't hesitate to seek some professional counseling. A good place to start is with your pediatrician or other trusted physician. Doctors are often neutral parties who won't make the decision for you; they won't talk you into choosing an abortion or opting to deliver the baby. That decision rests with your daughter and your family. However, pediatricians can help you sort out the alternatives and clarify the consequences. Ultimately they can also refer you to a physician or a clinic for an abortion or to an obstetrician who can begin providing prenatal care. No matter what your choice, they'll help you make an informed decision that best suits your own family's needs and circumstances.

And what about your son's obligations when he is the responsible male in the pregnancy? He has some legal liability, mostly financial in nature, such as child support. But he is not obligated to marry the mother of his child. By the way, if the pregnant girl names him as the father, but he believes he is not the responsible party, he may have to go to court to resolve this conflict.

Most families who have been through a teenage pregnancy find out there's really no good solution to this predicament. The best "solution" to a teenage pregnancy is never to have become pregnant at all. That's why sex education and contraception are essential for every sexually active adolescent.

18

WHEN YOUR TEENAGER IS HOMOSEXUAL

*E*ach year many hundreds of parents learn that their son or daughter is a homosexual. And in the overwhelming majority of instances parents find this news distressing. The statistics—the numbers showing that about 5 to 10 percent of adolescents are gay—don't cushion their anguish much. Statistics are apparently little comfort to parents whose dreams of their offspring's future have been shattered, particularly if those dreams included a traditional marriage and grandchildren.

Parents also often have to deal with their own guilt. Almost inevitably there are the questions that have no answers: "Did I do anything to cause this? If we had done something differently when he was a child, would he have turned out 'different'? Is it my fault?"

Although questions like these are almost inevitable, blaming yourself is not helpful. No one knows what causes a person to become a homosexual. In fact we know relatively little about teenage male homosexuality in general and even less about adolescent lesbians. As for what may cause this sexual orientation, there are probably a number of factors involved. Some may be biological. Others may be psychological. The reasons may vary from one person to another. No one really knows for sure why any particular individual is homosexual.

WHAT DO WE KNOW ABOUT HOMOSEXUALITY?

Most young people go through an anxious stage during which they wonder, "Am I gay?" It often happens at about age thirteen or fourteen, when a teenager admits to himself that he finds a friend of the same sex attractive, he develops a crush on a teacher of the same gender, or he engages in some individual or group homosexual activity.

But his anxiety is usually unwarranted. It's quite normal for boys and girls to go through a phase like this as their own sexual identity is evolving. During early or middle adolescence they may even experiment with some same-sex activity.

Once again, this type of *normal,* exploratory behavior is not an indication that a teenager is homosexual. Nor does it suggest that he or she will become a homosexual adult—whether the teenage homosexual experiences are voluntary or even forced. In much the same way, homosexual adults have usually experimented with heterosexual behavior earlier in life. Thus as youngsters go through their adolescence their parents should offer support as individual sexual orientations develop. Avoid labeling teenagers as they struggle with their sexual identity, as homosexual or heterosexual.

In fact, by middle adolescence most teenagers are asserting themselves heterosexually and have started to date. However, what about the boy or girl who, in *late* adolescence or early adulthood, defines himself as a homosexual? Is this behavior abnormal? And how should you react?

First, there's no evidence that homosexuals are mentally ill. Yes, there are many religious groups that still consider a homosexual lifestyle to be "immoral" or "contrary to nature." But in 1974 the American Psychiatric Association withdrew its classification of homosexuality as a mental disorder. Instead the APA now considers it an alternate choice for sexual expression. A year later the American Psychological Association adopted a similar position.

Although the evidence isn't conclusive, most researchers now believe that a homosexual orientation is established before adolescence. According to one theory, complex social learning that takes place early in childhood sets the youngster on a course toward homosexuality. This doesn't necessarily mean that these boys and girls participated in overt homosexual play early in life; however, the biological and/or psychological basis for their adolescent and adult sexuality is probably set very early.

Parents familiar with the homosexual stereotypes that permeate society sometimes begin to wonder on their own whether their adolescent son or daughter is a homosexual. In some cases, if a boy acts a bit effeminate or a girl acts somewhat masculine, that's all the "proof" that some parents need. But very likely this "evidence" is deceptive. Most homosexual males and females look and act just like their "straight" counterparts. No matter what you've heard, you usually can't tell a person's sexual orientation by the way he looks or acts.

The confusion is compounded by the common misconception that males who cross-dress (i.e., enjoy dressing in women's clothing) are necessarily homosexual. In fact, although some teenage boys do engage in so-called *transvestism,* most are heterosexual. If your own son cross-dresses, he probably finds some sexual excitement in doing so; but this behavior is *not* an indication of homosexuality, even though some young homosexual boys do engage in this behavior. As disturbing as you may find this activity, it appears to be psychologically harmless, particularly as young people sort out their sexual drives and interests. Even so, if this activity persists into late adolescence, you may want to consult your son's doctor for an evaluation.

For those teenagers who actually are homosexual, few actually "come out of the closet" in adolescence. Because of the social stigma associated with homosexuality, some will wrestle with the "coming out" decision for years before finally deciding to do so. Others will keep their homosexuality a secret for a lifetime. Yes, some teenagers do proclaim their homosexuality during the high school years, but most wait until their twenties or even later to confide in anyone other than their homosexual peers. Until then life can be difficult for these young people. Some go through periods of denial, shame, guilt, fear, and even thoughts of suicide. Some actually commit suicide.

Unfortunately, this emotional turmoil is not always resolved once a homosexual decides to announce publicly his or her sexual preference. Society has a definite negative bias against gays, making it difficult for them to accept their own identity. Peers may subject them to painful name-calling. Their self-esteem often suffers, they have to cope with a lack of sex education about their own orientation (including an explanation of sexually transmitted diseases), and they probably have no adult role models.

To make matters even worse, when homosexual adolescents make their sexual orientation known, their families often reject them. Perhaps that's how you think you'd react. But it's the *wrong response.* Your teenager may be having incredible difficulty coming to terms with his sexuality, and he may find it devastating if his parents reject him at the same time. *Your adolescent still needs you!*

So take a deep breath and think. Yes, you may need some time to come to grips with the news; you may need to adjust to your own lost dreams of your child marrying and having a traditional family; you may have to deal with your own negative stereotypes of homosexuality, if they exist. But in the process you must decide early on not to reject your teenager for his or her sexual orientation. He or she is still your youngster, and you should channel your energy toward providing love and support.

Your adolescent didn't choose homosexuality. Accept him or her and be there to help with any problems that arise, such as rejection in the world in which your youngster is growing up. If you think you or your child could benefit from some counseling, ask your pediatrician for a referral.

THE MEDICAL RISKS

Since the early 1980s male homosexuals have had to deal with more than just societal prejudice and classic STDs. (See Chapter 32.) They have also found themselves at high risk for AIDS, one of the most devastating diseases of modern times. The rapid spread of this lethal infection—often transmitted by sexual contact—has caused dramatic shifts toward more conservative sexual practices in the homosexual community.

No one knows just how prevalent AIDS is among adolescent homosexuals. However, one thing is clear: "safe sex" practices are essential for all sexually active gay males, no matter what their age. Condoms not only can protect against AIDS during anal intercourse but can also prevent the spread of many other sexually transmitted diseases that are common in the homosexual community.

Homosexual boys should also be advised that the more sexual partners they have, the greater the chance of exposure to someone infected with the AIDS virus.

If your homosexual (or heterosexual) son has any questions about protecting himself against AIDS (and other sexually transmitted diseases), your pediatrician should be able to answer them. Education about AIDS, herpes, gonorrhea, syphilis, hepatitis, and many other STDs is essential. (See Chapter 32.) Your youngster needs the facts about "safe sex" *before* he engages in sexual activity; after the fact it may be too late.

19

Protecting Your Teenager Against Sexual Abuse

"I met this boy at a high school football game. He was real cute and had a great sense of humor. After the game we went to a coffee shop, and then he offered to drive me home. But on the way he stopped on a dark road and told me that if I didn't have sex with him, he'd hurt me real bad. I was so scared that I did everything he asked me to do. I can't believe this happened to me. He seemed like such a nice guy."

*T*elevision, radio, and the newspapers are filled with unsettling news about the sexual exploitation of teenagers (and preteenagers). An eleven-year-old girl is a victim of sexual molestation by her stepfather. A thirteen-year-old male is molested by a neighbor. A seventeen-year-old girl is raped at a fraternity party. Judging by the media coverage, sexual abuse of adolescents appears almost epidemic in America.

Accurate statistics in this area are difficult to assemble since so many cases of sexual abuse never make the police blotters. For instance, girls rarely report "date rape," where a boy forces his date to have sex. But according to one estimate one in four girls and one in eleven boys will be molested before the age of eighteen—as the victim of incest, date rape, gang rape, or some other form of sexual abuse. About 40 percent of reported cases of sexual abuse involve boys, who are typically assaulted by older boys or men and sometimes by women.

Both young children and teenagers can become victims of sexual abuse, and the actual median age of sexually abused minors is nine to ten years old. For that reason you need to include an awareness of sexual abuse—including how to prevent it—as part of the sex education of your children. Still, learning how to deal with their own emerging sexuality, teenagers sometimes naively place themselves in social situations where sexual exploitation is likely to occur. Several studies show that nearly 50 percent of reported rape victims are teenagers.

DATE RAPE

If your daughter is the victim of rape—no matter what her age—there's a strong likelihood that she knows her attacker. More than half of all rapists are friends, casual acquaintances, or relatives of their victims.

Particularly in a dating situation, girls know at least something about the boy they're with, although familiarity doesn't necessarily provide them with safety. Date rapes have occurred at every stage of involvement, ranging from a pickup in a bar to a first date to a steady relationship.

Boys often say that they don't consider it rape when they use force on a date. Some believe it's "macho" to use aggression to get sex. Some even think that girls really want their boyfriends to force them into sex ("She may be saying no, but she really means yes").

One recent study uncovered some disturbing facts relative to this issue. Only 24 percent of males said that force was definitely unacceptable to obtain sex when "the girl got the guy sexually excited." Fewer girls agreed with that statement, but even so, 44 percent did not rule out the use of force in such a situation.

As a parent you may tell your daughter to "be careful." Most parents do. But she also needs some more specific guidance than that. Most teenagers just don't have the same fear of being sexually attacked that adult women do. Because of their immaturity and their lack of life experience, they don't expect other people to take advantage of them. But they need to know rape can happen to *them*.

Be sure your daughter understands that once she engages in certain sexual behavior in a dating situation, it may provoke other things. Petting may lead a boy to think that she is also receptive to intercourse. For that reason girls must be precise with their boyfriend, spelling out what they're willing to do and what they're not. They should know where the evening is headed and not allow things to get "out of control." And if a situation arises where he won't take no for an answer, she shouldn't hesitate to shout, scream, fight back, or run away to protect herself.

If you have a teenage son, make sure he understands that his dates have the right to say no. And when they say no, that means no.

WHEN A RAPE OCCURS . . .

Throughout society some myths about rape are quite prevalent. Here are three of the most common:

- The victim somehow provoked the attack. There are even girls who believe they somehow invited the rape or led the boy on. (But even if she did dress provocatively, does that give a male the right to rape her?)

- Rape is tied to sex and love rather than anger and loss of control.

- Rape happens only to certain people or in certain places.

All of these statements are false.

There's a lot of misunderstanding about rape, and that's at least partly why most female (and nearly all male) victims—no matter what their age—are reluctant to report this crime. If the rapist is a boyfriend or an acquaintance, your daughter may find it difficult to press charges against him. Most girls also have heard how stressful a rape trial can be for the victim, reliving the event again and again and being asked many personal questions. Still others fear retaliation from the rapist.

Many teenagers won't tell their parents what has happened. Some are embarrassed. Some feel that they may have provoked the attack and that they're somehow "dirty." Others are afraid their parents will punish them for getting into such a situation—perhaps they've hitchhiked despite their parents' warning against it. Still others have been threatened with harm if they do tell. However, your daughter needs your support at a time like this. So since she may be reluctant to divulge what has happened, you'll have to be alert for signs of rape.

For example, does your teenager show signs of physical trauma, perhaps bruises or torn clothing? Does she seem depressed? Does she sometimes cry for no apparent reason or seem unusually angry or nervous? Is she having trouble sleeping? Has she experienced unusual medical problems such as frequent fainting spells or prolonged hyperventilation episodes? Has she unexpectedly cut off a relationship with a particular boy? Is she suddenly upset when a certain male member of the family is around her, or does she avoid this individual?

Keep in mind that rape is a crime and should be reported. And the sooner, the better. Not only should you notify the police, but your daughter should see a doctor as well. She should have a physical exam, which will include an evaluation (and possible treatment) for sexually transmitted diseases. The doctor also may recommend a prescribed dose of a common birth control pill (Ovral) or other measures to protect against the possibility of pregnancy. He or she may recommend psychological counseling too. Most cities have rape crisis centers that can provide a range of useful medical and psychological services.

We can't overemphasize the importance of helping your teenager deal with the emotional aftereffects of rape. In the initial days after the assault the young person is typically quite upset, confused, and disorganized and appears almost to be in shock. After that she may experience fear, anxiety, and guilt. There may also be a period of denial, during which she may refuse to discuss the incident with anyone. Severe depression develops in many rape victims. And when issues remain unresolved, her future adult functioning can be impaired by sexual dysfunction, depression, and other psychological problems.

Obviously, then, rape can be a terrible experience for an adolescent. But your own reaction can influence how well—or how poorly—your daughter will get through it. Of course you'll probably feel some rage of your own, but expressing your anger to your teenager won't help her at all. Instead you may need to talk to a counselor about it.

Despite your own pain, support your teenager and sensitively help her deal with her fear, embarrassment, and anger. If she's allowed to express her grief and guilt, the lasting negative effects of this difficult experience can be minimized.

INCEST

As we explained earlier, a victim of sexual assault often knows her attacker. In some cases, he lives in the same house. He may be her father, stepfather, a brother, an uncle, or the boyfriend of her mother.

As if rape itself weren't traumatic enough, it becomes even more complicated and disruptive when it involves incest–sexual abuse committed by a relative. Studies note that incest accounts for 40 percent of identified child sexual abuse and that most incest cases (perhaps 90 percent!) are never reported.

The most common forms of incest are father (stepfather) -daughter and uncle-niece incest, though some experts feel that sibling (brother-sister) incest may be as, or even more common. Infrequently, father-son, mother-son, and other variations are reported as well.

Though incest can occur at any time during childhood or adolescence, it usually begins when the child is 10–12 years of age. It typically arises out of a very complex, poorly-understood pattern of severe family dysfunction. In father-daughter incest there is a poor father-mother marital relationship, frequently with a daughter taking on a "mother" role while the real mother reverses her position into that of a "daughter." The daughter can take over the mother's caretaker role in the home and eventually is molested by her father or stepfather. Many variations on this identified pattern are noted.

Parents who were sexually abused as children are more likely than those who were not to sexually abuse their own children. Once the incest begins, it often becomes a chronic pattern, lasting many years—even generations. If the incest is not identified and stopped early, numerous children within the family can be abused—one daughter replacing another, as each grows up and leaves the home. Grandchildren can even be abused by the grandfather who abused his own daughters.

Children and adolescents who are sexually abused by their own family members are caught up in a very tragic world. When they are violated by those whom they should trust, such victims become very confused. Whom can they trust? To whom do they turn for advice? They often fear being rejected by their family and that the family will break-up if they reveal what is or has occurred. Thus there is often a delay in telling others. Many will not reveal their terrible secret for many years; others never will.

Yet the emotional consequences of being sexually abused by family member(s) are very serious, and as noted, can last a lifetime. Incest victims can develop severe depression (with or without suicidal thoughts and attempts), anxiety, sexual promiscuity, drug and alcohol abuse, sleep disturbances, school failure, juvenile delinquency behavior, and other problems. They may argue bitterly with parents, run away from home, and develop an intense distrust for all adults—especially males. If these issues are not treated, they can persist and worsen in adulthood. This adult may have chronic depression, sexual difficulties, marital problems, and many other conflicts.

One should consider incest in the following situations (especially if they occur in combination):

- Running away behavior (often recurrent)

- Severe unexplained depression

- Families where the daughter acts as the mother, caring for other siblings, and there is known or uncovered marital difficulties

- Serious adolescent rebellion against any of the parents

- Families with drug-abusing parents

- Frequent, unexplained medical complaints in a youth (such as chest pain, abdominal pain, or fainting)

- Teenager who has been physically abused

- Teenager who sexually abuses other children

- Sexually transmitted disease in a young or retarded teenager

- Pregnancy in a young or retarded youth (especially when she insists she never had sex)

If you suspect that incest is occurring, it should be reported to local child-protective agencies. Physicians and school officials are *manditory reporters*—that is, they are required by law to report suspected cases of child abuse (physical, sexual, or neglect). However, *all of us* should report suspected cases and help break this vicious cycle. Anyone can report without fear that they will be subjected to legal consequences—even if a proper investigation eventually reveals no acceptable evidence of abuse. Incest is a crime! It should be thoroughly investigated by appropriate legal agencies.

Incest families need professional evaluation and treatment. Once the incest has been revealed, potentially overwhelming reactions may occur to all family members. Denial and anger are common. The victim may blame herself for what is happening. If she has been recently abused, medical evaluation, as noted for rape victims, is necessary. The possibility of sexually transmitted diseases (even AIDS) and pregnancy are quite real. Current and future emotional difficulties, as noted, are well-known—intense treatment is needed for *all* family members. Ideally, both victim and offender can be involved in expert psychological evaluation and treatment. The best outcome is where all family members receive treatment and the family unit can be saved and no further abuse occurs. Unfortunately, this is not always possible. As with other emotional situations, early treatment (versus delayed) usually provides the best outcome.

Remember, help is possible. Some families do eventually recover, but the healing process is a lengthy one. See your pediatrician for a referral to a local counseling agency. And don't give up on your teenager or yourself as a parent. If your teenager has signs of incest or suggests to you that incest is occurring, believe her! If incest has or is identified in your family, get help now for yourself and for others who are involved. You can help prevent or resolve problems that can impact on current and future generations of your family.

PART V

YOUR TEENAGER'S SOCIAL GROWTH AND DEVELOPMENT

20

THE NEED TO BELONG

*F*riends.

Most of us have them. All of us need them.

When your child was very young, you probably began to recognize just what a social being she was. Although her interactions with other people started within the family, she undoubtedly found friends to play with early in childhood, and that need for companionship has remained very important.

As an adolescent your youngster wants friends for many reasons. She needs to test her ideas, actions, and roles, and friends can help her do that. She also probably worries a lot about herself, particularly about whether she's normal—and friends can put those anxieties to rest. Most importantly, she just wants to *be accepted*—whether by a chosen peer group or by a special individual. And as she progresses from acquaintances to companions to friends, she'll be developing socially and evolving into adulthood.

MAKING FRIENDS

The need for friends doesn't suddenly begin at puberty. Individuals have been making friends long before adolescence, and they'll continue to use some of the same techniques to make new ones throughout life. This process, however, becomes somewhat more complicated during the teenage years. After all, adolescence is a time of many physical, cognitive, psychological, and social changes that can disrupt the perceptions adolescents have of themselves and their friends. As young teenagers rapidly change in physical size and appearance, they have new, often strange feelings that can cause uncertainty as to who they are and what they'll become. In short, they're unsure of themselves, and that often makes establishing new friendships harder.

By middle adolescence, after most of their physical changes are complete and as their self-concept and confidence improve, this will become less of a problem. They'll have more freedom of action and association with a greater number of peers—and friendships will often develop more easily. Then, in late adolescence, there will be a new twist to the scenario: in confronting the future, teenagers will face the prospect of leaving good friends behind and having to make new ones at a job or at college. These issues of attachment, separation, and loss arise normally on the road to adulthood.

Let's take a closer look at each of these developmental periods. When young adolescents are in the midst of their greatest growth spurt, they'll be preoccupied by themselves, wondering if they're maturing normally. At this stage of development they may or may not have many friends (most teenagers do), but they'll probably want one best friend, almost always of the same sex.

If this special relationship develops, these two special friends will bond tightly, implicitly trusting each other and sharing their hopes, fears, and problems. They'll often compare physical characteristics to convince themselves that their own growth is typical. And they'll have long discussions about their families or about things they've heard from older adolescents. When teenagers find this "true" best friend, they'll expect this individual to be loyal and to keep these intimate revelations completely confidential.

During middle adolescence (ages fourteen to sixteen), along with increases in self-confidence and a stronger interest in other people, they'll undergo a major life change—namely, they'll want to begin to form closer associations with members of the opposite sex. For some teenagers building these new friendships will be easy; for others it will be very difficult. At times during middle or late adolescence feelings of love may come into play, which can be either extremely supportive of these evolving friendships or potentially harmful to them. Some teenagers find out that as nice as it is to have a romantic relationship, it can get in the way of other friendships, causing conflicts of interest and complications in their participation in activities. You can support your youngster during these times by providing information and advice (if asked) and by showing your willingness to share her concerns.

By late adolescence (seventeen and over) teenagers may have established satisfactory relationships with a dating partner and also with one or more peer groups that may have members of both sexes. They will be more independent and more capable of maintaining friendships.

Despite these generalizations, bear in mind that each adolescent is unique. Yes, all teenagers have a need to belong and be accepted. They rely heavily on friends to facilitate their psychological separation from parents and family. But they differ in the number of friends they desire and in some of the reasons they want them. For some adolescents friendships provide primarily personal support. Others are looking for intimacy. Some are searching for acceptance that they feel is not being given to them in their own families. Still others find that friends enable them to participate in a greater array of activities.

Some adolescents hope to gain status through their friends and thus make selections based on appearance, accomplishments, or shared interests or opinions. Others unconsciously select friends who will *not* please their parents, as a way of asserting their autonomy. Frequently, however, they are attracted to another teenager for no definable reason.

Adolescents also vary in the style in which they make friends. Earlier in life they may have learned to attract friends in their own unique way—by being tolerant or aggressive, interested or uninterested in the views and rights of other people. Some adolescents make friends by being cooperative, others by being competitive, or in some cases by being creative. For example, your teenager may choose to associate with peers who have similar interests—perhaps in sports or in music.

Keep in mind that when your adolescent is cooperative, that's quite different from being submissive or congenial. If she's going to become friends with another person, the two of them must get along reasonably well and cooperate to achieve their mutual objectives. To go beyond being just acquaintances, associates, or classmates, they'll need to spend time together and participate in activities that they both enjoy. As they learn to appreciate each other, their companionship will evolve into friendship. And as a parent you need to allow this to happen without feeling that the family is being permanently replaced.

If your adolescent is competitive or even aggressive, she'll find that these qualities too can interest other teenagers. Creativity or intelligence can work to her advantage as well, particularly if it allows her to become a leader of a group or earn the respect of others.

Why do some teenagers have difficulty making friends? A number of factors can play a role. Shyness, low self-esteem, or feelings of inferiority can get in the way. Also, when an adolescent's past relationships or friendships have been unsatisfactory, or if a friend has betrayed her, she may be reluctant to make new friends, preferring that her relationships go no further than the acquaintance level, without the closeness or responsibility of friendship. On occasion a teenager won't want close friends because she's unwilling to reveal much about herself.

Other obstacles can arise as well. Consider that Americans are a mobile people, and as parents move to another city, state, or country their children obviously go with them. Not surprisingly, leaving friends behind is difficult for youngsters. Being the new kid on the block can be even harder. Most adolescents need time to evaluate their new environment and the teenagers there before trying to establish a place in the group. Their situation can become even more complicated if the family is settling into an unfamiliar cultural, racial, or ethnic community, where newcomers can be excluded because of being "different."

Divorce can also affect an adolescent's relationships with peers. Frequently, as the family structure changes when parents separate and divorce, teenagers can develop emotional or behavioral problems that disrupt their existing friendships. Then, just as they're settling in, accepting their new life situation, one of their parents may remarry, often forcing additional adjustments that can again affect their friendships.

By the way, even though your teenager will usually have one or two close friends, these friendships may change throughout adolescence. As youngsters move through each stage of development, they may find that a different friend meets their needs at that particular time.

Even so, some of the special attachments teenagers make will become lifelong friendships, although the individuals may have limited contact during adulthood. This permanent closeness really isn't surprising, however; after all, it's built on mutual appreciation, a sharing of personal information, hopes, and dreams, and a tolerance of one another's shortcomings. That's a great foundation for a lasting friendship.

PEER GROUPS AND CLIQUES

You've probably witnessed this scene a hundred times or more: teenagers just "hanging out," sometimes at a fast-food restaurant, other times at a shopping mall or the roller skating rink. They congregate to gossip, observe, attract attention, and pass the time. On occasion they might even get together with a specific purpose in mind, perhaps to attend a sports event or a church activity.

Let's face it: adolescents like to be with their contemporaries, and groups are part of their lives. They'll often form cliques or small circles of friends who attempt to set styles, rules, and modes of behavior—and may be perceived as snobbish by outsiders. There are all sorts of these cliques or "in" groups; some teenagers belong to several of them, each with a special importance or meaning.

Who's most likely to be part of a particular peer group? In theory peer groups are composed of persons of equal rank, ability, and interests. But in truth every group assigns a particular status and reputation to each member, and thus some adolescents are considered more equal than others. There are also unwritten rules for admission, one of which is unwavering loyalty to the group's activities and members.

At various ages teenagers will find these peer groups serving a different function in their life. When they're young adolescents, whose thinking and appearance are rapidly changing, a peer group provides a model to which they can conform and a place where they can feel at home. By being part of the group they'll also have "proof" of their acceptance by other teenagers.

As adolescents grow and develop, they may leave this peer group to join another one that better reflects their evolving beliefs and interests. But sometimes, after being accepted by this new group, they'll find that its activities are not what they had expected or are contrary to their own values. Then they'll have to make a difficult decision: either to conform or to abandon the peer group—fully aware of the obvious benefits but still the price to be paid for leaving.

As a parent you can understand your teenager's need to belong to a group. Your big concern, however, is probably the influence it will have. Some groups can have a positive effect, but others may have a negative impact.

Let's conclude this section with a little closer look at how these peer groups operate. Their value system will evolve from the opinions and actions of their members and will usually change very little. Those who belong know what's expected, they're comfortable with it, and they'll find support within the group. They'll conform to approved types of dress, hairstyles, and behavior, although some individuality may be permitted as long as it doesn't affect the group.

Research into teenage pregnancy has shown just how persuasive peer groups can be. These studies looked at the factors that influence whether a teenager becomes sexually active. Their conclusion: those adolescents who had a good friend who was sexually active or belonged to a peer group whose members were having sex were more likely to become sexually active themselves.

Some groups exert influence on other behaviors too—for example, encouraging young people to experiment with illegal drugs or to become involved in unlawful gang activities. These urban gangs and their negative impact have become much more visible in recent years, attracting young people who are seeking to make sense out of what they perceive to be their own chaotic family situation within a cold world. Belonging to a gang, even if it's involved in criminal activity, gives them a sense of acceptance and understanding.

These types of gangs are still more the exception than the rule, however, except in urban ghettos. In most cases peer-influenced behaviors are short-lived and do not involve serious unruliness. Many peer groups don't go far offtrack at all, often reflecting parental values. When this happens, your own standards will be reinforced and integrated into your teenager's personality. In fact your adolescent's choice of a peer group depends largely on her earlier life experiences, as well as her self-esteem, self-reliance, religious affiliation, ethnic background, and socioeconomic status.

Even so, peer groups do differ. For that reason you should participate in your adolescent's choice of friends, beginning in childhood and continuing in earnest during the early teenage years. That's part of being a parent.

21

LONELINESS, REJECTION, AND ISOLATION

"*T*here's absolutely nothing for me to do."

Sound familiar? Every teenager has recited this complaint from time to time. Most can't stand being alone and bored, longing instead to be with friends. They want to be active and doing something. It just comes with the territory of adolescence.

For most teenagers the purpose of life is to be happy—and when they're not, they'll let you know. There seems to be an urgency to their feeling that the time to be happy is running out. You can anticipate that your teenager will go through some mood swings, and you'll probably bear the brunt of most of them. Fortunately, as he becomes older, some emotional stability will return, but he'll still experience lonely and unhappy periods. Even so, these are *brief* mood spells—rarely lasting for days or weeks.

When this loneliness, rejection, and isolation occur, a number of internal and external factors can be working against your teenager. For example, as we suggested in the previous chapter, perhaps your teenager is extremely shy. As a result he may be reluctant even to try to form friendships or gain acceptance by a group. Even though he may yearn for companionship, he may be unsure of how to go about making friends, or he may fear rejection if he tries. On the other hand, he might be so overly aggressive or domineering that he's rejected by his contemporaries for that reason—while being perplexed as to why no one wants to be with him. Or if the family moves to a different city, he may frantically reach out for new friends and sometimes make the wrong choices.

Here's how a sixteen-year-old boy described what happened to him:

"We moved here a year ago. I joined a car pool to get to school, and we all ended up smoking pot together. We did it before school, at school, and when we came home. In the summer I went away on vacation, and when I came back I decided not to get into that situation again. I just didn't want to do it anymore. But now I feel left out, and I don't have any friends. I'm trying to make new ones, but that's been impossible because of the reputation I have for having spent so much time with those other guys. I'm so alone and unhappy that I'm almost ready to start back with them. I really don't want to—but I've got to do something!"

Circumstances like this occur now and then. When they do, you need to provide emotional support and understanding until your teenager adjusts to a new and better situation. He'll eventually begin making friends, although it may take longer than he'd like.

Teenagers also sometimes find themselves left out of a highly desired social situation, perhaps having been passed over for the cheerleading squad or a place on the football team. If this happens to your adolescent, he may feel depressed and inadequate. Offer him encouragement and help him recognize and appreciate his positive personal qualities. Guide him into other activities that he'll find fulfilling and where he'll be with peers.

Also remind your youngster that loneliness and rejection during adolescence are usually temporary. When a teenager is turned down for a date, when no one asks her to the school prom, when he's not chosen for the debate team, or when she's not selected for the lead in the school play, it can be devastating. But it's not the end of the world.

To help get your youngster through this "crisis," urge him to talk about his feelings with you. Perhaps he'll share these confidences while riding with you in the car just after school. No matter where the discussion takes place, however, find a time and a location where no one else is present and the two of you can give full attention to one another. As he talks about what's on his mind, listen attentively. Let him know that he's not the only adolescent experiencing such setbacks and that he's not alone in fighting these inner battles. Try to offer some suggestions for coping with the situation and provide a direction for the future.

Sometimes others in his life (teachers, other adults, peers) may have ideas as well. Tell him you love him and will support him. Do or share something special with him—a sports event, shopping, a special meal, a videotape. Sponsor a party for him with his friends. Each teenager is unique and will respond to different measures. If you become worried, check with your pediatrician for other suggestions and/or an evaluation.

If your teenager's anxiety centers around a romantic involvement, the communication between the two of you can be more important than ever. Love during adolescence is almost always intense, and encountering indifference or rejection from a boyfriend or a girlfriend can be terribly painful. Don't joke about it or minimize its importance. Adolescents often feel emotionally destroyed when a romance ends, and they'll need to talk about the hurt and why the breakup occurred.

Adolescents, of course, don't have the wisdom and the experiences of adults to fall back on. They must learn, through trial and error, about trust and betrayal, love and loyalty, stability and maturity. They must learn to interpret and integrate their growing experiences. Until they do, parents and other adults with whom the teenagers have rapport should be available to give support and assistance during troubling times.

Of course this isn't always what happens. In some cases family members are so busy that they just don't spend time with one another, and parents don't even notice when their teenager seems desperate for help. In divorced households one parent or the other usually isn't available to listen at any given time. Adolescents in these types of situations need to learn that it's not their fault that their parents are often inaccessible. Life isn't always fair—although adolescents have a difficult time accepting that reality. (Circumstances like these underscore the importance of an accessible and trusted doctor, school counselor, or member of the clergy to whom an adolescent can turn.)

With or without parental support a teenager will learn much about life during this time. These lessons, if they're learned well, can help an adolescent become a more successful and happier adult. And if you're there to lend a hand, you can assist your youngster in getting through the more difficult experiences.

One other important point: there's often more to adolescent isolation than just being alone. When teenagers feel emotionally as well as physically isolated, their pain can be overwhelming, particularly if it has built up over many months and years. If adolescents have made efforts to turn things around and break through their solitude (or whatever else is causing their distress) but have been unsuccessful, they may view the future as even worse than the present. Hope may turn to hopelessness, and when all seems lost, they may perceive suicide as the only solution. Unfortunately, these adolescents do *not* view suicide as a "permanent solution to their temporary problem."

How can you recognize teenagers in this kind of trouble? If their relationships with friends change, if their school performance radically deteriorates, or if other aspects of their life seem quite different to you, get them some professional help immediately. Don't disregard any signs that could indicate your teenager is contemplating ending his or her own life. Prolonged (or even brief but severe) mood swings should prompt you to arrange for a professional evaluation immediately. For a more thorough discussion of teenage suicide, see Chapter 12.

22

WHO ARE YOUR
TEENAGER'S FRIENDS?

"*M*y kid has a lousy group of friends!"

A lot of parents feel that way. And in most cases they might add, ". . . and I don't know what to do about it."

However, even if you do not approve of your teenager's friends, the situation may not be as bleak as you think. Here are some factors you should consider:

First, take some time to consider carefully what you don't like about these friends. Some parents find it helpful to jot down what they dislike and then try to rank these points in importance. Is it the appearance of these friends that bothers you? Or their opinions? Their reputation? Their behavior? The fact that you have not met many of them? Or are you apprehensive that these friends will have too much influence on your teenager in matters that are potentially dangerous or conflict with family beliefs?

Calmly evaluate this situation, paying particular attention to what these friends stand for and how they act. Once you've completed this process, only then should you arrive at a conclusion as to whether your child should continue to associate with them. Whatever decision you reach, base it on facts as much as possible rather than making an emotional judgment. Other parents may have concerns similar to yours, and it may help to talk with them. Particularly if a major problem exists, suggest that the school hold a parents' meeting to discuss the relevant issues and develop recommendations for improving the situation.

The second major step is to make a careful and objective evaluation of your own teenager. As a parent you've undoubtedly become used to your youngster, and you may not see him as others do or really know what goes on when he's away from home. But keep this fact in mind: if there have been difficulties with him within your own family, it's quite likely that his behavior outside the home has sometimes been objectionable, too. (If you should discover that his behavior is negative only at home, you need to evaluate carefully this environment.)

Of course finding out exactly what that behavior is can be difficult. After all, friends of your teenager will usually support him, and your own adult friends may be reluctant to criticize your child as well. Even so, don't give up. Take the time to seek out this kind of information. You may discover that you really have nothing to worry about. On the other hand, you might learn that your teenager is part of a group that has a reputation for making trouble.

If your teenager has been part of a clique that causes problems, ask yourself why he wants or needs to associate with these particular peers. What is he gaining by doing so? Is he using this group to psychologically distance himself from you, helping him to gain autonomy and independence? Is he trying to make up for low self-esteem? Again, school counselors and other adults who have contact with your adolescent may help provide some answers.

With all this information in hand you can look more closely at the precise problems that exist and how serious they are. In the process you also may find that the news isn't all bad. Although real, these problems will often be only temporary and of little or no importance for the future.

Even so, when your teenager's behavior is seriously antisocial, you can't take it lightly. Not only is it a sign of rejection of parental values, but it may also represent a danger to your adolescent's well-being.

When your teenager repudiates your ideals, you need to show some tolerance (although not necessarily approval); but if he's putting himself at peril, you need to give him immediate attention to prevent further risk taking and alienation from the family. If you think your teenager is on a dangerous course that won't improve soon on its own, you need to chart a plan of action to turn things around, perhaps with the help of a counselor or other professional.

What kinds of actions can you take? There are many options open to you, but here are some points to keep in mind. Just saying no to your teenager rarely works. Doing nothing more than criticizing his friends or forbidding future association with them will usually be ineffective. Instead you need to give him alternatives to choose from, providing him with some sense of control over his life.

So, for example, you can steer him in new directions at school that might discourage his association with one group of friends and bring him in contact with others—for example, by suggesting that he join school clubs or sports programs or change to a different car pool. Occasionally he might benefit from transferring to another class in school to decrease his contact with a particular group, and the school counselor can help you make this decision. But in addition to helping change your teenager's external circumstances, you must also help him develop some internal motivation for making wiser decisions in his life.

Incidentally, the summer can become an even more difficult time. Your teenager will have many idle hours to fill when school lets out, and in some communities there are few summer jobs for teenagers. To cope with his boredom, your youngster may become involved in group behaviors that you consider undesirable or potentially harmful.

That's when you need to offer your help. Again, you must provide your teenager with alternatives to "hanging out" with friends who also have "nothing to do." For instance, find some summer sports programs in your city that can provide outlets for energy for both boys and girls—and perhaps bring them some recognition in the process. See what summer youth activities your church or synagogue is planning or look into outings sponsored by the YMCA or YWCA.

If you think back to your own adolescence, you may be more sympathetic with your teenager's restlessness and his desire for exciting and interesting activities. But if he can find "nothing to do" during the summer, he'll probably look to someone else for suggestions—and if you don't take the initiative, his friends may step in and take over that role.

So encourage local community organizations to sponsor productive activities. If your youngster has developed skills in earlier years, have him put them to good use now, perhaps as a camp counselor or a teacher of younger children. Talk to other parents and plan ahead. Also, ask other adults to offer their suggestions to your adolescent, since he'll often respond to them more readily than he will to you.

If your teenager gets involved in serious trouble—drug abuse, for example—you need to become even more aggressive in your intervention. You may have to dramatically alter your family's lifestyle in order to be more available and to watch over your youngster much more closely. Or you might even have to obtain residential treatment for him. Yes, the latter is a drastic step, but to stop his negative behavior in its tracks he may need a completely different environment and some intensive, skilled therapy.

Incidentally, if this residential treatment is needed, it can be very expensive. So keep possibilities like this in mind when selecting health insurance. Too often people choose limited coverage, but in general you should select the best insurance protection you can find. Many parents are shocked to discover that their insurance ultimately turns out to be inadequate for their needs.

In the meantime, as important as any other step you take is trying to maintain trust and communication between you and your teenager. That's the best means of preventing him from getting into a mess now or in the future. Hopefully you've nurtured this relationship throughout his childhood and have created a strong foundation that you can build on in his adolescence. Make those extra efforts to spend more time listening to him, trying to understand what he's feeling, discussing his behaviors, and calmly giving reasons for your own opinions. Communication needs to become one of your top priorities. If you're a parent who doesn't really listen, who becomes angry too quickly, and who issues rules and makes judgments based on too few facts, you need to change.

However, there are no guarantees. Even under the best circumstances things don't always go right. Many excellent parents have done their best, and yet their adolescent rejects them and their advice. If you find yourself in that situation—that is, if you've seriously approached the problem at hand, sought help from health professionals, and tried to implement a reasonable solution, and your teenager has continued to rebel or associate with the wrong crowd—there may come a time when you need to conclude that you've done your best and can no longer accept responsibility. You can't blame yourself for everything that goes awry.

If your teenager has at least average intelligence, he'll gradually learn to think for himself, to differentiate right from wrong and change his lifestyle. Eventually he'll become responsible for himself. And certainly by the time late adolescence arrives, you must insist that he does.

23

WHEN YOUR TEENAGER STARTS DATING

*D*ating is part of growing up. And even though you assume your children will date during adolescence, you probably haven't thought much about it in advance. However, you really need to prepare for this time in your teenager's life.

Let's face it: times have changed. When you were dating as a teenager, things were different from now they are today. And if you've based your parental attitudes about dating on the past, you may need to adapt to what lies ahead. It's time for some personal investigating of current, local dating practices.

Depending on the social group to which your teenager belongs, she may already have strong views of her own on dating behaviors. She might have an opinion about the age that adolescents can start dating, when parents should expect their teenagers to be home, whether teens should date on school nights, the functions adolescents should be permitted to attend, whether a very young teenager should date someone much older, and so forth.

THE ROLE OF PARENTS

Not surprisingly, you probably have your own ideas on these matters. Before your adolescent begins to date, you and your spouse may find it useful to discuss these issues together and agree on rules that you will communicate to your youngster. If the dating practices common among your adolescent's peers are unacceptable to you, family members may need to reexamine their respective beliefs, and perhaps reach a compromise on what the family's dating rules will be. No matter what standards you ultimately decide on, make sure your teenager understands them clearly. If she still has some objections, listen to them and explain why you believe the rules should remain as they are.

Also, plan in advance what you'll do if your teenager violates these guidelines. Quite often parents react with anger when a teenager misses a curfew or attends a party they had designated as off-limits; in the heat of the moment they may dole out punishments or restrictions that are impractical or ineffective. But here's a better approach: discuss reasonable penalties with your adolescent at the time you establish the rules themselves; in that way she'll know beforehand the consequences of any unacceptable behavior.

Some families also adopt a "free-ride" policy—that is, if your teenager finds herself in a difficult situation, she can call you and get a "free" ride home with no questions asked until the next day. In short, you'll be encouraging your adolescent to call home for support and help.

But as smoothly as you try to make things run, they sometimes won't! Now and then you can expect some difficult circumstances to arise. Perhaps your daughter has chosen a new dating partner of whom you strongly disapprove. Or against your objections, maybe she wants to go with a group of friends on a weekend skiing trip. Your own decision may depend in large part on whether your child is in early, middle, or late adolescence. But if you ultimately refuse permission and she stubbornly rejects all your well-reasoned explanations, keep in mind that *the final decision is yours.*

During "crises" such as this, it's important for you to forbid unwise or potentially harmful activities. Undoubtedly you'll hear the argument that "Michelle's father is letting her go." But stand firm. Parents will differ on the amount of freedom they give their children, and you need to decide what's best for you and your family; you're ultimately responsible for your children—adolescents included.

The situation may become even more complicated when teenagers become old enough to drive an automobile. When that happens, they may feel some newfound independence and presume that they now have a wider geographical area for activities. A trip to the beach or lake, for example, is no longer the logistical problem it once was. As a parent, however, you might have a different point of view. Almost inevitably you'll have some worries about the dangers of your teenager driving and some added concerns if you don't know just how safely a dating partner may drive. And with each new friend and date the anxieties about who will be behind the wheel can start all over again.

That isn't all. Age differences in dating can add even further to your stress levels. In high school girls usually go out with older boys, while some boys may ask out girls who are still in junior high school. In a sense these matchups are understandable since girls develop earlier than boys and may be attracted to "older" males who seem more mature and "exciting." However, if there's a wide variation in age, you need to consider carefully whether to permit this dating situation. When an eighteen- or nineteen-year-old young man dates a fourteen-year-old girl, the potential for trouble exists, especially if it evolves into a steady relationship. (Page 137)

Many adolescents, incidentally, prefer steady dating, no matter what their ages. After all, this kind of relationship can provide a reliable partner for parties and other activities and prevent the anxiety-provoking situation of getting to know someone new. Not all steady dating is bad, but you should be sensitive to just how intense such relationships become.

One other point: bear in mind that children learn by example. If you don't want your teenager to use tobacco, alcohol, or other chemical substances in dating situations—or any other time, for that matter—don't use them yourself. Also, if you and your spouse demonstrate mutual respect for one another, that's the best example for your adolescent's own developing relationships. In much the same way, if you're a single parent, your adolescent will learn a lot by watching your own dating practices. If you're sexually permissive, or if you have a live-in partner or a succession of partners, you'll convey the impression that multiple sexual relationships are acceptable. It is not wise to assume that your teenager will embrace the notion that such an arrangement is good for adults but bad for adolescents. Examine your own lifestyle and either change it or communicate some very persuasive reasons why your adolescent shouldn't live by the same rules.

ADOLESCENTS AND DATING

Thus far in this chapter we've discussed how you can expect to react to your teenager's dating years. Now let's look more closely at this important part of adolescence, specifically from the teenager's point of view.

First, when youngsters are very early adolescents, they probably won't be dating at all. They'll be interested mostly in themselves, and forming a close association with someone of the opposite sex isn't yet a top priority. Yes, they'll watch older adolescents, learning what will be expected of them and how they should act later on. But for the present any interrelating of boys and girls will usually be in groups, thus providing safety without demanding any of the sophistication and actions of older teenagers.

By middle adolescence teenagers are still socializing in groups, but they also may be starting to form closer relationships with particular persons of the opposite sex. This can be a tumultuous, unpredictable stage of development; some teenagers will try to date many different partners, while others will choose to date rarely or not at all. Some boys will refuse to date until they can drive an automobile, embarrassed to have a parent chauffeur them on dates.

As middle adolescents grow older, they'll become more self-confident, perhaps have regular access to a car, and may date fairly often. Even so, dating patterns during this time can range from one extreme to the other: Some teenagers will have few (if any) dates, perhaps because they're busy with other endeavors such as sports or drama, or maybe because they simply don't feel ready yet. At the other end of the spectrum there are adolescents who have fallen in love with their dating partner as the end of high school approaches and start making plans to attend the same college and even begin thinking about marriage. (On the other hand, some young people in the same situation may recognize that continuing this serious relationship could interfere with their future, and they'll begin to unloosen their bonds.)

Let your adolescents know that as they begin and continue to date, you'll always be available to give advice. Few teenagers will want to discuss all their thoughts, feelings, and concerns with their parents, but when they turn instead to other adolescents for information, much of it will be inaccurate. So if your teenager doesn't raise sexual matters with you, it's appropriate for you to introduce the topic from time to time.

As we pointed out in Chapter 14, sexual feelings and curiosity are universal during the teenage years. And in dating situations adolescents will begin to experiment with their sexuality. In particular, try to keep an eye on an adolescent who has begun puberty earlier than her friends. She may be more eager to try experimenting sexually, while still lacking the judgment that only age can bring.

(Also, give some extra attention to late-maturing adolescents who may not wish to date when their companions do, as well as less attractive teenagers; you may have to channel these youngsters into more activities outside the home to improve their self-esteem.)

In addition to reckless sexual behavior, other risk-taking behaviors—smoking, drug abuse, and drinking and driving—can be part of dating as well. Ironically, almost all teenagers recognize that these activities are harmful and run counter to their parents' wishes—but they'll do them anyway. Much of this experimentation takes place to satisfy adolescent curiosity, but some of it may be a way of fitting into a group, of being accepted.

As a fifteen-year-old girl told her pediatrician, "You know, sitting here talking to you, it's simple to see what's right and wrong. But when I'm on a date and we really like each other, I just don't think like this."

To sum up, dating is an important part of an adolescent's social development. It's an opportunity to build skills in relating to persons of the opposite sex, to test one's ability to form friendships, to increase understanding and tolerance, and to experience relationships that may later lead to marriage. It's a learning process, and as it evolves teenagers will have successes and failures, happy moments and sad ones—and they'll have the need for advice and understanding from parents. However, be sure this advice comes before, not after, the dating process begins.

24

MANNERS AND
SOCIAL GRACES

*W*hat is your teenager's style of social behavior? Does he act the way you want him to most of the time? Or is he a constant source of embarrassment, as though he were a visitor from another planet?

Ask most adolescents, and they'll tell you that they resent parental instructions on social customs, whether it's about proper attire for a particular occasion or how to carry on a polite conversation. They'll say they don't care what other people think of them. But that's really not true. Teenagers do care—but only in situations where peers or adults they consider important would find their social behavior odd or unacceptable.

Small children are less of a problem. They usually imitate and accept the ways of the family, thus establishing some important traits long before puberty. But then comes adolescence. At least for a time, as they strive for freedom and individuality, teenagers will disregard many of these past parental instructions. They'll tend to be impudent, in a hurry, and oblivious to prevailing social graces. And that can send many parents into a frenzy.

However, don't despair. Just when you've decided that you shouldn't let him out in public ever again, he'll start to adopt some acceptable table manners, for example. Since you're one of his most important role models, make sure your own social skills (at home and in public) are up to par. As he sees how you (and other people) act and becomes familiar with the advantages of behaving in a certain way, he'll start to come around. Yes, he may still profess a lack of interest in manners and social graces—but he'll also hate being embarrassed in public, and thus he'll soon learn to conform.

Even the most stubborn teenagers usually know what to do and how to act—but they may need their memory refreshed from time to time. As ancient as it may sound, the Golden Rule does apply: we really should do to others what we want them to do to (or for) us.

By older adolescence youngsters will start to recognize the future value of manners in business or any other future vocation. Social graces affect getting a job, being successful in college, being accepted by a community organization, influencing associates and employees, and delivering a good speech. Once it becomes clear to them that good manners can contribute to success in life, teenagers will find a place for them.

There's one significant obstacle that can get in your adolescent's way, however. If he lives in one culture or socioeconomic group and has friends who belong to another group with different social mores, he may have trouble fitting in. He'll have to learn some new behaviors, but if he's determined to belong, he'll eventually conform (for better or worse) to these unfamiliar customs.

We can summarize this entire chapter this way: as a group adolescents probably do much better than adults suspect when it comes to social growth. Most of them do absorb principles from their parents and other respected adults, and although deviations from these standards certainly occur, the majority of teenagers will resemble their parents when they become adults.

Of course the road to adulthood may be a rocky one. All adolescents make mistakes. But teenagers will get through these difficult times by observing, imitating, and maturing enough to become responsible for themselves.

As a parent you may feel as if you're in a dilemma of your own. On the one hand, you don't want your child to be a clone—that is, an exact replica of you. Even so, the freedom to be different needs some limits, and your teenager must learn to stay within certain boundaries that you and other adults set. Naturally you're not the only influence in your adolescent's life; he's also affected by friends and the expectations of the society and culture in which he lives, not to mention his own genetic makeup. But in the long run you'll be one of his strongest influences. And when he finally reaches adulthood, you'll probably be quite proud of how he has turned out.

PART VI

EDUCATION:
NORMAL ASPECTS AND
PROBLEM AREAS

25

GOALS AND
EXPECTATIONS

*F*or today's adolescents, growing up in the latter part of the twentieth century is not always easy. Just ask the many researchers who have consistently written about the "external stressors" that influence young people now, from the threat of nuclear war to anxieties about the national economy.

You can't deny the potential impact of these concerns. Even so, in other parts of this book we've described some other matters that are much more immediate and personal and that may cause even greater adolescent anxiety. This is the time of life, after all, in which young people are asserting their independence, establishing a sense of self, finding a place in the world, dealing with their emerging sexuality, and looking ahead to career choices—all of which can be sources of stress. Then there are family concerns: interpersonal turmoil or even divorce . . . job changes by parents that force geographical relocation . . . financial pressures within the family.

These are the kinds of influences that can really raise the stress levels of adolescents and in the process disrupt nearly every aspect of their lives—including their performance at school. Add to that the growing pressures within the educational system itself—for instance, the mounting competition to get into the country's top colleges (or for some, any college) and the widespread prevalence of illegal drugs and the temptations to use them—and some teenagers find junior high and high school demanding, sometimes superfluous, and even intimidating.

Education, of course, is a dominant part of your adolescent's life. These crucial junior and senior high school years represent the transition from childhood to adulthood. Doing well in school can be the springboard to success later in life. But if your youngster has difficulties—and particularly if he drops out of school— a lot of doors to the future may be closed to him.

No wonder, then, that as a parent you may become disturbed if your adolescent brings home report cards with Cs and Ds rather than As and Bs. And if he isn't achieving academically, you may react with anger, anxiety, and even guilt.

However, don't jump to conclusions. When your adolescent isn't doing well in school, you may have to look beyond the obvious—beyond a lack of self-discipline, beyond an unwillingness to study. There are other contributing factors you may need to consider as well. For instance, as we suggested earlier, what are the other stresses in his life that could be preoccupying him? Is he being distracted by girlfriend problems? At school, are older, bigger students harassing him? Has he become involved with drugs? Does he have a health problem that's interfering with his ability to concentrate? Is he bored, and does he perceive school as irrelevant? Or does he have a learning disability that's gone unrecognized or untreated?

THE PURPOSE OF EDUCATION

William J. Bennett, U.S. secretary of education during the Reagan administration, capsulized the goals of a high school education this way:

> We want our students—whatever their plans for the future—to take from high school a shared body of knowledge and skills, a common language of ideas, a common moral and intellectual discipline. We want them to know math and science, history and literature. We want them to know how to think for them-

selves, to respond to important questions, to solve problems, to pursue an argument, to defend a point of view, to understand its opposite, and to weigh alternatives. We want them to develop, through example and experience, those habits of mind and traits of character properly prized by our society. And we want them to be prepared for entry into the community of responsible adults.

That's quite an ambitious agenda. And with all the potential obstacles that exist today—from drugs on campus to overcrowded classrooms—schools face a real challenge in preparing America's youth for adulthood. As a result you can't count on the schools to do it alone. If you want your teenager to do well, you need to get involved, too. In the midst of his search for independence and separation from his family, you remain an important influence in his life, still capable of giving him many of the tools he'll need for success in school.

With this in mind, ask yourself how well you've assumed the following responsibilities:

- Have you instilled in your adolescent the values that will help him in school, including a belief in the importance of education? While a good education requires hard work, does he realize that it's worth the effort?

- Do you set high (but realistic) expectations for your adolescent? Does he know that you expect him to work up to his capabilities?

- Do you take an active interest in your youngster's schoolwork, assisting him when problems occur and giving him an occasional ride to the library to study or do research?

- Do you praise and reward his achievements in school as well as help him get back on track when he falls short of what's expected of him?

- Do you give him responsibilities around the house that are not school-related but that develop personal qualities such as resourcefulness, self-reliance, and pride in his accomplishments—all of which will help him at school?

- Have you assisted your adolescent in prioritizing the tasks and activities in his life, making sure that his homework (and his home responsibilities) come first, *ahead* of television and phone calls?

- Have you visited the school to consult with his teachers—and to serve as an advocate for him?

Don't underestimate the value of these kinds of parental contributions. They are more important than influences like your own educational level or your family income. In fact studies show that college-bound children from low-income families are more than twice as likely to say that their parents expected them to achieve a higher education as those students not planning to reach beyond a high school diploma. Your values and expectations count!

GETTING HOMEWORK DONE

"Son, have you done your homework yet?"

"Homework? Oh, I don't think I have any tonight, Dad."

There's more to doing well in school than the six to seven hours that your adolescent spends on his junior high or high school campus each day. He'll also have homework to contend with, if not every night, then several nights a week.

Don't undervalue the significance of homework. As conscientious as he may be at school, if he's going to do well on tests and get his assignments finished on time, he'll need to get used to committing *some* time at home to his studies.

If you think back to your own school days, you may understand why your adolescent sometimes resists poring over his books in the late afternoon or evening. After all, other activities—meeting with friends, talking on the phone, watching TV—are much more enjoyable.

However, you can help make your adolescent's homework seem a lot less burdensome. Make sure he has a quiet place to study at home—in his room or at the dining room table before or after dinner. Suggest that he do his homework at a particular time each day—perhaps from 4:00 to 6:00 P.M. or from 7:30 to 9:30 P.M. Help him keep track of his assignments, perhaps with an assignment pad to carry from school to home or maybe with a flowchart on which he can list the due dates of his term papers and other reports and the dates of his exams.

If your adolescent learns good study habits early, he'll be able to fall back on them throughout high school and college. By taking his homework seriously, he'll not only bring home a better report card, but he'll develop self-discipline and perseverance. This self-discipline will rub off in other areas too, such as his work and hobbies. And although he may complain at times that his homework is overwhelming, studies show that schools that assign greater amounts of homework turn out students who perform better academically. It's as simple as that.

SETTING REALISTIC ACADEMIC GOALS

Some parents become obsessed with their children achieving—and overachieving—in life. A father may want his son or daughter to follow in his footsteps and become a lawyer. Or if a parent never fulfilled his own dreams—for example, if he never became the doctor or the engineer he had once set his sights on being—he may yearn for his youngster to achieve what he never did.

But imagine the pressures on a child in that type of environment. Yes, there are times when a parent's ambitious script for his adolescent's life may provide inspiration and motivation for the young person—if the dreams are really appropriate and realistic. However, if Mom and Dad want their child to pursue a career he has no interest in—or if he doesn't have the talent or the academic prowess to fulfill that dream—it can be devastating. Some youngsters may make the effort anyway, driven by the fear of disappointing their parents. In the process, however, they may build up a lot of resentment over not pursuing their own goals, feeling pushed in a direction that isn't right for them. For other adolescents unrealistic parental expectations can become the cornerstone of a power struggle in which the young person may rebel by not trying anymore.

Career choices aren't the only areas where parents often apply pressure. Mothers and fathers also sometimes demand unrealistic performance at school. These are the parents who always look for their youngster's name on the principal's honor roll or who expect English essays from their adolescent as finely crafted as a Hemingway novel. Maybe they're well intentioned, but those kinds of expectations can often do much more harm than good.

Imagine the sense of failure that an adolescent may have if he has very little aptitude in the sciences or in foreign languages, and yet his father scolds him when he brings home poor grades in those classes. These youngsters may do much better in other areas—perhaps excelling in music, literature, or athletics—but some mothers and fathers have high expectations for *every* subject. Parents like these don't realize that one of their roles is to help each child discover his special interests and talents.

"I can't figure my parents out," said one fifteen-year-old. "When I get a C, they ask why I didn't get a B. When I get a B, they wonder why it's not an A. They keep telling me that I'll never get into a good college unless I do better. But can't they see that I spend a lot of time studying? I really am trying, and I think I'm getting better at taking tests. My older brother was valedictorian of his class, and he got accepted to three different colleges. Maybe he's just smarter than I am. Why can't my mom and dad just accept me for what I am?"

It's not fair to compare your teenager to his siblings or friends. If you tell your adolescent that he isn't as smart or isn't as talented as his brother or classmates, he's very likely to react with anger—not only toward you but also toward those whom you've compared him to. Feeling less valued by you, he may experience some serious impairment of his self-esteem.

What kind of message should you be communicating to your adolescent? More than anything else, tell him you expect him to do his best in all his classes. If he can get As, that's great. If his best efforts produce Cs, that's all right too—but don't label him as only a C person. Encourage him to learn as much and do as well as he can, while reminding him that your love and approval won't hinge on how impressive his report card is.

No matter what grades your adolescent ultimately achieves, if he works hard, studies diligently, and accepts the challenge for doing the best he can, you should reward him for that. Particularly if he's struggling in school, despite his hard work, let him know that you appreciate his efforts and will continue to support him. By acknowledging his efforts—no matter what the outcome—you'll be boosting his self-esteem and motivating him to keep trying. As a parent you should not express disappointment when your youngster reaches his limits. Yes, other parents' children may do better, but you must accept and love your own adolescent for what he is, not what you dreamed he'd become.

On the other hand, you need to draw the line at certain times. For example, don't accept sloppy work that falls below your adolescent's capabilities. If he's been a consistent B student but suddenly brings home a report card with Ds, find out why. Is he encountering some distractions like those described at the beginning of this chapter—perhaps troubles with peers or drug abuse? Try to identify and correct the problem and redirect his attention back to his schoolwork. And avoid power struggles with school achievement in the middle.

Remember, if your adolescent has been a C student all along, maybe that's all you can realistically expect from him. It doesn't necessarily mean he's lazy or dumb. He might be living up to his capabilities. And that's all you can really expect.

Don't forget, too, that schools themselves differ in many respects and that some are more academically demanding than others. If you live in an urban community, your adolescent may have access to a number of schools. Evaluate them carefully and select the one best suited for your youngster based on reputation, educational philosophy, academic, fine arts, and sports programs, ability to deal with your child's specific educational needs, etc.

Then, if your adolescent is having problems at school, ask his teachers to help you assess what his abilities are and where his talents may lie. With this information in hand, you can help him set practical goals for the present and the future. Try pointing him in directions to maximize his potential. If he works well with his hands, perhaps he's more suited for a career as a car mechanic than as a physicist. *And that's okay.*

Keep in mind that when a vocational counselor evaluates a youngster, he's looking primarily at that individual's *interests* and *aptitudes,* not at the social prestige or the salary associated with them. If your adolescent moves into a vocation in which he has little interest or aptitude, this can be very stressful and perhaps detrimental to his mental and physical health. So to avoid harming your youngster's mind and body, make sure he understands that you want him to reach for goals that are achievable and that interest him.

Also, take a few minutes to evaluate yourself and your goals and experiences concerning your own education. Ask yourself pointed questions such as, "What were my educational goals? Did I reach them? How does reaching them [or not reaching them] affect my reaction to my youngster's schoolwork? Regarding the educational goals I have for my teenager, are they really for him—or for me? And are my teenager's own educational goals the same or different from mine?"

MAKING THE MOST OF EDUCATION

To benefit fully from his education, your adolescent will have to shed most of the sweat and tears. Even so, as we've already emphasized, you can make a significant difference. Your support is important, so from time to time, review the suggestions in this chapter and offer your youngster the encouragement to maximize his learning opportunities. More than anything else, make sure your teenager feels your presence and your interest when his education is concerned. This will take some time and effort, but as we discussed in earlier sections of this book, loving your child means spending time with him and finding out about his world. And when you do, the payoff can be substantial as your youngster moves from adolescence into adulthood.

That means showing your concern by conversing often with your adolescent about what's going on in school. What subjects does he enjoy? Which ones is he having trouble with? Is he having problems with any teachers? Ask to see his homework and his tests and take the time to sit down with him and discuss how he can solve any difficulties he's having. Encourage him to think and question what he's studying; the more actively involved he is in the subject, the more he'll learn and retain.

Also, show your interest by attending open houses at school and keeping in contact with your youngster's teachers. While it's nice to attend such meetings and hear glowing reports about your child, don't shy away because you expect negative feedback from the teachers. The school can alert you to difficulties and potential solutions—if you are listening. So get involved!

During your adolescent's leisure time, try to channel him into intellectually stimulating activities. Talking about current events over the dinner table can be very productive. Something positive can even come out of television viewing—if you make a point of discussing with your adolescent what he liked about the program and what he got out of it. At the same time, encourage reading rather than TV watching; during summer vacations in particular, make sure plenty of books—and a variety of books—are available. Also, let your youngster see *you* reading frequently.

Remind your adolescent that it's not easy to get a good education. However, there is a payoff—namely, a more productive, fulfilling, and successful adult life. Despite the obstacles and the challenges that he'll have to confront and conquer, his schooling will help him become independent—and make a mark in the world for himself.

26

WHEN YOUR TEENAGER
NEEDS SOME MOTIVATION

"*I* hate school. I don't like going to class, and I don't like studying. The sooner I get out of school, the better."

Some adolescents feel that their life would be perfect if only school didn't exist. They daydream during class. They rarely turn in homework assignments and try to "bluff" their way through tests that they didn't study for. They're unaffected by terrible report cards, don't seem to care about learning, and are indifferent to what the future may hold.

If this is a mini-profile of your adolescent, you've almost certainly felt frustrated by her lack of motivation and her lack of interest in turning things around. While many of her classmates are striving for As and Bs, why is she content never to open a book? When many of her fellow students are thinking about the SATs and the college they might choose, why is she dreaming only about putting school behind her and perhaps even dropping out?

As the preceding chapter pointed out, a lot of things can distract an adolescent from taking her schoolwork seriously. If your youngster is unmotivated, ask her about peer problems at school. Or difficulties with a particular teacher. Sometimes the problem is physical, from bad eyesight to poorly controlled diabetes (in these latter cases, perhaps a pair of glasses or more conscientious meal planning can go a long way toward getting her back on track). A careful medical evaluation can help identify and deal with any contributing medical difficulties.

Some adolescents are depressed or have problems with self-esteem that detract from their motivation. Because of limited expectations of themselves, they often don't even try to do well. Ironically, while achievement in school might boost that sagging self-confidence, they perceive themselves as being undeserving of success and don't even make an effort to attain it.

Some outside tutoring can often assist these adolescents, concentrating on the subjects giving them the most trouble. If they can start to feel competent in working with algebraic formulas or linguistic concepts, for instance, these positive experiences may give them enough motivation to work for success in other areas.

In the meantime, try extra hard to keep the communication channels open, no matter how passive and uninterested in talking your adolescent seems to be. Discuss what's on her mind and in her heart. If it's not a turnoff for her, even tell her stories about your own adolescence—for instance, about the problems you may have encountered in high school trying to learn a foreign language or make sense of a chemistry table. Encourage her to put out the effort and to set realistic goals and try to reach them.

Unfortunately, as a natural by-product of your teenager's search for independence he may instinctively say no whenever you say yes. School underachievement is a classic manifestation of this adolescent rebellion. When this happens, professional counseling may be necessary to get him headed in the right direction. A skilled counselor may be able to get through to him when you can't.

SCHOOL AVOIDANCE

Sometimes when an adolescent loses interest in school, the signs and symptoms of this apathy may go beyond a poor report card. He might have severe anxiety attacks whenever he approaches school. He may complain of stomach pains, backaches, chest pain, and fatigue. He'll probably tell you he's just unable to go to school or doesn't want to anymore.

The physical symptoms, although real, are occurring in response to psychological distress. Some of the factors that contribute to this school avoidance may be familiar to you by now—from an intimidating bully at school to a problem with a teacher, from relationships with parents and difficulties at home (marital strife) to stress about entering a new school environment (starting junior high or high school).

School violence in particular is a problem that you cannot afford to ignore. Some adolescents are afraid to go to school because they fear for their own safety. Violence on junior high and high school campuses has become almost epidemic in some parts of the country, particularly in urban centers. Not only does it threaten the physical well-being of youngsters, but it undermines the educational process. Gangs, assaults, and extortions have forced reading, writing, and arithmetic into a secondary role in too many schools.

If you suspect that anxiety may be keeping your own teenager away from school, you need to intervene *before* circumstances become completely out of control. Bring situations such as violence and intimidation to the attention of school authorities and work with them to make the school environment more comfortable for your youngster. Some school districts and principals have gotten tough with the troublemakers on their campuses and have restored order and discipline.

Once the environment is safe, insist that your youngster return to school. *The longer he stays away, the worse his anxieties are likely to become.* In the midst of his grumbling about how much his stomach hurts or how terrible his chest pains are, you need to insist that he get back into the classroom. Let him know that the circumstances that he dreads have been resolved. Although you may be tempted to be "gentle" and allow him to stay away from school until he feels completely comfortable going back, his anxiety may only intensify if that happens. Therefore, be firm! Remind him that school attendance is legally mandated. At the same time, however, be sure you have tackled this situation fully by getting to the root of the problem—that is, identifying the specific crises that are interfering with your youngster's normal adjustment and helping to resolve these difficulties as rapidly as possible.

Also, keep in mind that whether your youngster is concerned about violence or difficulties with a teacher, you may not be able to completely prevent him from experiencing pain in such a situation. But you might be able to help him see and choose alternatives that can ease his anxiety or make the problem less stressful. A school counselor might be able to help as well, as can a trusted professional; but you must seek their help early, and their advice must be followed. The longer your child avoids school, the more difficult it will be to put this problem behind him.

One more point about school violence: if your teenager is the aggressor in such situations, you need to intervene immediately. Teach your youngster, through your words and actions, that violence is *never* an acceptable form of behavior.

Limit his access to violent films and television programs, which have been associated with aggressive behavior. Adolescents who seem incapable of controlling their violent outbursts can often be helped by professional counseling.

IF HE WANTS TO DROP OUT . . .

Just how important is schooling? Ask the average parent, and he'll probably tell you that a college degree would be a wonderful asset to help carry his youngster through life. A high school education, he might add, would be the bare minimum.

No wonder most parents react with horror if their adolescent announces that he wants to drop out of school. It's like having the rug pulled out from under *their* dreams. They also can see hundreds of doors of opportunity slammed in their youngster's face.

Your adolescent may try to justify his decision to drop out in a number of ways. Perhaps he's not doing well in school, isn't getting along with teachers, and doesn't show any interest in learning. Or maybe he's yearning for more independence and is eager to enter the job market. Or he may want to get married. From one study, here are some of the responses teenagers gave for dropping out:

"I was mostly just discouraged because I wasn't passing."

"I was bored. I had the grades but was just bored. It was the teachers. They didn't make it interesting enough."

"School . . . didn't teach me how to cope with society once I got out of [the] school doors."

If your adolescent is serious about dropping out, here are some important points to keep in mind: First, your instincts are right about the value of a diploma. There are many jobs that require high school graduation, and by dropping out your youngster will immediately limit his employment options. There's also a real boost in self-esteem that comes on graduation day—a sense that he has accomplished something important.

On the other hand, some adolescents just aren't suited for academic life. For them, other opportunities are available. They can learn a trade, for example, and lead a life as happy and productive as someone with a diploma. Also, there may be other school options—perhaps work-study programs—in your community that better suit your youngster's academic (and social) needs. Enlist the help of the school staff; school districts are as concerned about dropouts as parents are. The school may have special counselors or alternative programs available for "at-risk" youth, and teachers often have insight into what the problems—and solutions—may be.

After unsuccessfully trying to talk their adolescent into staying in high school, some parents have chosen to support their youngster in his decision. "I didn't want to make it so hard on him that a wedge would be driven between us that would be very difficult to mend. I told him I'd back his decision, but that I hoped someday he'd go back and get his diploma. Three years later, he finally did."

For some dropouts, leaving school allows them to escape from what they perceive as a terrible rut that they've fallen into. Having accomplished little in school, they may find a job that's rewarding and satisfying. In the process they can often bolster their sagging self-esteem.

If your youngster fits this description, help him develop a specific plan so he can begin dealing with his life financially and socially, preferably *before* he actually leaves school. Offer to help him locate some job training or perhaps career counseling to find out what he may be best suited for. Also, encourage him to talk to others who have dropped out, especially those who have been away from school for several years. When he's ready, he can go back to school and/or pursue various educational opportunities. Discuss the situation fully with your adolescent—but allow him to make up *his own mind.*

THE "CURSE" OF INTELLIGENCE

"Sometimes I think she's too smart for her own good. She's bored and says school isn't challenging anymore."

As we've seen, problems with motivation can come from a variety of directions. One that baffles parents the most is the bright teenager who seems to have lost her desire to learn.

For youngsters such as this, work in the classroom is dull and dreary. Their curiosity seems untapped, their imagination unstimulated. Despite their intelligence, they become underachievers, frustrated by what they consider to be "busy-work." They may even develop discipline problems, rebelling against what they perceive to be an intolerable situation.

If your own adolescent is academically advanced beyond most of her peers—but is bored in class—how should you react? First, you should help her search for some additional learning experiences. Nearly all high schools have programs for "gifted" students designed to bring some stimulation and excitement into their academic lives. Also, look for after-school or Saturday programs, either at your teenager's school or at community colleges, that challenge her with subjects like astronomy or physics. Many colleges and universities have "special student" status that allows younger students to enroll in college-level curricula. Whether your youngster's special interests are in science, math, music, or literature, don't let her talents go to waste.

Also, don't neglect the home environment. Make sure your bookshelves are well stocked with novels and nonfiction books that appeal to your adolescent.

Her hobbies and games should be intellectually stimulating. Encourage her to associate with peers and role models with similar interests and intelligence; remember, she needs opportunities not only for developing her mind but also for improving her social skills. A bright child who has no social outlets can become very depressed.

Even once strategies like these are in place, there may still be another baffling obstacle to overcome. In brief, your gifted adolescent may tell you that she's not interested in studying because she "can't stand being different." She may say that she just wants to be like everyone else and avoid being identified as "a brain" by her classmates, for fear of being rejected or labeled as a "nerd."

Here is the typical situation you might face: Your adolescent is very bright and, in fact, actually enjoys the intellectual stimulation of school. Yet as much as she yearns for knowledge, she may want friends even more. And since school is the primary place where young people meet and form friendships, she'll do just about anything to avoid being singled out and ridiculed as an "egghead."

What a sad but all too real phenomenon! Imagine having the gift of intelligence but being embarrassed by it and thus not taking advantage of the opportunities it could open up.

With an adolescent like this, you need to encourage some balance in her life. Don't deny the importance of making and maintaining friendships; they are a critically important part of growing up. On the other hand, support her in the lifelong benefits of developing her intellectual abilities. Remind her how academic achievements today can result in a more fulfilling career. Point to admirable role models whom she can emulate. Help her find intellectual pursuits that are "fun," including imaginative games and hobbies. And reward her with praise when she excels at school, letting her know there's a payoff to learning.

GETTING YOUR ADOLESCENT BACK ON TRACK

It's one of the toughest positions for a parent to be in: you see the lack of motivation in your adolescent, and you recognize just how damaging that attitude can be. As he moves down this self-defeating path, your intervention may ultimately become essential.

This chapter has already given you some options to explore to help your adolescent. Here are some additional approaches:

- Even though your adolescent may resist your suggestions, encourage her to think about the future—not just short-term objectives but also goals for the decades ahead. What does she hope to do with her life? What kind of career does she look forward to in ten to twenty years? By setting her sights on the future, she may start to comprehend how her decisions today may influence whether she ever reaches those goals. If she doesn't apply herself, she'll have to put aside those dreams of being a lawyer, an accountant, a computer programmer, or a veterinarian. Many colleges and vocational schools have a "career day" each year, during which students can talk to representatives about various vocational opportunities; these meetings can provide motivation and direct young people toward pertinent outside classes and summer jobs.

- Tell your adolescent that you're going to treat her like a young adult and you expect her to assume responsibility for the task at hand. For the time being, her "job" is going to school, and she should take it seriously and make the most of this opportunity. Like everyone else in the family, she must be accountable for her performance at her "job."

- Ask your adolescent for some suggestions on how to get her out of the "motivation blahs." Why is she so unhappy? What are her solutions to the problem? What opportunities can you give her to encourage her to roll up her sleeves and get to work?

- Be sensitive to specific learning problems or a low IQ in your youngster. (See the next chapter.)

- Talk with your family's pediatrician or the school psychologist about whether some psychological counseling, or perhaps a battery of tests, might be in order. On occasion there could be an underlying depression driving your adolescent's behavior. Several sessions of therapy (or just "talking" with her pediatrician) might help her transform her self-defeating attitudes into productive ones.

A final reminder: *try not to overreact.* If you become too overbearing, if you try too hard to pressure and motivate your teenager, your best efforts may backfire. Be patient. Wait to see if she makes some changes on her own. Ultimately, if no shifts in attitude are forthcoming, it's time to intervene. It's your responsibility as a parent.

27

COPING WITH LEARNING PROBLEMS

*L*ouis is fifteen years old. According to a recent test, his IQ is 119. Even so, his grades are terribly disappointing—some Cs, even more Ds. Everybody agrees he should be doing better.

Some of Louis's problems are apparent to just about anyone who observes him. He can't sit still, constantly squirming in his seat. He doesn't pay attention to what his teachers say. He's disorderly in class. He can't seem to stop talking. His schoolwork—when he does it—is sloppy and messy. And his teachers have warned his parents that unless there's a major transformation in his behavior, his grades could deteriorate even further.

The challenge before Louis, however, is difficult. He's been diagnosed as having a problem that interferes with his ability to learn—he has a behavioral condition that goes by a number of names, including "attention-deficit hyperactivity disorder" (ADHD). And he's not alone.

Various studies have concluded that the incidence of learning difficulties in general ranges from 10 to 30 percent of the school population, depending on how these problems are defined. Some of these teenagers may have difficulty following instructions. Their problem-solving and perceptual skills may be in disarray. As a result they might have problems with reading, writing, spelling, speech, and mathematics. Ironically, as in the case of Louis, these youngsters tend to have normal or even above-normal intelligence. But probably since elementary school, they have demonstrated some signs of their learning problems.

In 1970 Public Law 94–230 defined a learning disability as an impairment of the psychological processes involved in the understanding or usage of language. It singled out difficulties in listening, speaking, reading, writing, and/or reasoning, including handling math concepts. Framers of this law recognized that learning is a very complex process and that if there are defects (subtle to obvious) in the way an individual sees, hears, or remembers, learning can be impaired.

Not surprisingly, then, learning disabilities can cause chronic problems in school. By adolescence many of these youngsters have had run-ins with their teachers and dissension with other students—and they're more likely to eventually drop out of school.

Some adolescents with learning problems will tend to seek out friendships with other kids with similar life experiences. Feeling rejected, defeated, and demoralized, these youngsters are more prone to antisocial behavior such as lying, truancy, substance abuse, vandalism, and aggression.

DIAGNOSING LEARNING PROBLEMS

As prevalent as learning difficulties are, teachers and school counselors cannot diagnose all of them. Children may slip through the diagnostic cracks, and their condition might not be identified properly until adolescence—if at all.

A number of tests are available, however, to help in the diagnostic process. They can measure overall intelligence (IQ tests), evaluate achievement (in reading, spelling, writing, mathematics, reasoning), identify behavioral problems, and test various auditory and visual learning skills. They are precise, and in the hands of a skilled diagnostician they often can differentiate one learning disorder from another.

When should you have your teenager evaluated? Here are some signs that could indicate a learning disorder or a behavioral problem that interferes with academic performance:

- He is not performing academically as well as his teachers say he should.

- He reads poorly and doesn't comprehend much of what he reads. He has sloppy work habits, poor handwriting, and trouble organizing his homework.

- He is clumsy, has difficulty with his balance, and shies away from sports and physical activity.

- He's overactive, fidgety, excitable, and distractible.

- He has a short attention span, is forgetful, daydreams, and completes tasks slowly.

If you suspect a problem, ask your adolescent's teachers if they perceive the situation in the same way. Request that a school psychologist evaluate your teenager or ask for a referral to a specialist in learning and/or behavioral problems for a battery of tests. Although the latter approach can be quite expensive, it may be necessary.

The sooner the diagnosis is made, the better. The longer your adolescent goes without help, the greater the likelihood of lasting scars. Some young people spend years (elementary through junior high and high school) suffering with an undiagnosed learning problem, resulting in depression and a major dislike of school. They can fall so far behind academically that catching up can become a monumental undertaking. Emotionally the wounds from feeling "stupid" and inadequate can persist for a lifetime. Unfortunately, poor self-esteem heals very slowly.

WHAT DISORDER DOES HE HAVE?

Educators and pediatricians don't always agree on what labels to apply to childhood learning problems. Some use the term *hyperactive behavioral syndrome,* a broad (and sometimes misused) expression that refers to specific behavioral and attention difficulties. You'll hear a number of other labels too, including minimal cerebral dysfunction, brain-injured, maturation lag, cognitive deficiencies, multisensory disorders, neurologically handicapped, neurologically immature, perceptually handicapped, specific learning disabled, invisibly handicapped, and word blindness or dyslexia. Because there are so many types of these disorders— some subtle and others more easily identifiable—a complete evaluation is necessary if a problem is suspected.

Let's briefly describe two of the most common disabilities:

Dyslexia

Does your adolescent have reading problems that cause him to reverse letters or numbers or see them upside down? Does he read at a slow rate, really struggle to decode words, or continually misspell fairly simple words?

These kinds of problems fall into a category commonly called dyslexia, which is a specific reading disorder. Even though dyslexia is more likely to be identified properly than many other learning deficiencies, it still sometimes goes undetected by both teachers and parents unless the child undergoes specific diagnostic tests.

What causes dyslexia? According to some specialists it may be due to a combination of delayed developmental factors—physical, emotional, motivational—that cumulatively influence the central nervous system and impede the brain's capacity to interpret the written word properly. In many cases it may run in families.

Whatever the cause, the symptoms are quite familiar to most teachers. A dyslexic adolescent often:

- confuses the order of letters in words

- doesn't look carefully at all the letters in a word, guessing what the word is from the first letter

- loses his place on a page while reading, sometimes in the middle of a line

- doesn't remember common words he's learned from one day to the next

- has no systematic way to figure out a word he doesn't know; instead, he guesses or says, "I don't know"

- reads word by word, struggling with almost every one of them

- reads without expression and ignores punctuation

- reads very slowly and tires significantly from reading

- adds, deletes, or substitutes words in a sentence

If your adolescent's teachers suspect dyslexia, make sure that any formal evaluation rules out other possible problems. For instance, does he have difficulties with his eyesight? Are there family problems that might be placing strains on his learning ability? Has he developed slowly on an emotional level?

Once dyslexia is diagnosed, several treatment options are available, and adolescents often make good progress.

Attention-Deficit
Hyperactivity Disorder

Many parents and even some doctors think of attention-deficit hyperactivity disorder as a learning disability, but it really isn't. More accurately, ADHD is a behavioral disorder. A youngster with ADHD may suffer from poor attention span, impulsive behavior, restlessness, and/or overactivity. He may have difficulty listening to the teacher, organizing his assignments, and completing his homework. He may blurt out answers in class when he's not called on or talk to other students at inappropriate times.

Although these symptoms often interfere with learning, some youngsters with ADHD still function well in the classroom, particularly if they happen to be bright. On the other hand, there are many teenagers with learning disabilities who do not have attention difficulties.

In recent years specialists have debated whether children eventually outgrow ADHD and whether it thus becomes much less of a problem by late adolescence and adulthood. In fact by adolescence some young people do seem to improve. However, many researchers now concur that the syndrome itself never really disappears but that the adolescents who have it may learn to better control or compensate for it. Or they may take medications that help keep their symptoms in check.

In a study of a hundred of these children (ages eleven to seventeen), their symptoms improved considerably with time. Even so, they were still more distractible and had more conduct difficulties than normal youngsters. Other studies have reached similar conclusions: although improvement is noted in many of these adolescents, a significant number continue to have problems.

For those youngsters whose ADHD symptoms persist, there's more bad news. One study found that after age sixteen nearly half (48 percent) of these adolescents act out in some way (for example, combativeness with peers, vandalism, or truancy), and about one-third become drug abusers.

If your youngster has been evaluated and diagnosed with ADHD, his doctor may recommend treatment with a medication called methylphenidate (commonly known by its trade name, Ritalin). Some doctors may prescribe other medications called dextroamphetamine (Dexedrine) and pemoline (Cylert) instead. These medications may permit your child to exercise more self-control over his behavior. About 70 to 80 percent of ADHD youngsters significantly improve on medication.

How much of the drug is enough? The most effective dose varies from person to person; thus it must be individualized. Once that happens, the drug can often improve the youth's ability to concentrate and thus to learn better.

Incidentally, in recent years, perhaps you've heard some criticism of methylphenidate when it's used in ADHD children and adolescents. Some drug side effects have been reported, although for most youngsters methylphenidate is safe at recommended dosages. There may be some minor sleep disruptions or appetite suppression, but not enough to bother most teenagers or their parents. This drug also may worsen Tourette's disorder, a condition characterized by a combination of motor and vocal tics. Several studies have also suggested that the drug might interfere with adolescent growth, but this finding remains controversial, and you should check with your teenager's doctor for the most up-to-date information.

With the help of the physician you can decide whether or not medication is indicated. Also, keep in mind that in some cases ADHD can occur along with other behavioral conditions, such as an antisocial personality, depression, or an anxiety disorder; thus, don't blame methylphenidate or ADHD for these other problems that might be present.

In addition to stimulants, doctors sometimes prescribe other types of medications, most notably antidepressant drugs, particularly for adolescents and young adults. These individuals may have become depressed after years of school problems associated with their ADHD, and for them counseling and occasionally antidepressants can be useful.

No matter what type of medication the doctor prescribes, however, it should *never* be utilized as the *sole* treatment. The pediatrician should recommend it only in conjunction with other approaches, including behavioral techniques (e.g., imposing rewards and punishment) as well as counseling and physical education programs.

Because teenagers with ADHD frequently act before thinking, any treatment approach should incorporate a component to help these youngsters identify situations that may get out of control and assist them in dealing effectively with these circumstances *before* a problem develops. If your ADHD adolescent has trouble coping with periods of idle time, for instance, help him find constructive ways to occupy himself.

These young people can be very difficult in the classroom. But help them set small goals for themselves and reward them for small accomplishments. They are *not* bad kids. Don't blame your ADHD youngster for his problems; instead, concentrate your energy on developing strategies for dealing effectively with them.

One last thought about treatments: several highly touted therapies for ADHD haven't fared well when carefully studied by researchers, even though they're still sometimes recommended. For instance, the so-called Feingold diet—which cuts out sugar and other specific food items from a child's meals—hasn't stood up to scientific scrutiny. Even so, because the Feingold diet and other modalities add structure to the lives of these young people, some do improve on these regimens. Nevertheless, carefully evaluate any claims about the successful management of this common and perplexing problem.

Other Learning Problems

As we've already noted, many types of learning problems can occur, with multiple difficulties sometimes present in the same youngster. For instance, when adolescents have specific reading disabilities, problems with spelling and mathematical concepts can also occur as manifestations of the same problem. Although we've already given some guidelines about when to have your youngster evaluated, here are some other clues, based on the specific types of difficulties that may be present. They are adapted from Sally L. Smith's book, *No Easy Answers: The Learning Disabled Child* (Bantam, 1981). Some testing is in order if you answer yes to some of these questions:

Spelling Problems. Does he transpose the order of letters? Does he write only isolated parts of a word, as if he doesn't hear the sequence of sounds? Does he have no memory for common words that are spelled in an unusual way? Does he use neither capital letters nor punctuation? Does he leave words out of sentences and express himself in incomplete sentences? Does he avoid writing as much as possible because he finds it so demanding? Does he frequently disguise his poor spelling with deliberately illegible handwriting?

Handwriting Problems. Does he hold his pencil awkwardly or too tightly? Is his writing unusually large because he can't control the pencil? Is his spacing poor

---

Learning Disability Resources

Learning Disabilities: A Family Affair, by Betty B. Osman (Warner Books, 1985)

No One to Play With: The Social Side of Learning Disabilities, by Betty B. Osman (Academic Therapy Publications, 1989)

Something's Wrong with My Child, by B. M. Richardson and C. Mangel (Harcourt Brace Jovanovich, 1979)

The Misunderstood Child: A Guide for Parents of Learning Disabled Children, by Larry B. Silver (McGraw-Hill, 1988)

No Easy Answers: The Learning Disabled Child, by Sally L. Smith (Bantam Books, 1981)

The FCLD Learning Disabilities Resource Guide: A State-By-State Directory of Programs & Services, by the Foundation for Children with Learning Disabilities (NYU Press, 1985)

between words, usually running words together and leaving no margin? Are his letters written backward or upside down? Does he improperly mix lowercase letters with capitals? Does he write very slowly (for example, taking five minutes for a single sentence)? Due to his poor memory, does he frequently form the same letters differently?

Math Problems. Does he count on his fingers? Does he have trouble memorizing multiplication tables? Does he often understand concepts but find it impossible to solve the problems with paper and pencil? Does he solve problems left to right instead of right to left? Does he have difficulty solving math problems in daily life, such as making change?

Reasoning or Thinking Problems. Does he have difficulty sticking to the main point in a discussion or an essay? Are cause-and-effect relationships difficult for him to grasp? Is his memory poor, often sidetracking his reasoning? Does he have difficulty organizing facts and concepts, complicating his efforts to solve problems? Does he approach concepts too broadly or too narrowly?

THE MENTALLY RETARDED ADOLESCENT

There is another reason for school failure we haven't discussed yet: some youngsters do poorly because they are less capable intellectually than average teenagers. Mental testing usually provides what is called an IQ, or intelligence quotient; this number is an *estimate* of how an individual compares intellectually with other persons. About 3 percent of children fall into the category of "mental retardation," so their numbers are not small. Some children have great difficulty at a very young age, and their parents recognize early this handicapped thinking. For others the differences are not apparent until about the third grade or even not until adolescence, when it becomes obvious that the teenager is not keeping up with peers. Though some of these children will test in the mentally retarded range of intelligence, others will be classified with borderline intellectual ability or as slow learners.

These mentally retarded children can be classified in one of three general groups:

- *Mild mental retardation.* About 90 to 96 percent of retarded teenagers fall into this category. They are educable, and some are potentially literate (usually up to a fourth- to sixth-grade reading/math level). They can typically speak in sentences and follow fairly complex directions. Thus with proper vocational training they can function at semiskilled (and unskilled) jobs. Many of them later marry and live independently.

- *Moderate mental retardation.* These teenagers require considerable help since it is very difficult to teach them even basic skills. They can learn some aspects of self-care, socialization, and verbal communication. They can also perform useful, simple chores. Frequently, as they enter adulthood, they still live in their parents' home or a group facility. They rarely marry.

- *Severe mental retardation.* These teenagers are "untrainable." They need constant custodial care and are totally dependent.

Although these categories are useful guidelines, bear in mind that children and adolescents with the same IQ are not the same in their actions, abilities, and potential for the future. Each adolescent must be considered individually and helped to cope with this handicap and become as independent as possible.

If Your Teenager Is Mildly Retarded . . .

Since most retarded adolescents fall into the first of these three groups, let's look more closely at it. First, the cause of retardation in these (and other) youngsters is usually not known. However, doctors have linked retardation with factors such as infections during pregnancy (rubella or measles), problems before or at the time of birth (premature birth, lack of oxygen), severe central nervous system infections (meningitis), trauma, genetic conditions (Down's syndrome), and thyroid deficiencies (cretinism). Also, severe emotional deprivation after birth can cause an impairment in intellectual capabilities.

If your teenager is mildly retarded, he and your family will likely have many problems. About 40 percent or more of these youngsters have significant emotional and psychological difficulties: depression, ADHD, other learning problems, and aggressive tendencies. They may also have a variety of medical problems as well as cosmetic difficulties (a small head, an unusual facial appearance, short stature).

These adolescents are intelligent enough to recognize their own shortcomings, their rejection by "normal" peers, and their parents' (and society's) disappointment in and frustration with them. They also usually feel a growing frustration regarding their own limitations. After all, they can't realistically pursue the goals that drive much of the "normal" population—the desire for love and romance, wealth, power, popularity, and intellectual achievement. Yet they have the same needs as other teenagers, including a desire for independence and for sexual expression, although they're usually deprived of outlets for them.

The cosmetic difficulties of these adolescents only aggravate their rejection by peers and the rest of society. In social settings these teenagers often feel they can get attention only by being aggressive or behaving in other inappropriate ways—which further alienates them from others. All the while they find themselves dependent on parents who have difficulty coping with the fact that their child is retarded or who devote themselves so totally to their care (sometimes out of guilt for having given birth to them) that independent living, marriage, and jobs are often jeopardized.

Despite such difficulties the situation need not be so bleak. If a youngster receives good education and comes from a good family situation, he will fare much better than many of his mentally retarded peers. Some of these adolescents do quite well in a supportive home environment.

As a parent, how should you approach caring for a mildly retarded adolescent? As well as you can, try to work around the difficulties described above. Become familiar with your community's resources—and use them. Look for support and information from your family's pediatrician and from local groups such as the Association for Retarded Citizens. Take advantage of summer camps for the retarded, the Special Olympics, and other organized peer activities. Governmental agencies, including Children's Rehabilitative Services (formerly called the Crippled Children's Program), can help, too.

Remember, federal law mandates that children under age twenty-one receive educational services in the least restrictive environment (i.e., school settings), either by mainstreaming them in regular schools or by placing them in special classes. This education should emphasize social skills and vocational training. Get your youngster into the program he needs and keep in mind that he has rights.

Also, insist that your teenager behave properly in social settings whenever possible. Teach him simple life skills, personal grooming, and social etiquette. Make sure he has proper dental and medical care. Provide him with sex education and repeat this information regularly so he will remember it. Your teenager's pediatrician can help with many of these matters. (See Page 144.)

Importantly, don't sacrifice all other aspects of your own life. Many communities have group home settings (not institutions) or camps where your youngster can "vacation" briefly, allowing you to temporarily get away from the constant stress of his total dependence. Seek professional help if his behavior is out of control and overly aggressive. Counseling (individual, group, and family) is available to deal with his depression, personality disorders, and interpersonal problems. Seek out this kind of assistance early.

In some cases your teenager will require residential placement. When that becomes obvious, remain his strongest advocate, but do what is necessary. Don't let your guilt prevent appropriate actions.

Like all other teenagers, your retarded youngster will have an array of growing pains and problems. Other parts of this book will help you deal with many of them.

SOME FINAL THOUGHTS

Fortunately, most parents aren't confronted with the reality of a mentally retarded child. Nevertheless, they often fare quite poorly in helping their adolescent of normal intelligence deal with a learning disorder. Even when parents suspect that their teenager has a learning problem, some of them prefer not to rock the boat. Not trusting their own instincts, they don't mention their concerns to teachers or school counselors, hoping that the disorder will somehow be resolved on its own. As one parent said, "I'm not qualified to know if there's anything wrong. I'm embarrassed to even bring it up. Anyway, my kid is learning to cope the best he can."

That approach, however, is not in the best interest of anyone—your adolescent, you, or the school staff. As we've already pointed out, the earlier a learning deficiency is diagnosed, the better off your child will be. Don't let him live with the frustration and low self-esteem that often accompany disorders like this.

Once a teenager has been properly diagnosed with a learning disability, help is available so he can adapt successfully to his learning environment. In addition to those strategies we've already mentioned, many school districts have specialized learning programs for these adolescents. As with mentally retarded children, those of normal intelligence with learning disabilities have also been guaranteed by federal law a free, appropriate education that meets their specific needs.

In your parenting role you need to make certain that your teenager's school has assessed his learning difficulties and is providing him with necessary services. As closely as possible, monitor his progress in the classroom. If he doesn't seem to be showing much improvement, talk with his teachers and the school principal.

Particularly if your school district has limited academic and financial resources, consider seeking some outside professional help. Don't ignore the problem or pretend that it doesn't exist or that it will go away by itself. With the proper care most of these children eventually do quite well. Without it, however, a learning disability can become a lifetime disability.

Even if your school district has excellent programs, there will be some complex decisions to make about the type of learning environment most helpful for your youngster. For instance, does he belong in the regular classroom with an individualized program? On the positive side, this regular classroom will reduce disruptions for him in nonacademic areas and expose him to material appropriate for his age. He'll also be around his peers. On the other hand, he may need some extra time and effort from the teacher, which he often may not get in the regular classroom. At the same time, he may feel academically inferior to his classmates, and his self-esteem may suffer.

You need to weigh similar types of pros and cons with the other options that are available. For instance:

Should he spend part of the day with a remedial teacher, getting more individual attention? This will permit him to work on his areas of weakness, and his progress and problems are more likely to be carefully monitored. However, some youngsters feel stigmatized when they're singled out this way, and they may miss important new material that their classmates are receiving. Also, there may be poor communication between the regular and remedial teachers, which can make matters worse and create even a larger learning gap.

Does he belong in a special class with other adolescents with particular learning problems? The program in this type of setting can be intense and extremely beneficial, with a well-trained teacher who can aggressively tackle his learning difficulties. But if he's in the same class with disruptive youngsters, or if he feels stigmatized by this placement, the effort can become counterproductive.

Should he be held back to repeat the same grade? By being kept back, the slow-maturing adolescent will have more time to learn the material, and he's more likely to experience success dealing with familiar subject matter. However, if he has a true learning disability, this may not be an effective strategy and may interfere with the proper diagnosis of the learning problem.

Does he belong in a special school (often a residential one)? In this setting the adolescent will be removed from a family environment that may have been causing difficulties, and his learning problems can be the focus of most of the attention he receives. However, this is an expensive option, with drawbacks that include possible difficulties when he tries to return to regular school.

When making these decisions, ask for input from school officials, counselors, your pediatrician or other involved doctor, and the teenager himself. Schedule a conference with all interested parties and weigh the pros and cons of each option. Join support groups of parents with learning disabled teenagers; you'll be able to share your experiences with them and get some input as well.

No matter what choice you ultimately make, try to give your adolescent positive, out-of-the-classroom experiences to counterbalance the negative episodes he may continue to confront from time to time. Can he excel in sports? Or the arts? Might he enjoy hobbies? Or does he do well when he plays computer games?

Throughout this entire process, don't blame yourself for your teenager's learning problems. It may be tempting to do so, but don't let yourself lapse into thoughts like these: "Maybe I did something while I was pregnant. If only I had taken better care of myself." "I had the same kinds of learning problems when I was a child. I must have passed this disability on to him, and I feel just terrible about it."

In all likelihood nothing you did or didn't do is playing a role in his learning problems today. And letting guilt or anger get the best of you can interfere with your own efforts to make sure your adolescent gets the help he needs. For instance, when you feel guilty, you may hesitate to impose rules and restrictions on your youngster that might help him deal more effectively with his disability. Put the guilt aside and channel your energy into helping him conquer his learning disorder.

Some adolescents express anger or depression upon being labeled with a learning disorder. And that's not surprising. No teenager wants to be different. Listen to him carefully. Find out what's on his mind. And keep the lines of communication open.

Finally, learning disabilities are complex and poorly understood. No one has all the answers. If you want more information, see page 213 for a few good resources.

PART VII

THE CARE AND FEEDING
OF YOUR ADOLESCENT

28

PUTTING RESPONSIBILITY
INTO PERSPECTIVE

A baby is born. In the minutes after his birth his parents ask the inevitable question, "Is the baby normal?" In most instances the newborn is healthy, and once this initial concern has been alleviated, the joyful parents ask, "Is it a boy or a girl?" They also often find themselves beginning to think about the future and what they want their baby to become.

At the same time, Mom and Dad also quickly noticed that they now have increased responsibilities. After all, they are beginning a long period of child rearing, during which they'll have obligations and rewards, joys and sorrows.

Through the years both children and parents will learn, adapt, and grow according to their own characteristics and the culture in which they live. While an infant will be completely dependent, his parents' responsibility for his care will gradually decline, eventually almost ceasing with the independence of maturity.

Until that time arrives, however, there will be a seemingly endless number of anxieties and issues that will have to be confronted, particularly during adolescence: "Is my teenager eating properly? Is he getting enough exercise? What kinds of diseases is he susceptible to, and how can I prevent them?" These are the types of issues that we'll deal with later in this section.

Of course every age through which children pass presents its own share of parental stresses. But many mothers and fathers dread the uncertainty and potential turmoil of adolescence more than any other. They don't know quite what to expect. They're unsure about exactly what changes lie ahead. Fortunately, the transition from childhood to early adulthood takes place gradually (even though physical growth may be rapid), and both parents and adolescents can usually adapt to the evolving circumstances successfully.

Without a doubt, however, the teenage years are a demanding time. After all, while you're trying to get your youngster to eat balanced meals or to adhere to his treatment schedule for diabetes, for example, he's feeling a need for greater freedom and self-determination. At times it may seem that a constant war is under way in the household.

Ironically, without even realizing it a parent may sometimes push his teenager away from rational life choices. Here is how this might occur in your own family: As your youngster grows and you dream about his future, you'll almost certainly think of him as—and want him to be—special. This is an almost universal parental feeling, but it may be dangerous if he becomes especially sensitive to this expectation. If he feels a need to always be special, he may be unwilling to pursue a goal (e.g., weight loss or participation in sports) if he believes he can't excel. Meanwhile, you may have difficulty understanding this attitude, particularly when you also see him struggling for freedom and individuality—yet being unwilling to strive for particular goals.

The parenting of an adolescent, then, is a series of challenges. The duty of a mother and father is to provide an environment to promote the most positive physical, emotional, cognitive, and psychosocial growth in their youngster. This is a big task, but earlier parts of this book have already helped guide you through some of these areas. In this section we'll discuss several others.

RESPONSIBILITIES OF PARENTS

Throughout these pages we've discussed many of the responsibilities of parenting. Some of them should be quite obvious by now, but let's reiterate the most important ones here:

Physical Growth

One of the most basic responsibilities of parents is to provide food for their children. With appropriate and adequate nutrition—along with efforts to prevent handicapping illnesses and injuries—infants, children, and adolescents can enjoy the best possible physical growth. Later in this section we'll help you get your teenager on track in these areas.

In adolescence, of course, the body changes in size and shape, and teenagers should understand the significance of this transformation and develop respect for their bodies and health. Also, remind your youngster that there are many variations in normal growth and that some of his peers will begin to mature before he does, while others will start after him. These differences are usually genetic and are *not* related to the quality of care provided by parents. Even so, your teenager shares some of the responsibility in making sure he eats well and cares for his body in a protective and nurturing way.

Cognitive and Psychosocial Changes

Thought processes also change in adolescence, and as a parent you'll need to be tolerant of your teenager's questioning, rejecting, or promoting of ideas and principles that may or may not coincide with your own. During these years your youngster will develop his abstract thinking capabilities, learn to comprehend more adult concepts, and start to realistically evaluate his own well-being and his future. Through it all he'll need your patience and guidance to help him solve problems and establish health-promoting habits.

Yes, he'll learn a lot—and sharpen his thinking skills—in school. But the classroom isn't the only source of his education. He'll also acquire knowledge and values from his family and from the culture in which he grows. His race, ethnic origin, community, and country all will exert strong influences on who he is and what he'll become. In this process you'll need to assist him in sorting out the customs, beliefs, and information that he's exposed to and help him understand how the choices he makes intimately affect his life.

LOOKING TO THE FUTURE

Adolescents are restless and often filled with contradictions. They want freedom but frequently retreat into dependency. They test limits set by parents but are often hesitant to go beyond certain boundaries of unacceptable behavior. They are unsure of themselves and the future yet try to project an aura of complete self-confidence.

Fortunately, teenagers do eventually move out of this confusing time of indecision. Most settle down and accept greater responsibility for their own self-care; as a result family life becomes more peaceful. Until that happens, however, the turmoil within the household can sometimes become almost unbearable—often exacerbated by a parent's own personal unrest. Not surprisingly, if you're like most parents of adolescents, you're probably dealing with some changes and problems of your own, brought on by middle age. In fact sometimes adolescents are blamed for family disruptions when the real root of the trouble actually lies with Mom or Dad. Most adults are not aware of how they're changing, and all of us need to look at ourselves before instinctively censuring our teenagers.

You can also help matters proceed more smoothly during your child's adolescence by laying some groundwork in the years leading up to this time. When you're helping him through a crisis like a chronic illness, for example, he'll probably be much more responsive to your advice and guidance if you've made an effort to become "friendly" with him as he matured. This doesn't mean forsaking your parental role and substituting friendship for it; but you should begin to generate a feeling of camaraderie based on mutual respect. This special relationship may not be fully developed until your youngster is an adult, but it should begin during late childhood and continue throughout adolescence.

IT'S NOT ALL YOUR FAULT

Throughout this book we've emphasized the important role parents play in their teenager's life. Even so, a parent is just one of many influences that mold an adolescent into the person he's becoming.

Nevertheless, if you ask some people—young and old—who's to blame for their problems, "Mom and Dad" will often be the first words out of their mouths. There's a real tendency to attribute many of an individual's problems or difficulties to his parents. If he's overweight, "He's just like his dad"; if she has an eating disorder, "It's Mom's fault." Less frequently, parents are given credit for what they did right.

While it's true there are incompetent parents—and some truly terrible ones—most do their best to help their children. Yes, if they had a second chance, all parents would do many things differently; like everyone, parents sometimes err, making the wrong choices on occasion. However, these mistakes are unlikely to be the sole cause of a youngster's personal troubles. Instead a teenager's problems are usually the result of a number of factors and experiences, not an individual act.

Thus, in spite of parental mistakes—even very unfortunate ones of long duration—people can weather the storm and bring change to their lives. When they mature and learn to think and reason better, young adults can make their own decisions and self-direct their lives more clearly. If they suffer from an eating disorder, for example, they may also need the help of professionals, and sometimes this counseling will be most productive if other family members participate in the process, too. But here's the essential point: with maturity and resolve your youngster can change if he really wants to do so. He can't blame his continuing difficulties on his parents forever.

REMEMBER YOURSELF

Some parents (perhaps mothers more often than fathers) believe they should dedicate their lives to caring for their youngster. For them this means always being available to meet the child's every request.

This is a mistake, however, even in the special circumstances of a teenager who has a chronic illness. When parents live this way, their youngster's demands inevitably escalate rather than shifting in a direction toward the adolescent's assuming more responsibility for his own care and well-being. If your youngster has diabetes, for instance, don't allow yourself to become overly immersed in his illness and the way he cares for himself. Yes, you should make sure he's not putting himself in any danger. But you also need to let him start accepting more control over his own well-being—while you save some energy for yourself and your spouse. If you don't, everyone will suffer in the long run.

Yes, you're a parent, and a concerned one. However, fathers should also be husbands, and mothers should also be wives. While being responsible for rearing your children, you also need to nurture your own spousal relationship. And if you keep things in perspective and realize you cannot do everything all the time, rearing an adolescent—even during difficult periods—can be a satisfying and rewarding experience.

You also need to continue developing yourself in other aspects of your life, such as work, hobbies, and volunteer activities. Take care of yourself—which will present your children with a good role model. Also, once you have truly done your best to raise your children, get on with your life without guilt feelings! Don't let your adolescents blame you for all their difficulties and sink you into a quagmire of unending guilt. Enjoy relating to your youngsters as special adults, but also get on with your own life. You've earned this precious right!

Keep in mind, however, that even though your children are now young adults, they may occasionally have to turn to you, asking for temporary help, guidance, or haven during a setback or time of need. Because of your special relationship with them, your door should always remain open, within reasonable limits.

Now, let's get down to specifics. There are many areas of concern that this book still hasn't dealt with in detail—topics such as nutrition, eating disorders, physical exercise and sports, gynecological problems, and acute and chronic medical disorders. The following chapters will serve as a guide to these subjects.

29

NUTRITION AND EATING DISORDERS

*A*fter drugs and sex the issue that most concerns parents (particularly mothers) of adolescents is teenage eating habits.

"How can she grow when she eats so little?"

"What can I do to stop him from eating fast foods?"

"Don't you think she has anorexia nervosa?"

Pediatricians frequently hear questions like these from moms and dads. Many such parental anxieties, however, are unwarranted. When it comes to nutrition, some parents just worry too much, largely because of misunderstandings about the dietary needs of their kids.

In this chapter, let's take a look at the nutritional requirements of the growing adolescent. With this information in hand you can help your teenager maintain her good health without making any unreasonable demands on her eating behavior.

EATING RIGHT
DURING ADOLESCENCE

As we pointed out in Chapter 5, the teenage growth spurt is one of the most dramatic, rapid changes that the human body ever experiences. Imagine: within a period of just two to three years a child perhaps four-and-a-half feet tall, weighing about seventy-five pounds, is transformed into a tall, strong, and muscular man or a shapely and attractive woman.

To support this major physical transformation, the body requires increased energy (i.e., calories), protein, nutrients, vitamins, and, yes, even fat! As the table on the following page shows, during the year of the greatest rate of growth in height (about age twelve in most girls and age fourteen in most boys) the average male teenager requires about 2,800 to 3,000 calories per day and the female 2,400 calories. When this growth spurt ebbs, your adolescent's energy needs will gradually decline; girls, for example, will require about 300 fewer calories a day by the end of puberty.

These adolescent caloric requirements, although much greater than the needs of younger children or older adults, were actually revised downward by nutritionists in the late 1970s, largely in response to an increase in television watching and thus a decline in caloric expenditure by these youngsters. However, many pediatricians believe those adjustments may no longer be applicable. After all, many of today's adolescents, particularly females, have become more, rather than less, physically active in the past decade.

No matter what the official guidelines state, however, keep this important fact in mind: these figures represent *averages,* and the precise energy demands for your particular teenager may vary, depending on her growth phase, physical activity, metabolic rate, and illnesses. Thus, unless your adolescent is under- or overweight, let her eat in accordance with her own appetite rather than adhering to any general recommendations. Just make sure that there are sufficient amounts of protein, fats, and carbohydrates in her diet.

Let's look at some of the specific concerns that parents have about their youngster's nutritional needs:

Protein

"My teenager eats so poorly . . . Cokes, potato chips, an occasional balanced meal. She can't possibly be getting all the protein she needs, can she?"

Without a doubt adequate amounts of high-quality, digestible protein are essential during puberty. But even though we've grown up with the idea that the best protein comes from beef and other animals, teenagers can draw their protein

RECOMMENDED DAILY DIETARY ALLOWANCES

Calories and Protein

	Age (years)	Energy (kcal)	Protein (g)
Males	11–14	2,800	45
	15–18	3,000	56
Females	11–14	2,400	46
	15–18	2,100	46
Pregnant		+300	+30
Lactating		+500	+20

Fat-Soluble Vitamins

	Age (years)	Vitamin A (mcg)	Vitamin D (mcg)	Vitamin E (mg)
Males	11–14	1,000	10	8
	15–18	1,000	10	10
Females	11–14	800	10	8
	15–18	800	10	8
Pregnant		+200	+5	+2
Lactating		+400	+5	+3

Water-Soluble Vitamins

		Ascorbic acid (mg)	Thiamine (mg)	Riboflavin (mg)	Niacin (mg)	Vitamin B (mg)	Vitamin B_{12} (mcg)	Folacin (mcg)
Males	11–14	50	1.4	1.6	18	1.8	3.0	400
	15–18	60	1.4	1.7	18	2.0	3.0	400
Females	11–14	50	1.1	1.3	15	1.8	3.0	400
	15–18	60	1.1	1.3	14	2.0	3.0	400
Pregnant		+20	+0.4	+0.3	+2	+0.6	+1.0	+400
Lactating		+40	+0.5	+0.5	+5	+0.5	+1.0	+100

Minerals

		Calcium (mg)	Phosphorus (mg)	Iodine (mcg)	Iron (mg)	Magnesium (mg)	Zinc (mg)
Males	11–14	1,200	1,200	150	18	350	15
	15–18	1,200	1,200	150	18	400	15
Females	11–14	1,200	1,200	150	18	300	15
	15–18	1,200	1,200	150	18	300	15
Pregnant		+400	+400	+25	*	+150	+5
Lactating		+400	+400	+50	+50	+150	+10

*Use of supplemental iron recommended.

from a number of other sources too—milk and milk products (such as cheese), and eggs. Foods such as milk and eggs tend to have higher-quality protein than items such as rice and beans. Dried peas and beans are the richest sources of vegetable proteins.

So while a lot of parents worry that their adolescents are protein-deficient, few teenagers really do have a genuine shortage. Even so, there is a complicating factor in all of this: while animal proteins tend to contain all the amino acids essential for growth, vegetable sources (except soybeans) tend to be "incomplete." Thus, if your teenager is a vegetarian and doesn't include any animal proteins in her diet (even milk and milk products), she needs to consume some "complementary" proteins—that is, by eating two or more vegetable proteins she'll create a complete protein that her body can use efficiently.

What are some complementary proteins? In this category are rice with beans, corn with beans, and wheat germ with rice or corn.

At the peak of their growth spurt girls require about eighty grams of protein daily and boys about one hundred grams. That's about 15 percent of their caloric expenditure. Many teenage athletes, however, try to consume much more, convinced that extra protein will give them a competitive edge. But the special (and expensive) powdered protein supplements that they usually turn to are worthless unless their diet is protein-deficient. Yes, adolescent athletes need protein—two grams of protein for each kilogram of body weight—but a well-balanced diet can meet that requirement.

Incidentally, some sources of protein are foods that are also rich in carbohydrates—specifically, complex carbohydrates such as legumes (peas and beans). Most nutritionists recommend that complex carbohydrates make up 50 to 60 percent of your teenager's caloric intake.

Fats

In these weight-conscious times the mere mention of the word *fat* sends shudders through a lot of teenagers. Many adolescents, particularly females and athletes, conscientiously and fanatically avoid foods containing fats.

Ironically, however, these well-intentioned efforts may be counterproductive. Even in the healthiest diets fats should comprise up to 30 percent of total calories, with 10 percent of those total calories derived from saturated fats.

Why fats? They fulfill several important roles in the body. For instance, they're essential for the production of important chemicals, including the hormones that stimulate puberty itself. They're also necessary to transport certain vitamins (A, D, E, K) into the body.

Even so, your adolescent shouldn't consume fats to an extreme either, because

Types of Fat

SATURATED	MONOUNSATURATED	POLYUNSATURATED
Butter	Cashews	Almonds
Cheese	Olives and olive oil	Corn oil
Chocolate	Peanuts and peanut oil	Cottonseed oil
Coconut and coconut oil	Peanut butter	Fish
Egg yolk		Safflower oil
Meat		Sesame seed oil
Milk		Soybean oil
Palm oil		Sunflower seed oil
Poultry		
Vegetable shortening		

in excess they're intimately tied to heart disease. Although teenagers consider themselves invulnerable to serious illness, they can significantly increase their chances of having a heart attack later in life by eating a high-fat diet. Researchers also have singled out such a diet as a potential cause of breast cancer in adult women.

Since it's the so-called saturated fats that can potentially cause problems, your teenager's fat consumption should come primarily from monounsaturated or polyunsaturated sources. The chart above can help your teenager make the healthiest choices.

Minerals

As your child grows during adolescence, the most important minerals in her diet will be *zinc, iron, and calcium*—each for a very different reason. *Zinc,* for example, is necessary for normal development of the gonads (the testes and ovaries). It's also essential for healthy skin, as well as for general overall growth. If your teenager's intake of zinc is low, she may experience some emotional difficulties as well.

In general, your teenager should consume about fifteen milligrams of zinc a day. However, many adolescents don't even come close to meeting this recommendation. Studies of adolescent girls show that one-third consume significantly less than fifteen milligrams.

One of the best ways for your teenager to obtain an adequate supply of zinc is

Nutrition and Prescribed Medications: Do You Need to Worry?

All medications have side effects, and in some cases they can interfere with normal nutritional processes. Some oral contraceptives, for instance, can cause a variety of nutritional problems, including a lowering of the blood levels of vitamins C, B$_{12}$, riboflavin, folacin, pyridoxine, and zinc and an increase in the levels of vitamin A, copper, and iron. Even so, young women who are taking these oral contraceptives can compensate for such changes by eating a well-balanced diet. Fortunately, nutritional deficiency appears to be less of a problem with lower-dose birth control pills, but check with your teenager's doctor.

Also, ask the pediatrician if the specific medications he or she has prescribed for your youngster can have an impact on vitamin absorption or production. Long-term use of certain antibiotics, for instance, can alter the bacterial content of the gastrointestinal tract and as a result can produce a deficiency in vitamin K and biotin. Isoniazid, a drug given to treat or prevent active tuberculosis, is associated with a pyridoxine deficiency.

to make animal protein a regular part of the diet; every hundred grams of protein (or three ounces of meat) provides fifteen milligrams of zinc (the daily requirement). Beans, wheat germ, and nuts are other sources of zinc.

There are several circumstances that should send up warning flags of a possible zinc deficiency. For example, a vegetarian diet—particularly if it's devoid of milk and eggs as well as meat—is generally deficient in zinc. Certain higher-dose, estrogen-containing birth control pills can also cause a decline in zinc levels, as can the abuse of alcohol.

As important as zinc is to normal growth, it's no easy task to accurately determine zinc levels in the body. Precise measurement in a given individual requires special collection and handling of blood and urine.

Some labs claim that by analyzing hair or other body substances they can quickly determine levels of zinc and other trace elements. They might even promise to diagnose complicated behavioral problems allegedly tied to trace element deficiencies. You should approach these claims with caution, however. Most labs aren't capable of reliable and valid measurements of zinc, much less evaluating a still unproven connection with behavioral disorders.

Now, what about *iron*? Adolescents of both sexes require eighteen milligrams of iron daily. The body needs this iron for the proper functioning of its enzymes. Boys especially use iron in their diets for muscle development and expansion. Girls particularly need iron to replace what they've lost through menses (averaging 1.5 milligrams of iron daily). The sweating associated with vigorous exercise can also cause a reduction of iron at levels comparable to that lost during menses.

Unfortunately, as you try to add iron-rich foods to your teenager's diet, you may find that girls in particular dislike the foods with the highest iron content (e.g., red meats and green vegetables). That's why adolescents (especially girls) have a high incidence of iron deficiency anemia. Sophisticated tests evaluating the levels of iron in the body have documented that even when adolescents' blood counts are not low, many may still have some iron deficiency.

You need to encourage your teenager to keep her consumption of iron up. Have some iron-fortified cereals on hand in your cupboard. Make snacks such as peanut butter, dried fruits, and even burritos available. To enhance the absorption of iron, have her eat foods containing generous amounts of vitamin C (citrus fruits and green vegetables) in combination with high-iron foods.

The third vital mineral—*calcium*—is necessary for normal adolescent growth of the skeletal system. At the peak of their growth spurt both boys and girls need a daily calcium intake of 1,200 milligrams. That's an amount far more than the levels ordinarily provided by the typical American diet.

What's the best way for your teenager to meet her calcium requirements? She should consume four to six servings of dairy products each day. That may not be as easy as it sounds, however. Some adolescents simply refuse to consume milk or other dairy items; a few actually *can't* because they have trouble digesting milk and related products. For these adolescents the family's pediatrician may suggest supplementation with a product containing calcium carbonate, which is absorbed well by most individuals (antacids such as Tums can be used, providing 300 milligrams of calcium per tablet).

Two final notes: Keep in mind that phosphorus and calcium compete with one another in the digestive process. By consuming nonessential foods high in phosphorus (such as soft drinks), you'll lower the level of calcium that's absorbed. Also, female athletes and girls who have stopped menstruating (and ovulating) are at special risk for calcium deficiency.

Vitamins

During the pubertal growth spurt your teenager needs increased amounts of certain vitamins. For skeletal growth, for example, she'll require vitamins A, C, D, and E. Folacin (folic acid) and Vitamin B_{12} are necessary for increased tissue synthesis. She'll need greater levels of thiamine, niacin, and riboflavin to help release energy from carbohydrates. Vitamin B_6 or pyridoxine is needed for many body functions, as transport of amino acids and proper central nervous system functioning.

Can Certain
Foods Cause Acne?

We've all grown up with the same myth: chocolate and greasy foods cause acne.

However, there's no scientific evidence to support this widely held belief. Except in rare individuals who are actually allergic to certain foods, there is *no* relationship between diet and acne.

Then what causes acne? The real culprit is the increased production of sebum (an oily secretion) by the sebaceous follicles of the skin; this is a natural response to increased levels of particular hormones during puberty.

Incidentally, even though chocolate and greasy foods won't cause acne in your teenager, let her know that they're still high in fat and thus should not be eaten in excess. For further information about acne, see page 291.

Unfortunately, though, certain teenagers aren't getting the vitamins that are so essential for their good health. Studies have shown that many adolescents who are dieting or otherwise restricting their food intake have inadequate blood levels of vitamins A, B_6, C, and folacin. Chronic alcohol abuse in teenagers sometimes leads to vitamin A and folacin deficiencies, while certain birth control pills can cause a deficit of various vitamins, too. Crash dieting and severe food restriction are also sometimes associated with vitamin deficiencies.

How can you help ensure appropriate intake of these vitamins? Your teenager should be eating the following foods:

Vitamin A: Whole milk, fruits, yellow vegetables, fortified margarine, butter, liver, some green leafy vegetables.

Vitamin C: Citrus fruits, lettuce, green leafy vegetables, broccoli, uncooked potatoes, tomatoes, strawberries, and currants.

Vitamin D: Milk, canned fish, egg yolk (and sunlight).

Vitamin B_{12}: Fish, eggs, milk, fortified soy milk.

Vitamin B_6: Fish, whole grains, corn, soybeans, liver.

Thiamine: Beans, nuts, peas, pork, wheat products (enriched and whole grain).

Niacin: Fish, whole grains, green vegetables, meat.

Riboflavin: Milk, eggs, meat, whole grains, green vegetables.

Folacin: Fresh oranges, nuts, liver, navy beans, dark green leafy vegetables, and whole wheat products.

While a good diet should supply all the vitamins an adolescent needs, those who eat very poorly or who have chronic illnesses may benefit from vitamin supplements under their pediatrician's guidance. Caution your teenager against consuming vitamin supplements in excess of accepted daily requirements. Vitamins A and D—the so-called fat-soluble vitamins—are stored in the body, and thus there's a danger of overdosing if your adolescent exceeds the suggested consumption levels. The water-soluble vitamins—vitamin C and the B vitamins—are not quite as risky since they're excreted out of the body. Again, consult your youngster's pediatrician about appropriate vitamin dosages.

Teenagers being treated for acne with a drug called Accutane (13-cis-retinoic acid) should be particularly wary about consuming vitamin A supplements at the same time; this drug is derived from vitamin A, and when teenagers take both Accutane and the vitamin, they may be more susceptible to overdosing and side effects such as severe headaches. (See Page 291.)

FOOD SELECTION TIPS

"Mom, I can't always eat the way you want me to. I'm very busy, you know. I just can't take the time to have three well-balanced meals a day."

If you've heard that lament from your teenager, here are some guidelines to help you cope with the special nutritional difficulties associated with modern adolescence:

Snacking

If your teenager is like most others, her eating patterns are probably something like this: skip breakfast, have a snack at lunchtime, eat another snack upon returning home from school, then have dinner, followed by some additional snacking with homework.

It's not an ideal schedule, is it? But despite wishes that it were otherwise, this is the reality for most busy teenagers.

Even so, there might be some encouraging news in all of this. If your teenager is still able to meet the basic dietary requirements mentioned earlier in this chapter—adequate protein, fats, and carbohydrates—there's no evidence that her eating-on-the-run lifestyle necessarily causes any nutritional problems.

Of course meeting those essential needs is not always easy. After all, 50 percent of teenagers don't eat breakfast, and many snack on the most readily available foods no matter how poor their nutritional content. To help your adolescent sidestep potential difficulties, encourage her to choose snacks that are low in both sugar and fat and high in vitamins, minerals, and protein. That means selecting fresh and dried fruits, fruit juices, raw vegetables, nuts, cheese, crackers (whole grain), and yogurt. Don't buy any snack foods that aren't nutritious, such as candy, cake, potato chips, cookies, and soft drinks.

Fast Foods

When you mention "fast foods," does the word *adolescents* immediately come to mind? Probably so, along with concerns over just how unwholesome these foods may be for your teenagers. Those anxieties, however, may be unwarranted. Contrary to conventional wisdom, eating fast foods need not be detrimental to your health—even though it's not gourmet dining either.

In a study conducted by the Committee on Nutrition of the American Academy of Pediatrics, researchers found that when adolescents dined at fast-food restaurants they could meet the recommended daily allowances for most foods—particularly when they also consumed a green salad sometime during the day. Even so, your teenager will have to pick and choose her fast foods carefully. Too many items at these restaurants are still high in both calories and fat, particularly if the food has been cooked at high temperatures in frying oils. You might suggest that your teenager replace french fries with an apple and thus fashion a very healthy diet at fast-food restaurants. Now that many of these restaurants have salad bars, this kind of dining has become quite possible.

Vegetarians

In recent years vegetarianism has become popular among many people. Particularly during adolescence, when idealism is the name of the game, a vegetarian diet seems like the perfect alternative to the customary high-fat, high-cholesterol fare.

But pediatricians have a lot of nutritional concerns about this kind of eating. More than anything, it may not provide enough protein, calcium, iron, zinc, and vitamins (particularly riboflavin, B_6, and B_{12}) to sustain a teenager's growth spurt. You can make some adjustments in a vegetarian diet, however, to minimize these risks. For instance, as we suggested in the earlier discussion of protein, your adolescent is more likely to meet her nutritional requirements if she allows dairy products and eggs in her diet (a lacto-ovo-vegetarian diet). Also, have your teenager add a vitamin B$_{12}$ supplement to her diet—either with pills or with fermented soybean products or fortified soybean milk.

Athletes

Every winning athlete, it seems, has her own favorite nutritional program that she credits for much of her success. However, the folklore about diet and exercise is replete with myths and inaccuracies about what competitors should eat and when and the foods "guaranteed" to improve sports performance. Some of the nutritional advice that abounds simply doesn't work (e.g., "carbohydrate loading" before an event); others are quite dangerous (e.g., "Don't drink any water before a long run").

So what should teenagers believe? There are some important and valid points they should keep in mind relative to food and athletics. First, their energy needs clearly increase during exercise. (See Page 255.) The chart on page 249 shows some examples of the energy expenditure associated with different activities. And where should they look for this additional energy? Fat is the food source that provides the most energy (nine calories per gram), compared to only four calories per gram in carbohydrates and protein. Remember, though, that the best way to obtain this extra energy is through food itself, not through "energy capsules" and other expensive supplements. These pills don't deliver the promised energy, largely because they lack enough volume to do so.

Your teenage athlete also shouldn't overlook the importance of consuming adequate protein, although training doesn't require an excessively high intake. A moderate increase in daily protein consumption is all that's recommended by most sports nutritionists. However, as we pointed out earlier, avoid powdered protein supplements in favor of protein from food sources themselves.

There's no evidence that other nutrients—such as vitamin and mineral supplements—taken just before a sports event will improve endurance and/or performance. Even so, female athletes in particular can become deficient in iron during the course of a playing season; this iron deficiency could impair their performance, although it's sometimes so subtle that it's not detected. In any case, make sure your daughter is eating foods rich in iron.

As a general rule, female athletes should have their iron status assessed before the season and then rechecked periodically. They need supplementation if there's evidence of a deficiency. Some pediatricians recommend a daily iron supplement as a preventive measure.

If your teenager participates in intensive athletic training and competition, he'll probably experience a loss of water, sodium, and potassium, particularly during hot weather. Have him eat generous amounts of potassium-containing foods (such as citrus fruits and bananas) during the season and drink plenty of water during training and the competition itself. As a general rule athletes should be well hydrated before an event and then should ingest small amounts of water throughout the activity. Also, although some athletes (especially wrestlers) turn to diuretics or even vomiting to lose weight for their sports, you must forcefully warn your youngster to refrain from these behaviors; they can cause a severe loss of potassium and other necessary electrolytes. If you find out that his coach is advising fluid or food restriction, or vomiting, to "make weight," make sure he doesn't adhere to such inappropriate advice.

Finally, if your teenage athlete insists on giving vitamins a try, remind him that ingestion of excessive amounts of vitamins A and D can cause serious side effects, including brain swelling and liver or bone damage.

DIETING: AN AMERICAN OBSESSION

Dieting is part of the American way of life. There's not a fashion magazine on the newsstands that doesn't feature models who are almost impossibly thin. They are the role models with whom our teenage girls grow up.

No wonder, then, that when adolescence begins, so does dieting. Girls often view their normal deposits of adipose tissue during puberty as offensive. Boys too usually wish to become thinner, taller, and more muscular.

Some of the statistics about dieting are truly alarming. For instance, one-half of all tenth-grade female students diet on a regular basis. And the particular diets they're selecting may be hazardous to their health. Many of these weight-loss diets provide 1,000 calories or less per day; with a caloric intake that low they're clearly designed only for *adult* women who have completed their growth. They're entirely inadequate to support the many changes of puberty.

If your teenager is dieting, encourage her to limit herself to a weight-loss goal of one to two pounds per week. Remind your youngster that each pound is equivalent to 3,500 calories, and thus such a timetable requires either a decrease of caloric intake of 500 calories per day or an increase in physical activity to "burn off" an equivalent number of calories. The most effective strategy, however, is to combine these approaches—increasing activity *and* decreasing caloric intake.

By taking it slowly and sensibly, your teenager will take the weight off safely—and it will be much more likely to stay off.

Eating Disorders

In an era so fixated on thinness, it's not surprising that eating disorders (anorexia nervosa, bulimia nervosa) are on the increase in the United States, as well as in all of the industrialized nations of the world. A lot has been written about the causes of these syndromes. Some researchers have postulated that anorexia is incited by family problems; others believe that its victims are rejecting the concept of growing up; still others insist that a physical abnormality is involved, perhaps in the connections between the brain and the pituitary gland.

Actually, we don't yet know which—if any—of these theories is correct. However, the common characteristic in nearly all cases is extreme dieting in order to lose weight. In some youngsters a medical illness with resultant weight loss has inspired their interest in an excessive shedding of pounds.

Anorexia Nervosa. Does your son or daughter have anorexia nervosa? This condition is characterized by the following:

1. Intense fear of being or becoming obese. This anxiety doesn't decrease as weight loss progresses.

2. A disturbed way in which body weight, size, or shape is perceived by the teenager (e.g., he or she claims to be too fat even while emaciated).

3. A refusal to maintain body weight at a minimal normal weight for one's age and height. These individuals typically keep their weight at more than 15 percent below a normal level, and any gains in weight are usually short-lived.

4. The absence of at least three consecutive menstrual periods, without any other explanations for why this has occurred. (There are other reasons for the cessation of menses as well, and your daughter should consult a doctor to sort them out. See Chapter 32.)

How do these girls (yes, it usually is females) lose their weight? They'll typically restrict their caloric intake to an extreme level (200 to 400 calories per day!). As if that weren't enough, about half of these girls also exercise vigorously several times a day; the other half may engage in "purging" behaviors (either self-induced vomiting or the use of laxatives) to accelerate their weight loss. (This latter subgroup, incidentally, is different from teenagers with bulimia nervosa, in that these youngsters are severely malnourished; by contrast, bulimics are at normal or even above-normal weights.)

Girls with anorexia nervosa often employ other "strategies" as well. Many, for example, consume huge amounts of water ("water loading") in hopes of deceiving their doctor into believing that they're really gaining weight. Others, however, diligently avoid drinking any water after experiencing a "bulging" tummy and therefore a "fat feeling" following water ingestion.

Is your daughter likely to become anorexic? These girls are commonly bright, self-driven, and high-achieving, and their parents often think of them as "perfect children." They typically range from fourteen to seventeen years old.

In addition to looking for extreme thinness, exhaustive exercise programs, and a lot of mirror gazing, you might be able to recognize anorexia in your daughter by looking for hair loss, brittle nails, insomnia—and unusual rituals related to food. Surprisingly, even though these girls eat very little, they're actually quite preoccupied by food. They often cook for hours for other family members and work at restaurants or grocery stores. They may even become involved in writing cookbooks!

Anorexics can probably answer almost any question you have about food composition (especially caloric content), and they may espouse healthy attitudes toward food such as avoidance of red meat and high-cholesterol foods. Quite a few are vegetarians, and the mainstay of their diets is often nonfat yogurt (low in carbohydrates and fat, high in protein and calcium). Many aspire to careers as nutritionists or other health professionals.

Not unexpectedly, there are many medical complications associated with this starvation syndrome. In fact anorexia nervosa has the highest death rate of any psychiatric illness—approximately 5 percent of all individuals with this disorder. What causes these fatalities? A number of factors can play a role, including abnormalities in the blood's electrolytes (caused by purging, water loading, or inadequate food intake), heart failure (following attempts at weight rehabilitation that are too rapid), or abnormalities in the electrical conduction through the heart (arrhythmias). Some deaths among these individuals in later life are the result of suicide.

In addition to life-threatening complications, these patients can develop many other medical problems, potentially involving virtually every organ system of the body. These may include abnormalities of the skin, gastrointestinal tract, endocrine system, temperature-controlling mechanism, blood, and urinary tract. Even after they've gained weight, some of these young women may have to wait years before their menstrual periods and ovulation return to normal again.

As you can tell, anorexia is not a disease you should take lightly. Early recognition and treatment of this disorder are important. Your teenager should be under the care of a physician with experience in treating this condition. The ideal treatment team should consist of the medical specialist, a psychotherapist, and a nutritionist. Group and family counseling and a behavioral modification program can add to the effectiveness of this approach. With a comprehensive treatment program doctors can achieve permanent improvement in 70 percent of patients. Of the remainder some become bulimic, others have relapses during times of stress, and a few actually become obese.

Incidentally, not only has anorexia nervosa become more common, but it is occurring at a younger age and is no longer restricted to members of the higher socioeconomic strata where this disease was once concentrated. More girls are also being mislabeled as anorexics when, in fact, they really have other conditions (such as depression) associated with weight loss and an absence of menstrual periods. For that reason every teenager suspected of having anorexia nervosa must see a medical doctor who specializes in treating this disorder.

Bulimia Nervosa. Doctors use the following criteria for making a diagnosis of bulimia:

1. Recurrent episodes of binge eating (rapid consumption of a large amount of food in a relatively short time, usually less than two hours).

2. A fear of not being able to stop eating during these binges.

3. Regularly engaging in self-induced vomiting, use of laxatives, rigorous dieting or fasting to counteract the effects of binge eating.

4. An average of at least two binge eating episodes per week for at least three months.

Unfortunately, purging has become a very popular method of weight control among some adolescents. This alone, however, does not constitute a diagnosis of bulimia nervosa; it must also include evidence of uncontrollable, repetitive binge eating (usually more than 2,000 calories of high-fat, high-sugar food). These teenagers usually binge in private, and each episode may continue until they develop terrible stomach pains, induce vomiting, or fall asleep.

Patients with bulimia typically are of normal weight, and thus they're less likely to be noticed and referred for medical treatment. Even so, their practice of purging can cause serious medical complications: rupture of the esophagus from self-induced vomiting, cardiac arrest from the use of ipecac syrup to induce vomiting, and a severe electrolyte imbalance that can cause death. Bulimics also experience many other problems, including swelling of the salivary glands, erosion of the enamel of the teeth, and dehydration from constant vomiting.

You might suspect bulimia in your daughter if she becomes overly concerned with her appearance. She may eat large dinners, then retreat immediately to the bathroom, where she may be overheard vomiting. She might also have disturbances in her menstrual periods or a bruised finger or knuckle if she uses it to induce vomiting. She might also have periods of depression and self-deprecation, particularly after a binging episode.

As with anorexia nervosa, teenagers with bulimia need medical attention. Get them under a doctor's care immediately and early. The treatment of both of these eating disorders must be intensive enough to reverse the medical and psychological consequences that may accompany these problems. Hospitalization is often necessary if the youngster's condition is serious. Without effective treatment the teenager may face a lifetime of problems, including poor relationships, depression—and even death.

30

WHEN YOUR TEENAGER
IS OBESE

*I*f your teenager is overweight, he or she is not alone. According to one estimate about 10 percent of preadolescents and 15 percent of adolescents are obese. And the ranks of the overweight are on the rise: there has been almost a 40 percent increase in obesity among adolescents over the past fifteen years.

Who's most likely to be overweight? There's some variation between the sexes as well as among socioeconomic and ethnic groups. For instance, obesity is more common among females, although both sexes are affected. It's also more prevalent in whites than blacks and in adolescents from lower- rather than high-income families. Children are more likely to end up as overweight adults if they have a family history of obesity and if they tend to be physically inactive. To date, however, there is no evidence that obesity during infancy automatically leads to adult weight problems; a fat baby will not necessarily become a fat adult.

Before going further, let's define the word *obesity*. It is a condition in which there is an excess of fat tissue in the body. Because it's difficult to measure the actual amount of this so-called adipose tissue without painful tests, doctors use indirect measures instead. For example, some doctors make the diagnosis of obesity when an adolescent's weight is more than 20 percent above what researchers have determined to be desirable for his height, age, and sex. This criterion, however, has some problems. It ignores the fact that tissues other than fat contribute to body weight and that large-boned or very muscular adolescents may weigh more than other teenagers of the same height, even though the former group doesn't have excess fat.

Doctors often use other indirect techniques in conjunction with height/weight charts to assess body fat. One common approach, for example, is skinfold measurement, a technique in which the thickness of a fold of fat is assessed at seven standard sites of the body, such as the hips and the upper arm (the triceps). Adolescents are usually considered obese if their triceps skinfold thickness is above the eighty-fifth percentile for their age and sex. But again, this technique, like others, has some limitations, and it should not be used as the sole basis for a diagnosis of obesity.

THE ROLE OF FAT CELLS

How many fat cells are too many? At birth, full-term, healthy infants have about five billion fat cells (or adipocytes). As immense as this figure sounds, babies have only about one-sixth of the number of fat cells they'll eventually have as adults. As they grow during childhood, generally the number of these cells will increase slowly and steadily and then will proliferate rapidly during puberty. Studies have found, however, that obese youngsters experience significant increases in early childhood as well, unlike their nonobese peers.

Genetic factors also seem to influence the number of fat cells that individuals have. As a result, by the age of seventeen years the offspring of two *obese* parents are likely to be three times as fat as those with two *lean* parents.

Fat tissue makes up about 7 percent of a youngster's body. There are some variations between the sexes, however, just before and during adolescence. For boys a temporary increase in body fat occurs just before puberty, followed by a decrease as muscle tissue enlarges. For girls, although some fat is added during the prepubertal time, there actually is a decline in the *rate* of fat accumulation;

this is then followed by a steady increase in the percentage of body fat during puberty itself, reaching 22 to 25 percent at its completion.

To repeat, the number of fat cells increases dramatically during adolescence. However, the size of each cell doesn't grow with the rest of the body. Instead these cells actually approximate adult dimensions by one year of age and then decrease slightly during the second year of life. If youngsters are overweight early in life, their fat cells will be large from that point forward: according to one study, obese two-year-olds had significantly bigger fat cells than those who were non-obese. Later in childhood—between ages two and sixteen—neither the thin nor the overweight youngsters in this study experienced a change in cell size, although after age sixteen the obese adolescents did demonstrate size increases.

As you can probably guess, an individual's diet can affect the number and size of his fat cells. For instance, a diet high in sucrose or saturated fat will increase both the number and size of these cells. By contrast, meals high in *un*saturated fat will increase only the size of the fat cells.

THE FAMILY
AND OTHER FACTORS

Although we've mentioned that the family can affect a child's likelihood of becoming obese, there are still unanswered questions about this particular influence. Some researchers firmly believe that overweight teenagers may have inherited a "set point" for body weight and fatness, probably determined by certain defects in their body's ability to burn or conserve calories. But others disagree, contending that a family's eating habits are the real culprit.

There's also little evidence to support the claim that certain metabolic or endocrine disorders cause obesity. Less than 5 percent of obese younger children fall into this category, and among adolescents this figure is even lower (less than 2 percent). Most adolescent obesity, therefore, is exogenous (caused by outside factors), including hereditary, physical, social, and behavioral influences—like poor family eating habits.

According to one researcher "progressive" obesity is generally related to diet and exercise patterns within families, resulting in steady weight gain throughout childhood. On the other hand, so-called reactive or emotional overeating occurs in depressed or passive adolescents who eat while under stress; as a result they often engage in binge eating, and their weight gain is episodic. Some research suggests that this second subtype predominates in adolescence.

There's one myth that we need to explode, however. Contrary to popular belief, obese adolescents do *not* necessarily eat more than their lean peers. Then what differentiates the thin from the overweight? The obese appear to have a pattern of eating that's faster than normal and very irregular. Obese adolescents also are clearly less physically active (although this may be more effect than cause). Television watching is greater among overweight adolescents, too; studies, in fact, show that the incidence of obesity increases by 2 percent for each hour of television viewing.

IS OBESITY HARMFUL TO
YOUR TEENAGER'S HEALTH?

The health hazards associated with obesity in *adulthood* are well known. Obesity clearly shortens life expectancy by increasing the risk of developing life-threatening diseases.

However, what about obesity during the teenage years? Despite the fact that obesity in adolescence predisposes an individual to being overweight as an adult, this adolescent obesity per se does not appear to present major health hazards. Even so, because obesity is often associated with high blood cholesterol and triglyceride (blood fat) levels, and occasionally with high blood pressure, a doctor should evaluate your overweight teenager for these conditions.

Adolescent obesity may also cause stress on certain parts of your youngster's skeletal system, increasing the risk of problems with the hips, knees, and other joints. Obesity also accelerates the pubertal process: obese girls generally begin menstruating earlier than those who are lean. Along with this acceleration of puberty, these obese adolescents experience an earlier growth spurt and, in turn, a shorter ultimate height.

But the most significant health-related problem of obese children and adolescents is not physical. Instead it's related to the psychological and social consequences of growing up in a society that abhors and fears fatness. Studies have found that as early as the kindergarten years children dislike chubbiness, ranking their obese peers as less likable than those with physical deformities. Adults have an equally unfair view of overweight individuals; for example, in the days when pictures or interviews were required for college entrance, research showed that obese teenagers were discriminated against in the selection process.

With prejudice like this so rampant, the findings of one study of middle-class children and adolescents are not surprising: it concluded that the self-esteem of obese youngsters is lower than that of their normal-weight counterparts and that they are more likely to suffer from depression. Interestingly, however, these results may not be applicable to all obese children; research into black inner-city obese children and adolescents found that their self-esteem was within the normal range.

CONTROLLING WEIGHT

Most successful weight-reduction strategies for obese teenagers have concentrated not only on dietary control and exercise but also on improving self-esteem. In programs combining these approaches adolescents can frequently achieve slow but steady weight loss of two pounds per week. That's the kind of realistic goal your teenager should set. In the process she should stay away from starvation diets, self-induced vomiting, and the use of diuretics, appetite-suppressant drugs, and laxatives.

An effective weight-loss program must deal with a number of problems common to adolescents, including:

- eating too much (such as second helpings, keeping food in the bedroom for snacking);

- having irregular eating habits (some teenagers eat one large meal a day and then snack frequently at other times);

- making unhealthy food choices, such as sweets, fried/oily foods, sodas, etc.;

- eating while bored or depressed and eating alone;

- getting limited exercise.

Bear in mind that while very-low-calorie diets may sometimes be perfectly acceptable for adults, adolescents must avoid them. Between 2,500 and 3,000 calories a day are necessary to support pubertal growth for physically active female and male teenagers respectively. That means staying away from the 1,000- or 1,500-calorie diets that magazines and weight-loss books often promote. Also, when an adolescent begins to lose too much weight too quickly—and becomes obsessed with it—anorexia nervosa and all its complications may develop (see Chapter 29).

Under the guidance of your pediatrician, your overweight youngster needs to adopt long-term lifestyle changes, including a sensible approach to the way she eats. If she goes on a "crash" diet instead—whether for two weeks, two months, or longer—she's doomed to fail and runs the risk of impairing her growth. These types of programs slow down your teenager's metabolic rate, and then, when she resumes normal eating after her diet, rapid increases in weight are all but inevitable. Thus a roller-coaster weight-loss/weight-gain pattern is established, which clearly should be avoided.

As your teenager tries to lose weight, be as supportive as you can without trying to take complete control of the situation. Don't buy "junk food" (cakes, pies, candy, ice cream, french fries). Instead, shop for low-calorie, low-fat, health-

ENERGY EXPENDITURE OF
PHYSICAL ACTIVITY

Activity	Men (kcal/hour)	Women (kcal/hour)
Sitting quietly	83	69
Walking (3 mph)	222	180
Light activity (bowling, golf, sailing)	150–300	120–240
Moderate activity (dancing, tennis, horseback riding)	300–450	240–360
Heavy activity (basketball, football, rowing)	450 +	360 +

promoting items such as chicken, turkey, tuna (canned in water), fruit, vegetables, clear soups, bread, plain spaghetti, rice, wheat germ, and unsweetened cereals.

Make healthy eating a family affair, which will improve your teenager's chances of success. In fact the family should try to eat together as much as possible— and as parents you should offer praise and encouragement when your youngster sticks to her dietary plan.

Also, don't forget regular exercise. To make physical activity a routine part of her life, your adolescent needs to enjoy getting her body moving. Exercise can be fun—if she carefully selects the type of activity. Encourage her to exercise with friends and remind her that physical activity will help suppress her hunger pangs, make her feel good about herself, and take away the normal teenage "blues."

The best forms of exercise use major muscles of the body. And there are a lot to choose from: tennis, dancing, handball, swimming, bicycling, skiing (snow and water), basketball, football, gymnastics, running, hockey, ice skating, surfing, soccer, the martial arts, and many others. (See Chapter 31.)

To get the most out of her exercise periods, your youngster should be physically active for at least thirty minutes, three to four times a week. Each time, she should warm up slowly and do some appropriate muscle stretching before exerting herself fully. And after a while, if she loses interest in a particular activity, help her find another one—and perhaps an optional indoor plan that will allow her to exercise even in inclement weather.

For any weight-reduction program to be successful, your teenager must be motivated. Trying to force an unmotivated adolescent to lose weight will not only strain the parent–child relationship but will almost assure failure and frustration. That, in turn, will further damage her self-esteem—and make the next attempt at weight loss even more difficult. The family pediatrician can direct your adolescent into programs that can stimulate enthusiasm and offer peer support. These groups encourage teenagers to think about how their excess pounds affect them and why they do (or don't) want to lose weight.

Once motivated, teenagers should begin working on changing their daily habits (e.g., their poor food choices, lack of exercise) that have led to their obesity. Encourage them to keep a meal and exercise log for at least several days. Then both parent and pediatrician can go over it with them and point out any problems. (They'll probably enjoy this extra attention!)

If teenagers are experiencing continuing difficulties, consider having a qualified nutritionist structure better meal plans for them. They should also learn to relax while eating, take small bites, enjoy each bite, chew slowly, and always leave some food on the table. Make sure you keep a bowl of low-calorie foods (e.g., celery, cauliflower, unbuttered popcorn, fruit) in the kitchen for snacking. Encourage your teenager to try harder to avoid unnecessary eating during certain times of the day, such as right after school to pass the time, while watching television, or while trying to postpone doing homework or chores.

No matter how conscientious your teenager is, some backsliding is almost inevitable from time to time. Warn her that she could experience a roller-coaster pattern of loss, gain, loss, and gain. She should also expect plateaus, where there is no change even when she's following all the rules. Nevertheless, with the proper motivation and guidance, many teenagers stick with it and eventually lose the excess weight they may have carried around for years.

For some additional help and information, see below.

Weight-Loss Resources

For teenagers: *Shapedown: Weight Management Program for Adolescents,* by Laurel Mellin (Balboa Publishing, 4th ed., 1987)
For parents: *Child of Mine: Feeding with Love and Good Sense,* by Ellyn Satter (Bull Publishing Co., 1986)

31

SPORTS AND PHYSICAL EXERCISE

*I*n large numbers teenagers are exercising. Some are jogging. Others are playing tennis. Or ice skating. Skiing. Shooting basketballs. Swimming.

Competitive sports are popular. At the high school level nearly seven million teenagers participate in them. And that's an encouraging sign.

Even so, this positive phenomenon is far from universal. Many adolescents are still much too sedentary. When school physical education programs aren't well rounded enough to give teenagers the exercise they need, a lot of them don't have the self-motivation to get their bodies moving on their own. Yes, the mass media continues to bombard us with campaigns about the importance of exercise, but a significant number of adolescents remain quite content to live as so-called "couch potatoes" or "armchair quarterbacks," preferring to watch others play sports on TV or at the local stadium.

That lifestyle, however, can be hazardous to your teenager's health. As a parent you need to take the initiative in urging your own adolescent to exercise, even though the battle to do so may seem difficult at times.

Here's part of the problem: teenagers feel invulnerable, and they live "for the moment." They can't imagine anything coming between themselves and good health. Thus they aren't impressed by the argument that by exercising they can do something *now* to prevent heart disease from developing three or four decades in the *future.* And since most inactive kids select friends who are just as sedentary as they are, you can't count on their peers getting them off the couch and into the parks and playgrounds.

Nevertheless, some parents have been quite successful in persuading their teenagers to adopt a more active lifestyle. True, in the final analysis your youngster will make the ultimate decisions about his physical activity or lack of it. But there are ways to try bringing the issues of exercise closer to home and make him more aware of the importance of finding a form of exercise that he enjoys.

How many teenagers know that high blood pressure, for example, sometimes begins in the adolescent and even preadolescent years—and that physical activity can help combat it? How many are conscious that exercise can be as important a factor in weight control as diet? Make sure your own teenager understands that physical activity is relevant to his life *now,* with some immediate payoffs.

At the same time, however, avoid placing excessive pressure on your adolescent, which could cause your efforts to backfire. Some teenagers start to exercise, only to suffer psychological "burnout" because their father or mother pushes them too hard, particularly in a competitive situation. You can also set a good example yourself by being physically active and acting as a good role model in this important area.

WHAT ABOUT ORGANIZED SPORTS?

From time to time parenting magazines publish articles warning about the pitfalls of organized sports: the "must win" attitudes, the pressures to excel from parents and coaches, the stresses that cause some kids to "crack" if their performance isn't up to their own (or someone else's) expectations. Some overinvolved parents, often unconsciously, convey the message that their offspring are loved and valued only if they win, and these adults often embarrass their children by yelling at coaches and umpires.

Those are the horror stories that make the headlines. But, in general, just how emotionally perilous are organized sports? Do the benefits usually outweigh the potential problems?

Under the best of circumstances—when there are no hurdles like parental pressures to deal with—organized sports can provide a positive learning experience. In a sense adolescents will be competing in a "microsociety" of the real world. As they do, they'll subtly learn the importance of dedication, discipline, practice, and cooperation with others in a team effort. Leadership qualities can also evolve from this peer group interaction. Even the emotional ups and downs associated with winning and losing can be instructive. Most adults who participated in sports as teenagers still have vivid memories of those experiences, many of them positive.

But the highly competitive "win at all cost" kind of competition should be unacceptable to you, and it certainly can interfere with the enjoyment of physical activity—negating the positive aspects of sports and exercise. As an alternative some teenagers turn to intramural sports or even school physical education classes, where they can still enhance their coordination, personality development, and personal confidence. And through intramural activities (or less competitive sports) many young athletes (and nonathletes) have discovered an aptitude for a particular sport that eventually turned into a lifelong form of recreation.

Your own teenager won't have to compete on a high school track-and-field team, for instance, to discover that running can be enjoyable. And as this or any other sport with an aerobic component (from swimming to bicycle riding) becomes a routine part of his life, it will help keep his cardiovascular, musculoskeletal, and respiratory systems healthy for decades.

Even so, some teenagers are drawn to the structure (and perhaps prestige) of organized sports. And for them this may be the best choice. But again, if your own adolescent is contemplating becoming involved in competitive sports or any other athletic environment, *he* should make the final decision about his participation. When a parent or a coach chooses for him, he may eventually begin to dread the activity. In some cases he'll react so negatively to the pressure that he'll decide to leave behind physical activity altogether.

Many teenagers, of course, enter organized sports very enthusiastically but are unprepared for some of the struggles they might encounter. For example, before the first game of the high school football or baseball season is ever played, the coach will probably cut some athletes from the team as he narrows down his roster to the allowable limit of players. Not surprisingly, that can be devastating for the boys or girls who learn that they're not good enough to make the squad. It's a tough experience for a youngster who truly loves the game and has closely tied his ego to winning a place on the squad and playing regularly.

Even when teenagers make the team—and excel in the sport—their conflicts may not be over. In many cases youth sports become so time-consuming that something ends up suffering—and it's usually schoolwork. There's often just not enough time for lengthy team practices and games—*and* writing term papers and studying for tests. These youngsters may have an A on the football field but might be fumbling their way through English, history, and algebra.

In an ideal world sports should complement academic subjects, forcing student-athletes to use their time more efficiently, set priorities, and adopt better study habits. And, in fact, some—but certainly not all—teenagers learn to do these things, thus achieving a positive balance between sports and schoolwork. Just as some adolescents are able to integrate other extracurricular activities into their day—such as band, other music, and dance—others find a way to enjoy sports without ignoring their other responsibilities. Their task is often easier if good communication and coordination exist between coaches and other teachers—and if both understand the benefits of doing well in sports as well as in academic subjects.

Finally, team sports can create a different problem; specifically, they usually don't foster participation in most traditional recreational activities. The individual sports that teenagers might be drawn to for lifelong exercise (perhaps swimming or brisk walking) are usually relegated to a subordinate (if any) role during adolescence, when teenagers are often concentrating on organized activities. For that reason some people believe our societal priorities are out of kilter, giving too much attention to team sports at the expense of individual activities that might keep us fit for life.

MAKING THE
MOST OF SPORTS

Everyone can benefit from exercise. Whether your teenagers are tall or short, fat or thin, well coordinated or a little awkward, they can find a sport that fits their abilities and interests—from racquetball to rock climbing, from badminton to brisk walking.

Running is popular among many teenagers, and for good reason. In addition to its well-documented benefits for the cardiovascular system, some research shows that joggers produce increased levels of chemicals called *endorphins,* which actually create a euphoric feeling or a "runner's high." This pleasant sensation is, in a sense, addictive, keeping runners coming back for more—a real advantage when a teenager is using jogging to help him stay healthy and perhaps lose weight. As we pointed out earlier, exercise is one of the best weapons your adolescent has for shedding his excess pounds.

You don't need to run, however, to experience a psychological boost from sports. Most people, young and old, feel a real mental lift when they're active, no matter what the precise form of exercise is. That's the case not only for healthy and able-bodied boys and girls but also for those with illnesses such as diabetes, bronchial asthma, mild or moderate hypertension, cystic fibrosis, and epilepsy. Adolescents just feel better—and feel better *about themselves*—when they go outside and get their bodies in motion.

Even so, parents need to be aware of the potential problems associated with specific types of physical activity. For example, long-distance runners, especially females, can often develop a mild running-related anemia, for which routine treatment is required. In activities that mandate weight control for good performance—such as gymnastics, ballet, and wrestling—teenage participants sometimes suffer from anorexia nervosa (an excessive weight-loss syndrome described in Chapter 29). More often, very active girls will stop menstruating when their body fat drops below a critical level, usually due to overtraining, undereating, or both.

Bear in mind that adolescents playing competitive sports generally need to consume more calories than their less active and sedentary peers—frequently many more calories. If you suspect that your teenager is not eating enough, you need to begin monitoring his or her eating habits. While a noncompeting athlete may need only 2,000 to 2,500 calories per day to maintain his weight, some athletes require 4,000 to 6,000 calories to keep their weight constant.

You also must be attentive to your children's level of physical maturity, making certain that coaches don't push them beyond what their bodies are ready for. Especially in the junior high school years, boys in particular sometimes find themselves competing with and against other adolescents whose physical growth and development are far ahead of their own, setting them up for possible injuries. All types of physical activity—from weight training to running to throwing—need to be modified to a level appropriate for each teenager's level of physical maturity.

Ideally youth of similar sex maturity ratings or SMRs (see Part II) should compete against one another. For example, a thirteen-year-old boy with a rating of SMR 2 may risk a more serious injury if he plays a contact sport such as competitive football with a thirteen-year-old peer with a rating of SMR 4. We suggest that teenagers see their pediatrician for a preparticipation exam, during which the doctor can help place these youngsters in a proper grouping as well as determine their fitness for their desired sport(s).

This physical should include a careful medical history (looking particularly for fainting episodes, family and personal cardiac problems, and previous injuries). The doctor should then carefully examine the youngster's cardiovascular and musculoskeletal systems and abdominal and genital structures. The American Academy of Pediatrics recommends such an examination every two years, and more often if there is a history of injury or another specific reason for doing so. Scheduling this evaluation several weeks before the desired sport begins will allow time to treat and rehabilitate any problems the doctor identifies.

COMMON SPORTS DISORDERS AND INJURIES

When it comes to sports injuries, no part of the body is immune. Pediatricians and sports medicine doctors frequently treat injuries to the eyes, ears, nose, and facial areas. Long bones and major joints (including the fingers, toes, and wrists) are also especially susceptible to problems. In some sports damage to the skin such as abrasions and blisters can occur (for instance, blisters on a baseball pitcher's first and second fingers).

Let's take a closer look at some of the problems your teenager might encounter:

Facial and Neck Injuries

As with injuries to all other parts of the body, facial injuries must be prevented whenever possible. A good place to start is for your teenager to wear a well-fitted helmet (in sports such as football, hockey, and lacrosse) to minimize the chances of injuries to the eyes, ears, and nose. The mouthpieces and face guards often attached to these helmets can cut down on mouth and teeth injuries too. If your teenager is playing racquet sports, he or she should also wear protective eye gear (made of polycarbonate) to avoid serious eye injuries. Some people think that contact lenses provide some degree of protection, but they're wrong: an adolescent wearing contacts also needs polycarbonate eye gear. As for external ear injuries, they can usually be prevented by using ear guards, not only during competition but for practices too.

When injuries do occur in the facial region, especially the eyes, have them properly diagnosed as rapidly as possible. Not only can this hasten the start of any necessary treatment but, based on these findings, your doctor can help you and your teenager decide whether your youngster needs to stop participating in the sport during the healing process.

Let's briefly look at some of the more common facial and neck injuries. Nasal injuries, for instance, are quite common, occurring when there has been a blow to the nose. They are most often seen in sports such as basketball, wrestling, boxing, volleyball, and skiing. Ear injuries can be serious and painful. Even so, your teenager's doctor should also look beyond them to determine if more severe trauma has occurred; for instance, when ear injuries take place, particularly when spinal fluid is draining from the ear canal, a skull fracture may be present as well.

Facial fractures and neck injuries do sometimes occur, but fortunately quite rarely. The most serious damage to the neck usually happens in sports such as football, hockey, and diving. Gymnasts and wrestlers also have experienced a recent increase in neck injuries. Ironically, football helmets—more specifically, the face guards attached to these helmets—are responsible for some serious injuries, occurring when another player grabs and twists them—which, in turn, twists the neck of the athletes wearing them. Even so, because most neck injuries in football are associated with dangerous tackling methods, recent rule changes that prohibit "spearing" and other risky tackling techniques have reduced this problem at least to some extent.

When neck trauma does occur, teenagers may experience sensations such as burning hands or "stingers." If the nerves in the neck were subjected to extreme stretching or compression, youngsters may have a so-called pinched nerve. If their neck underwent sudden twisting, such as in the face-guard situation described above, a number of additional, serious symptoms might be present, including bleeding under the skin, visual difficulties, weakness in the arms, and trouble concentrating. Studies show that wrestlers too can experience dizziness and changes in their visual and hearing capabilities in the aftermath of a prolonged rotation of the head.

Whiplash-type injuries are also common in many sports. When your teenager's neck is hyperextended suddenly in a sport like football, soccer, hockey, rugby, or diving, there could be an injury to the chief artery (the carotid artery) that runs along the neck. A doctor may order some tests to determine the extent of the damage.

Although a blow to the windpipe can cause anxiety in both teenagers and their parents, this concern is usually not really warranted, as long as the airway itself continues to function properly.

However, to repeat, any facial or neck injury should receive prompt attention from a doctor. If you or your teenager suspects that he or she may have suffered such an injury, assume that it actually has occurred until proven otherwise.

Head and Central Nervous System Injuries

"Gee, he really got his bell rung!"

You hear that phrase a lot in youth sports, usually when a teenager has suffered a blow to the head, resulting in a mild concussion, often in a sport such as football. The proper use of helmets for football and other types of headgear for other sports is essential to minimize the chances of sustaining head injury. Cerebral concussions are the most common head injuries in sports. Each year about one in five high school football players suffers a concussion.

And just what is a concussion? By definition it's a jarring injury to the brain that causes a change in responsiveness, even though this change can clear up with minimal if any noticeable damage. Some amnesia or loss of memory, however, can occur from the moment of the injury. Despite myths to the contrary, the teenager does not need to lose consciousness to have suffered a concussion.

What are the symptoms of a concussion? A headache is almost always present, often accompanied by dizziness, confusion, nausea, and irritability during the first two to three days. Although these symptoms will rarely persist for much longer, the teenager may have problems concentrating for up to seven days after the event and occasionally for even longer.

Sometimes teenagers will have a seizure in conjunction with a blow to the head. When that happens, they probably experienced a brain contusion or bruising rather than a concussion. The attending physician may order a CAT scan (a special X ray) to better diagnose this condition.

Any kind of blow to the head, however, warrants close medical observation for at least two to three days, when brain swelling can occur. Adolescents also should not return to sports practice or competition until their headache has *completely* subsided. And if they have repeated concussions, they might ultimately need to stop playing contact sports altogether, due to potential brain injury. (When your teenager has been disqualified from a sport for medical reasons, discuss it fully with a doctor. But don't allow anxiety over your youngster's not participating in the sport to overshadow the larger issue—namely, his future! This is true for any medical disqualification; evaluate the entire picture before insisting that your teenager get back into the sport. Serious heart, musculoskeletal, neurological, and other problems can have a negative impact on his future.)

Teenagers who have a known seizure disorder, such as epilepsy, can often still participate in most athletics, although their pediatricians should be advised of this activity. If their seizures are well controlled, the limitations on these youngsters need only be minimal. Also, tell their coach and team physician about the seizures as well as the type of anticonvulsant medication being used and the possible side effects.

Now, what about central nervous system (CNS) impairment? When athletes have CNS problems, they may suffer from severe dehydration, impaired by the effects of a condition such as hyperthermia (dangerously high body temperature). The symptoms: they may feel weak, tired, and dizzy and perspire heavily. To prevent these symptoms, make sure teenagers consume lots of liquids, particularly during hot weather. Thirst is not a reliable indicator of how much water the human body requires; remind your youngsters to drink periodically while they're exercising, even if they don't feel that they need the water.

Your teenager's coach should carefully adhere to well-established guidelines for exercising in hot weather and make sure his or her players are getting adequate fluids. Failure to do this can lead to heat-related problems that include fainting, seizures, coma, and even death!

Low Back and Abdominal Injuries

Doctors used to believe that low back injuries were uncommon in teenagers. But their thinking has changed. These types of problems do occur, frequently related to twisting maneuvers, improper warm-up, overstretching, and improper use of "sled blocking" (during football practice). Overuse injuries involving the low back are particularly common in weight training due to faulty lifting techniques. For these reasons your adolescent needs to learn to adhere closely to proper training techniques for the sports in which he participates.

Abdominal injuries are common, too, occurring in both contact and noncontact sports. Fortunately, though, such injuries are rarely serious. When there's been a blow to your teenager's abdomen (or back), a doctor should check to make sure that organs such as the spleen and kidneys have not been injured, since this type of damage can be serious. Injuries to the liver and stomach—caused by abdominal trauma—are uncommon, and stomach and bladder injuries are even rarer if these organs are relatively "empty" during competition.

Serious chest injuries, incidentally, are uncommon in most sports. Even so, bruising of the breastbone (sternum) is seen frequently in contact sports such as football, but perhaps surprisingly, breast injuries in female adolescents are rare (and certainly do not cause breast cancer).

Genital Injuries

Injuries to female genitals occur infrequently in competition. However, that's not the case with boys. Make sure your son wears the proper protective cup and appropriate padding to help shield his testicles from this type of injury. Fortunately, when a blow does occur to this region of the body, symptomatic treatment is usually all that's necessary. However, if there is continued pain, especially if it's associated with swelling and redness, he should be checked by his pediatrician. When the injury is accompanied by spasms of the muscles leading down to the testicles, seek a doctor's care immediately.

Wrist and Hand Injuries

Injuries to the wrist are common in teenage athletes. Adolescents might fracture their wrist in a variety of circumstances: in a fall, by making contact with a helmet or a face mask, while catching a ball, by resisting an opponent, or when handling a bat or a racquet. Although mildly incapacitating, these injuries can usually be encased in a silicone-type "soft" cast for sports or other modifications, which allow teenagers to carry on with most of their everyday activities.

Even so, the healing process may not be as rapid as the teenager desires. If the youngster has a navicular fracture, for instance—that is, a break of the bone at the base of his thumb—a full year may be needed for healing, even with the best therapy available. Obviously this can be quite distressing for a teenager involved in a sport that uses the wrist extensively, such as gymnastics.

Fingers are also susceptible to problems. If the injured finger appears only to be sprained, check its strengthening and bending abilities and then "buddy-tape" it to the one next to it to provide better protection. If you suspect a fracture, see a doctor promptly. The doctor will evaluate damage to the growth plate—the specialized parts of bone in which the growth actually occurs—which can be a special problem in children and adolescents.

A dislocated finger (accompanied by pain, swelling, and stiffness) can often be treated on the playing field, with a trainer or a doctor putting the finger back in place. Once it pops into position, the doctor will check the finger's circulation and range of motion, and in some cases he may order an X ray. If the doctor suspects a tendon injury, he may recommend early surgery, although some cases require only strict immobilization by taping and frequent monitoring over several days. If this tendon problem is related to a bite, cut, or laceration, the physician may dress (but not suture) the wound and buddy-tape the finger; then the doctor will observe the injury for infection over a period of one to three days.

Major Musculoskeletal Injuries

Many of the joint fractures, dislocations, or other injuries we've already discussed—involving the wrist and fingers, for instance—can be painful and are very susceptible to reinjury. As common as they are, however, they are still considered minor injuries. But that isn't the case with injuries to the knee, ankle, shoulder, or elbow, which generally cause a lot more concern because these injuries significantly influence performance in many sports.

Here are some of the more common major musculoskeletal injuries:

- The shoulder muscle area is often injured in contact sports such as football and hockey. Adolescents who participate in weight training, gymnastics, swimming, volleyball, and baseball also frequently injure this shoulder muscle group.

- The rotator cuff muscles, located in the shoulder area where it meets the upper arm, are susceptible to strains, particularly in the throwing sports (baseball, football). Swimmers and weight lifters also sometimes have chronically injured rotator cuffs. These injuries can also happen in falls on the shoulder in sports such as wrestling and gymnastics.

- Elbow injuries occur frequently in racquet sports such as tennis and racquetball. These are typically "overuse" injuries rather than being related directly to trauma. Some adolescent and preadolescent baseball players develop them as well (often called "Little League elbow"). Although elbow injuries are uncommon in wrestlers, they can occur when referees don't closely monitor potentially dangerous holds.

- A deep thigh bruise or contusion can occur to the quadriceps (the muscles in the front of the thighs). It requires aggressive treatment, including taping with adhesive strapping. Your teenager's doctor may warn her that because of the balanced relationship between the quadriceps and the hamstring muscles (the latter run from the buttocks across the back of the thigh), weakness in one muscle group can increase the chances of injury to the other. That's why a doctor will commonly prescribe restriction of activity for teenagers with such a quadriceps injury. Hamstring injuries, incidentally, usually occur in running events that involve a sudden burst of motion or when an athlete changes directions quickly; they can cause severe, disabling pain, but proper stretching and warm-up can prevent them. A persistent lump in the muscle may indicate bleeding in the area, and it should be checked by a doctor.

- Knee injuries are common in sports: More than 6,000 boys playing high school football suffer knee injuries during *each week* of football season—and 10 percent of these individuals require surgery! If your youngster experiences a knee injury, close medical supervision is necessary. Most of these injuries are the result of a specific incident of direct trauma to the tendon, ligament, or other knee structures, causing pain, swelling, and/or limitations in motion.

- When teenagers experience pain just below the kneecap, they probably have "jumper's knee" (also called "runner's knee" or *patellar tendon swelling*). This is a swelling of the tendon where it attaches to the lower part of the kneecap. The cause: a chronic stressor—e.g., the foot striking pavement— that moves up the leg and is absorbed by the knee.

- A condition called Osgood-Schlatter disease can also cause pain in the knee area among physically active teenagers. This common condition involves swelling with tenderness of the tibial tubercle (an obvious projection or bump of the tibia, below the kneecap). With rest and the passage of time, considerable improvement in the pain usually takes place. Still another disorder, chondromalacia patellae (or patellofemoral pain syndrome), is characterized by a softening of the kneecap cartilage and is often seen in female athletes. (See pages 305–306 for more information on both of these conditions.)

- Achilles tendinitis occurs when the tendons in the calf become overused and inflamed. It is quite common in adolescent athletes, particularly those who have undergone recent rapid growth periods. There also is an increased incidence of it early in the sport season, when intense training may involve additional running on hard surfaces. Doctors usually prescribe conservative treatment with ice, rest, and compression.

- Ankle sprains are common, and the intensity and pain associated with them can vary. With ice, compression (such as with an Ace bandage or even a cast), rest, and elevation over several days, the injury will usually resolve itself completely. If your teenager suffers an ankle injury, be sure he's examined by a doctor and keep him from returning to his sport until the physician gives him medical clearance; if he returns too soon, there's a risk of reinjury and possible chronic ankle instability.

Nerve Injuries

A number of different nerve injuries can complicate matters for the teenage athlete. For instance, when baseball pitchers throw or swimmers use a recurrent twisting motion of the shoulder, the nerve that runs between the collarbone and the shoulder blade may stretch, causing pain and weakness in the shoulder.

Problems also can develop with the long nerve that begins in the armpit and continues down the chest. Sharp downward shoulder motions—or hard blows to the neck or shoulder area—can injure it. The resulting pain may be concentrated in the neck, radiating to the chest and shoulder.

The median nerve, located in the lower arm and the first three fingers of the hand, can be injured by direct and repeated trauma to this area of the body. Baseball catchers often develop this problem, as do handball players, bicycle riders, and weight lifters. So-called carpal tunnel injuries, in which the nerve becomes compressed at the wrist, commonly involve the same median nerve, causing numbness, weakness, and pain. To test for possible injury to this nerve, doctors will ask the teenager to make a circle with his thumb and index finger;

if he's able to perform this well, he has normal median nerve function; but if he's unable to do so, he has a nerve injury.

When a knee dislocation occurs, or a fall on the knee takes place, the peroneal nerve between the knee and the ankle can become injured. Ankle sprains and tight ski boots can cause this type of nerve damage. These tight boots can produce a loss of sensation in the big toe as well as numbness on the backs and soles of the feet.

Some nerve injuries, incidentally, are extremely short-lived. For instance, a blow to the head or the neck may cause numbness, burning, or loss of sensation in the arm, forearm, and thumb; however, these symptoms may last only a few seconds, and any weakness that accompanies the injury may not last long either.

Other Sports Injuries

Perhaps you've heard of "weight lifter's blackout." This is a temporary loss of consciousness that can occur not only in weight lifters but in other athletes as well. Even when a fainting episode itself doesn't take place, the athlete may experience dizziness and confusion.

When does this syndrome occur? In weight training it often happens as the lifter is elevating a barbell or other weights from the floor, as he moves from a squatting to a standing position. A combination of factors is responsible, including hyperventilation before lifting and a decreased output of blood volume from the ventricles of the heart during this movement.

There are even more serious conditions you need to keep in mind. The sudden death of a teenage athlete is rare, but it nevertheless occurs from time to time. For example, death occurs in one in 81,000 high school football players a year (compared to one in 33,000 college football players and one in 4,000 in automobile accidents). Cardiovascular (heart and blood vessel) abnormalities are the most common cause of an unexpected sports fatality, usually because of a condition called *hypertrophic cardiomyopathy* (an enlargement of the septal heart muscle). Much less frequently, sudden death might be related to central nervous system or lung abnormalities.

When your teenager undergoes his physical exam before participating in sports, the doctor may inquire about a family history of unexpected sudden death in adolescence or the twenties. The physician may also be concerned when a teenager has experienced severe chest pain with dizziness or episodes of fainting. The doctor will also look for any other sign of heart problems. Although irregular heartbeats (arrhythmias) do occur in adolescents, they rarely require restriction of physical activity. Even so, if the doctor is concerned about any cardiovascular abnormality he uncovers, the teenager may be referred to a pediatric cardiologist for a thorough examination before being granted final approval to participate in sports.

DIAGNOSING SPORTS INJURIES

The previous sections of this chapter have provided you with some clues to help in the diagnosis of a sports injury. But chronic injuries in particular are sometimes difficult to diagnose and monitor properly. "Overuse" injuries often fall into this troublesome category. They are associated with running, swimming, baseball, dance, gymnastics, and cheerleading—and the symptoms can be subtle. In fact an athlete can sometimes become chronically incapacitated before a doctor finally identifies the precise problem. Under these circumstances the recovery period for treatment and rehabilitation can be lengthy.

You need to help protect your adolescent from "too much-too soon" situations. If he's allowed to train improperly or excessively, he may develop chronic problems with his hips, knees, heels, feet, or lower back.

Adolescence itself creates some extra physiological difficulties. In the midst of a growth spurt, for example, adolescent bodies will experience significant imbalances between the muscles and bones. These will place some stress on the spinal column and major joints. The result: a greater susceptibility to overuse injuries.

No wonder, then, that gymnasts—who have often barely started puberty—develop low back pain or hip or toe problems. Or that young adolescents who play baseball develop "Little League elbow." During the same rapid growth periods the risk of injuries is heightened further by delays in the coordination of a teenager's bodily movements and by any existing poor nutritional habits.

Fortunately, thanks to better coaching techniques and rule changes in contact sports (football, wrestling, hockey), there's now greater emphasis on the safety and well-being of the teenage athlete and thus a reduced chance of both acute and chronic injuries. Equipment is improving, too, including better helmets, face masks, mouthpieces, chest protectors, shin guards, and even shoes. The importance of proper equipment cannot be overemphasized in the prevention of sports injuries.

Ask your adolescent's pediatrician for help in creating a conditioning program for your teenager appropriate for his age and level of physical development. An adolescent who really enjoys an active lifestyle—with a minimum of aches and pains—is more likely to make exercise a lifelong habit. This can have an enormous health payoff in the years to come. Also, learn what types of injuries are common in your teenager's specific sport(s); although proper conditioning (and nutrition) can reduce the risks of encountering these problems, stay alert for them.

You also need to be wary of teenagers who seek to improve their athletic performance by using drugs. Some take "uppers" or speed (amphetamines) with the mistaken notion that these substances will give them an "edge" in competition. Some use synthetic male hormone products (anabolic steroids) because of the erroneous belief that these drugs are a harmless way of gaining strength and improving muscular development. What kinds of side effects are associated with steriods? They include damage to the testicles, development of breasts in males (gynecomastia), masculinization of females, increases in lipid (or fat) levels in the blood, and liver cancer (although the last occurs only rarely).

Make your teenager aware that using these drugs can potentially inflict long-term serious harm. Also, strongly discourage him from taking any of the other illicit drugs (such as alcohol and marijuana) that are not necessarily linked with sports but are widely accessible today. (See Chapter 11 for more information.) With new drug-testing procedures detection is likely, which could result in the teenager being banned from further competition. One of your most important roles as a parent is to educate your adolescent about the dangers of drugs—and to be a good role model too.

One last point: the human athlete—along with the race horse and the grey-hound—are the only animal species that exercises relentlessly despite pain. When teenagers overtrain, they're asking for trouble. At the first sign of discomfort they should rest, and if the pain persists, they should see a doctor. The frequently heard maxim "No pain, no gain" just doesn't make sense. If exercise is causing pain, not pleasure, the teenager is doing something wrong.

32

GYNECOLOGICAL PROBLEMS AND SEXUALLY TRANSMITTED DISEASES

"When my daughter began menstruating, a lot of things seemed to change, at least in my own mind," a mother recently recalled. "She no longer seemed like a little girl. It was as though she had crossed the threshold into adulthood. In fact she said to me, 'I guess I'm a woman now, Mom.' It was real emotional for me."

For teenage girls—and their parents—the beginning of menstruation is a momentous event. Many girls feel they have grown up overnight. At the same time, some are confused by the changes happening to them and wish all of this would just go away.

To add to the anxiety, this important time of life can become complicated by any number of common gynecological problems. For instance, are your daughter's periods irregular? Is she experiencing heavy bleeding? Or very painful periods?

Some teenage girls also notice lumps in their breasts—and they often think the worst ("It's cancer!"). Or they might notice a vaginal discharge or worry that they have contracted a sexually transmitted disease.

Many of these conditions are minor and relatively insignificant. Some, however, are serious and, on occasion, even potentially life-threatening. True, more than ever before, physicians have the ability to diagnose and effectively treat these difficulties—but in many cases they never get the chance. Too often teenage girls never go to their physician's office to seek help.

DEALING WITH MENSTRUAL DISORDERS

In Chapter 5 of this book, in a discussion of the physical changes of adolescence, we described some of what can go wrong—or at least cause anxiety—during teenage menstruation. Let's elaborate a little more on some of these disorders and discuss a few new ones as well.

For instance, what about a girl's *first* period? While most females begin menstruation (called *menarche*) between the ages of twelve and thirteen, it can start much earlier or later in some adolescents. If your daughter's development has been slow, and her periods have not started by age fifteen-and-a-half to sixteen years, this is called *delayed menarche*. It is probably due to heredity and is normal. But if her periods have not begun by age sixteen or seventeen, she needs to see her pediatrician; this so-called "primary amenorrhea" can have a number of causes, including stress, depression, eating disorders, obesity, drug use, or intense athletic training. Genetic abnormalities can play a role as well, as can endocrine problems or, in rare instances, serious diseases such as ovarian tumors.

Depending on the cause, your pediatrician can recommend a number of options to treat this absence of menstruation. If the problem seems particularly complex, he might refer your daughter to a gynecologist or an endocrinologist for some specialized care.

Most girls, though, never need to get this far. For them menstruation does eventually start on its own, even if it does begin later than average. However, whether the first period comes early or late (with a normal range of ten to sixteen years of age), many young females have one thing in common: they experience this dramatic change in their body's functioning without really being prepared for what's taking place.

"I knew I was going to get my period someday," recalled one teenage girl, "but my mom and I never really talked much about it. Then one day at school, there was this flow of blood from between my legs. My initial reaction was horror. I thought if I couldn't stop the bleeding, I might die! I was so scared."

As a parent you need to make sure your daughter understands fully what awaits her. Menstruation does not need to be traumatic. It doesn't deserve to be labeled "the curse." Rather, it is a normal bodily function, as much a part of a healthy body as breathing or the beating of the heart. Menstruation is a sign that the body is working just right.

Does your daughter really comprehend that? Or does she dread her period every month? For many girls even the most regular periods are an absolute "crisis." And if something should go awry with their menstrual cycle, that only makes things worse.

Here are some of the more common menstrual concerns that confront many teenage girls:

Irregular Periods

Beginning with their first period, many adolescents expect their menstrual cycles to occur precisely on schedule. But that rarely happens. During the first year (and perhaps more) of menstruation some teenagers have periods that are quite irregular. Some cycles are as short as three weeks; others are as lengthy as six weeks—or occasionally even longer. One girl recalled, "I had my first period, and then almost three months went by before my second one. I was sure something was wrong with me. If I had been having sex, I probably would have been really scared that I was pregnant."

Should your daughter become worried about this kind of menstrual irregularity? In general, no. There's really no reason for her concern, as long as her periods (when they occur) don't last longer than five to seven days, and as long as she's not soaking a new sanitary pad every hour. If she's patient, her cycle will usually become quite regular (every three to five weeks). Menstruation is a complex physiological process coordinated by several bodily organs, including the hypothalamus, the pituitary gland, the uterus, and the ovaries; and it will take a few months (sometimes one to three years) for these many interactions to become fine-tuned.

Incidentally, don't get the impression that this menstrual irregularity is a universal phenomenon. True, many girls do experience it in their first few periods, but it doesn't happen with everybody. Some studies show that as many as 45 percent of adolescent females begin having regular, ovulatory periods from the beginning. Everyone is different.

After a teenager's menstrual cycles finally become regular, a number of factors can still disturb their timing now and then. Of course, more than any other reason, pregnancy can cause her periods to stop. But there can be other disruptive influences as well, such as high stress levels, athletics, poor diet, and illnesses such as the flu.

Heavy Bleeding

Some girls bleed more heavily than others during their menstrual periods. But only a few bleed enough to cause problems. The normal adolescent female has about five quarts of blood in her body and loses only one to three fluid ounces of it with an average period.

When does your daughter have to worry about excessive bleeding? If she soaks more than six to eight pads or tampons in a single day, if she continues bleeding for more than seven to ten consecutive days, or if she discovers particularly large clots of blood, consult a pediatrician or gynecologist, who will most likely want to examine her. She may be so anxious herself that she'll readily agree to a visit to the doctor.

On occasion girls bleed abnormally because of a specific disease or condition— such as blood or clotting disorders, diabetes, thyroid or kidney disease, a pelvic infection, ovarian abnormalities, or forgotten tampons left in the vagina. Bleeding due to a threatened or impending miscarriage or a tubal pregnancy must be considered, too. But most times there is no physical cause for this bleeding, and the condition will be referred to as *dysfunctional uterine bleeding*. In this last case, unless anemia has occurred or the bleeding is very irregular, doctors will not prescribe any special treatment, and most girls will eventually outgrow this excessive bleeding. In the more severe cases, however, your teenager's doctor could recommend placing your daughter on birth control pills or other hormonal treatment to control the bleeding, as well as some supplemental iron tablets to manage the anemia (see Chapters 29 and 33).

Keep in mind that birth control pills are hormones and thus are prescribed for reasons in addition to contraception; in this case they can be used to regulate cycles until your daughter is mature enough to menstruate cyclically on her own. In other cases the pill can even treat dysfunctional uterine bleeding, ovarian cysts, or painful periods (dysmenorrhea). Some parents become concerned when a doctor prescribes the pill for their daughter to treat a gynecological condition, fearing it will give her license or a reason to become sexually active. However, this simply doesn't occur (See Chapter 14).

Painful Periods

"Every month when I get my period, I have such terrible cramps that I'm absolutely miserable. I stay home from school, and I don't feel like doing anything. I just wish my periods would go away."

It's not all that surprising that some teenage girls—particularly those in middle or late adolescence—dread their periods. After all, they routinely experience abdominal cramps and other symptoms, usually beginning within four hours before their menstrual period and continuing for about twenty-four hours or more.

Not too many years ago teenage girls who had these painful periods didn't receive much understanding or help from their doctor. In fact they were occasionally referred for psychotherapy, with some people believing that this female discomfort was nothing more than a psychological response to the monthly changes in their body. Some theorists even claimed that these girls were rebelling—that is, they didn't want to be women at all, but rather wanted to stay little girls, or perhaps they even would have preferred being male!

However, this kind of thinking is now unwarranted. A better understanding of female physiology has shown that painful periods almost never are psychological or psychosomatic. We now know that dysmenorrhea has a *physiological* basis. The discomfort is usually caused by chemical changes that occur in the uterus. The endometrium (uterine lining) releases hormonelike substances called *prostaglandins,* causing contractions of the uterine muscle tissues. And that provokes abdominal pain or cramps. Although this discomfort is quite mild in some girls, it can be disabling in others. To make matters worse, they can experience other symptoms as well, such as nausea, vomiting, headaches, and diarrhea.

But there's some good news for your daughter even if she experiences severe cramps along with her period. More than ever before, doctors have a wider array of preventive and pain-limiting drugs at their disposal to help control this discomfort. The most widely used medications are prostaglandin inhibitors, and they include drugs such as ibuprofen (Motrin, Advil, Medipren), mefenamic acid (Ponstel), and naproxen (Naprosyn). If these medications prove ineffective for your daughter, her doctor can turn to hormonal pills (birth control pills) to relieve the pain. She might also find exercise or a heating pad helpful. Bed rest is usually unnecessary.

Before moving on, let's mention an exception to the rule that we've been discussing. In a few cases of dysmenorrhea the pain is *not* caused by an imbalance of prostaglandins, but rather by a disease process—for instance, pelvic inflammatory disease (an inflammation of the fallopian tubes and other pelvic organs) or endometriosis (the latter is an unusual disorder in which the endometrium—that is, the tissue that normally grows in the uterine lining—grows outside the uterus, resulting in severe menstrual cramps and/or menstrual irregularity). That's why your daughter should see her physician if she's experiencing painful periods. The doctor can determine the cause and recommend a treatment. There's no reason for her to suffer.

When to See a Doctor

We've already described certain menstrual disorders that might call for a trip to the doctor's office. Let's briefly review when you should seek her physician's care. You and your daughter should be alert for the following menstrual symptoms, which should prompt a call to her doctor:

- an unexpected absence or irregularity in her period that doesn't have an obvious cause (such as illness)

- extremely heavy menstrual bleeding that persists beyond seven to ten days

- bleeding that occurs at a time other than during the period itself

- severe abdominal pain that lasts for more than two days and is not early in her period

- the possibility or suspicion of pregnancy

- any other concern you and/or your daughter have that something is wrong with her menstrual cycles

BREAST AND PELVIC DISORDERS

Let's face it: few women, no matter what their age, look forward to pelvic examinations. However, as we emphasized in Chapter 6, these pelvic exams are essential at times.

For instance, any teenager who is having sexual intercourse should have a pelvic exam at least once a year. Even those who are not having sex should begin having regular examinations (and Pap smears) at about the time they graduate from high school and are entering either college or the job market. Some physicians recommend that the first pelvic exam take place earlier to answer the teenage girl's questions, reassure her that this important bodily system is normal, and detect abnormalities as early as possible. Many girls find it easier to have their first exam when they're symptom-free than when they're in pain or have other concerns.

Discuss these options with both your daughter and her doctor. The decision to have the first "routine" pelvic exam is complex and depends a lot on your daughter's comfort with the idea, the family's cultural background, and her feelings about being examined by a male or female physician.

There are still other special circumstances that should bring your daughter to the doctor's office for a pelvic exam. We've already mentioned some of them, such as irregular bleeding, severe dysmenorrhea, and a lack of periods. Also, the presence of sexually transmitted diseases and vaginal discharges—which we will discuss later in this chapter—usually requires a pelvic exam. Girls also need a careful examination when they're beginning to use birth control methods or if they've been sexually molested or raped.

Growths such as ovarian cysts should be checked regularly by a doctor. Fortunately, most of these cysts stay small and thus they may not cause problems. But sometimes they can seriously disrupt menstrual periods—increasing blood flow in some girls and stopping it in others.

Now, what about cancer? Yes, cancer of the female reproductive organs *does* occur in teenagers, although *very rarely.* If cancer does develop in your youngster, it needs to be detected early (by parent and daughter responding to symptoms and daughter undergoing appropriate examinations, including a Pap smear) and treated early. Also, girls whose mothers took DES (diethylstilbestrol) or other hormones during pregnancy (to prevent abortion, to control bleeding or spotting) need a pelvic exam shortly after starting their own period; these teenagers may be more susceptible to a rare form of vaginal cancer. Fortunately, treatment with DES was stopped about twenty years ago, but your daughter's doctor should be told about any hormones or special medications that you took while pregnant.

One other important caution is in order: although cancer itself is unusual in this age group, the intermediate stages leading up to some forms of cancer are more common. Specifically, cervical dysplasia—an abnormality in cell growth that may lead to cancer—occurs in .7 percent of teenagers (7 in 1,000) having sexual intercourse. This condition arises when the lining of the cervix meets its outside surface and can be seen during a pelvic exam. If your daughter has been having sex since her early teens and has had multiple partners, she may be at *particular* risk. If untreated, this dysplasia may evolve into cancer, so it must be detected and cared for early. Thus girls most prone to this condition need regular Pap smears. In the past generation physicians have noted an increased incidence of cervical dysplasia in teenagers. Doctors have also recently discovered a link between cervical dysplasia and venereal warts caused by the papilloma virus.

Incidentally, as part of every gynecological exam (and any other general adolescent health checkup), your daughter's doctor should conduct a breast examination. Breast malignancies are uncommon in teenagers; less than 1 percent of all breast cancers occur in women under the age of twenty-five. Even so, her pediatrician should regularly check for any lumps in the breasts as well as moles, sores, swelling, and enlargements of the lymph nodes.

The doctor should also teach your daughter how to conduct breast self-examinations at home (see below), beginning with the onset of puberty. True, some physicians believe that teenage girls should *not* perform regular breast self-exams, since cancer is so rare in this age group and such routine attention may raise anxiety unnecessarily; however, most doctors disagree, arguing that these monthly exams will encourage girls to be more aware of and knowledgeable about their body and will prepare them for adulthood, when breast cancer is more common and regular self-examination of the breasts is so important.

Nonmalignant masses (called *benign breast disease*) are much more common during adolescence. If your daughter has a condition termed *fibrocystic disease,* her entire breast (or both breasts) may be lumpy and tender, most obviously just before she gets her periods. Pain usually accompanies this disease, too, and it is sometimes severe.

When your teenager has fibrocystic breast disease, she probably should avoid caffeine and chocolate, since they may make the condition worse. Some doctors also recommend taking vitamin E pills and treatment with hormonal drugs. Although several studies show that women with fibrocystic disease might be more susceptible to breast cancer later in life, the disease itself is *not* cancer.

Now, what if your daughter detects a single mass in the breast that persists for several weeks? Once again, her doctor should check it out. The physician may

How to Conduct a Breast Self-Examination

Once a month in the shower, when she's all soaped up, your daughter should perform an examination of her breasts. Tell her to think of each breast as a pie divided into four segments or quarters. Beginning with the right breast, she should feel each segment separately with the left hand and then feel the center of the "pie" (the nipple area). Then she should reverse the procedure, feeling the left breast with the right hand.

Let your daughter know that most teenage breasts normally have fibrous elements and some texture to them; they are not just soft tissue. She should become familiar with her own normal texture—and then be alert for any lumps or other irregularities if they should ever appear. As well as lumps, she should be looking for knots, depressions, an irregular shape or texture, or nipple discharge. Lumps sometimes come and go, but a doctor should examine those that persist.

Your daughter should conduct this breast self-examination once a month, preferably right after her menstrual period.

withdraw some fluid from the mass if it is a cyst and send it to the laboratory for examination. Most likely, it will be a fibroadenoma (a nonmalignant thickening or lump of breast tissue). But the mass could also be caused by a bruise or a contusion. In most cases the lump will go away on its own. If it doesn't, however, the doctor may have to perform a biopsy and perhaps excise it. Through this ordeal, reassure your daughter that in 99 percent of cases breast lumps in adolescents are *not* cancerous. Again, breast cancer is extremely rare in teenagers.

A number of other breast conditions may occur in adolescence and can be evaluated by a physician. For instance, your daughter may have concerns over breasts that she feels are too small, too large, or too asymmetrical. If she considers her breasts "too big," her doctor may explain that explosive breast growth (called *virginal* or *juvenile breast hypertrophy*) does occur in a few girls at puberty. As for breast asymmetry, various degrees of it can occur in teenage girls, sometimes causing considerable anxiety. Breast atrophy is often the result of severe weight loss, whether due to anorexia nervosa or chronic illness.

Should plastic surgery be considered for girls concerned about their breast size, whether too small, too large, or asymmetrical? In general a decision about such surgery should be deferred until late adolescence or early adulthood, when these girls are more mature physically as well as better able to evaluate these sensitive matters. Occasionally, however, when a younger teenager develops severe psychological problems associated with very large breasts, surgery to reduce the breast size may be warranted.

Breast infections, such as abscesses and mastitis (often pregnancy-related), can also occur in teenagers. Any discharge from the breast (aside from that associated with pregnancy) is called *galactorrhea* and warrants an evaluation by a doctor.

One final comment on breast disorders: teenagers can sometimes develop painful breasts—a condition that doctors label *mastalgia* or *mastodynia*. This painful disorder can occur for a number of reasons, although it is rarely a serious problem. For instance, it can be associated with a girl's menstrual cycle. It might be linked with breast swelling and lumpiness (nodularity) and be part of fibrocystic breast disease.

Quite often a doctor can't identify a specific cause for this breast pain and usually considers it a normal condition. The doctor may recommend a variety of measures to deal with the problem—perhaps well-fitting bras, mild pain-limiting drugs (analgesics), and occasionally hormonal drugs.

Painful breasts can also be part of the premenstrual tension syndrome (PMS), a condition often confused with painful menstrual cramps (or dysmenorrhea). By definition PMS refers to a number of symptoms that occur just before the menstrual period and persist for a few days or more after the blood flow actually begins. For instance, your teenage girl might complain not only of breast swelling and tenderness but also of nausea, vomiting, weight gain, diarrhea, constipation, and/

or mood changes. These symptoms may occur for only a few days but can continue for up to a week or more each month.

What's the cause of PMS? No one knows for certain, and this is a controversial topic in medical circles. Some doctors blame an excess of estrogen, a deficiency of progesterone, and/or a lack of the vitamin pyridoxine. There are a variety of other hypotheses too, but all are only theories at this point.

Check with your daughter's physician to discuss treatment options for PMS, while keeping in mind that many are unproven at this point. Diuretics ("water pills") may help some teenagers with severe breast swelling and weight gain. Analgesics may be useful to ease severe pain, and doctors sometimes prescribe various hormonal drugs to improve the patient's overall condition. Antidepressant drugs have been used for controlling severe mood changes, as have medications for dysmenorrhea. Certain dietary limitations (of caffeine, sugar) have been suggested as well.

SEXUALLY TRANSMITTED DISEASES

"It's silly for me to talk to my teenagers about sexually transmitted diseases. I know they're not having sexual intercourse yet."

Maybe they're not. But are you absolutely sure? It's risky to make those kinds of assumptions about adolescent behavior. First, perhaps your teenagers *are* having sex, without your knowledge. Yet even if they're not, they'll eventually begin doing so—whether it's next year, in five years, or once they're married. And before they do, they need to know how to protect themselves from sexually transmitted diseases. Remember, STDs can be transmitted the *first* time a boy or a girl has sex.

Here are some general facts your adolescent should know about STDs:

- Most STDs are easy to contract during intimate sexual contact.

- Some STDs (such as gonorrhea and syphilis) can be transmitted through oral sex. Your teenager need not engage in sexual intercourse to contract one.

- Individuals can catch an STD only from an infected sexual partner. Therefore, the more partners they have, the greater their risk of coming in contact with an infected person.

- An individual can be a carrier of an STD without knowing it. That's because these infections often don't cause any symptoms. With gonorrhea, for example, about 75 percent of infected females and from 10 to 20 percent of infected males aren't even aware they have the disease. But a word of caution: even though teenagers may not be able to see or feel the infection, they are still contagious and can pass it on to someone else during sexual intercourse.

- If any symptoms appear, consult a doctor immediately. Tell your teenager to be on the lookout for penile or vaginal discharges, a burning sensation during urination, lower abdominal pain, a shift from regular to irregular periods, increasingly painful periods, and painful intercourse or bleeding after sex. These are all signs that an STD could be present.

When teenagers contract a sexually transmitted disease, it won't disappear on its own. So while they may find it embarrassing to tell you or their pediatrician about a possible STD infection, it's essential that they do so. Most STDs are curable (herpes and AIDS are notable exceptions)—but only if a doctor treats the infection. And if no therapy is administered, STDs can cause serious health problems. They can be disabling. They can even kill.

There are more than twenty STDs that can be passed from one person to another, but in recent years gonorrhea and chlamydia have been the most prevalent among teenagers, reaching epidemic proportions. Let's spend a few moments discussing these two infections, and then we'll move on to some of the other common STDs.

Gonorrhea

The news about gonorrhea is very disturbing. Since 1960 the incidence of this STD has tripled among adolescents from ages fifteen to nineteen. Except for chlamydia (see next section), it is now the most common STD.

What causes gonorrhea? The *gonococcus* bacterium is to blame. This infectious organism can grow in the vagina and the penis as well as the throat and anus. In males it most often causes an inflammation of the urethra (the tube that runs the length of the penis); in girls it can inflame the cervix, the ovaries, and the fallopian tubes. And remember, it's transmitted through sexual contact—*not* via toilet seats or doorknobs!

When girls contract gonorrhea, they are usually symptom-free (although some may have a cloudy vaginal discharge or abdominal pain). Most females find out that they have the infection only if their sexual partner tells them that he's been diagnosed with the disease. Unlike girls, however, most boys do experience some symptoms—namely, painful or burning urination, bloody urine, or a puslike discharge from the penis—which may appear several days after transmission of the infection. When such symptoms appear, adolescents need to undergo a test at their doctor's office or a clinic for presence of the disease—and they must refrain from intercourse until they find out the exact cause. If they do have gonorrhea, they should inform their sexual contacts immediately.

What's the treatment for gonorrhea? In the past doctors would prescribe a drug such as penicillin, ampicillin, or tetracycline. But penicillin-resistant strains have developed over the last twenty-five years, and now alternative antibiotics must be used.

But when a teenager doesn't even know she has the disease—and thus she goes without treatment—the outcome can be disastrous. If the infection advances, both boys and girls can become sterile, due to scarring of the female fallopian tubes or the male epididymis (the tiny tubes at the back of the testicles). The infection can also move beyond the reproductive organs into the bloodstream, where it can cause havoc in other parts of the body (joint infections, skin rashes, and, less frequently, infections of the heart and central nervous system).

Chlamydia

Chlamydia is caused by a bacterium-like parasite called *Chlamydia trachomatis.* In the U.S. alone there are a staggering three million cases of chlamydia a year. Most often it causes an inflammation of the urethra. Like gonorrhea, chlamydia spreads via sexual contact, not through toilet seats or towels.

The similarities with gonorrhea don't end there, however. Although symptoms (vaginal discharge, painful urination) may begin to appear within a month after exposure to chlamydia, girls in particular are often asymptomatic, even when the organism is flourishing in the vagina or cervix. Also, chlamydia and gonorrhea often appear together; when one STD is detected, a search for others should occur since mixed infections are common.

When doctors diagnose chlamydia, an antibiotic is required, usually for one week but longer if complications have developed. Sexual partners need treatment as well. Also, infected teenagers should be advised not to engage in sex until the completion of therapy.

Now, what if chlamydia is untreated? As with gonorrhea, the chlamydia infection in girls can lead to pelvic inflammatory disease, which can damage the reproductive system drastically enough to cause sterility. Boys might also become sterile, and urinary difficulties can occur in both sexes.

Other STDs

Although this book could devote an entire chapter to STDs alone, two other infections—AIDS and herpes—need mention here.

AIDS (acquired immunodeficiency syndrome) is one of the newest and most ominous diseases of our time. It's caused by a virus—the human immunodeficiency virus (HIV)—that impairs the human immune system so severely that it makes the individual vulnerable to a number of potentially fatal infections.

HIV is not an easy virus to transmit. You can't catch it by shaking the hand of an AIDS patient. You can't get infected sitting next to someone with AIDS in a classroom. Even people living in the same household with family members who have AIDS haven't contracted the disease.

However, AIDS *is* spread through sexual contact—specifically the exchange of bodily fluids during intercourse and other forms of sexual activity. By coming in contact with the semen or vaginal secretions (as well as the blood and blood products) of an infected person, your teenager could get AIDS. The sharing of infected needles among drug users is another common means of contracting AIDS. (In the past blood transfusions and the use of blood products were responsible for some AIDS cases, but rigorous screening techniques have nearly eliminated this risk.) Once the infection is present, this is a disease that shows little or no mercy. AIDS has claimed tens of thousands of lives in the U.S. alone, and many more will die unless researchers find a cure.

As of 1991 children and adolescents make up only about 3 percent of all AIDS cases. However, we don't know just how prevalent the AIDS virus itself may be among adolescents. Is there a large, silent group of infected teenagers who will develop the full-blown disease in the years ahead? Researchers don't yet have the answer. We do know that the incubation period (the time from contracting the infectious agent until actual symptoms appear) can be several years; thus a teenager coming in contact with HIV may not manifest the disease until adulthood.

Homosexual males are at a particularly high risk for contracting AIDS, since the virus has spread so widely throughout that community (via rectal coitus). But *no one* is immune. If your teenager is heterosexual and having sex, he or she needs to practice "safe sex." That includes the proper use of a condom (even better when combined with a spermicide), which seems to offer the best protection against transmission of the virus. It also means limiting the number of sexual partners to cut down the chances of coming into contact with an HIV carrier.

Dr. C. Everett Koop, the U.S. surgeon general during the Reagan administration, sent a booklet on the AIDS epidemic to every household in America. New facts about AIDS are constantly being uncovered, so check with your physician to stay up to date. It is literally a matter of life and death!

Perhaps a bit less frightening than AIDS is still another STD—herpes. In the early 1980s herpes was splashed on magazine covers and across the front pages of newspapers. Because of the AIDS epidemic, we don't hear much about herpes anymore. But it's still around. And people are still catching it through sexual contact.

There are two herpes simplex viruses—Types 1 and 2 (HSV-1, HSV-2). Type 1 gets the blame for so-called "cold sores" in and around the mouth, and is not usually transmitted sexually. Type 2 is generally considered the agent responsible for blisterlike sores on the genitals. However, both types can actually cause lesions at either site.

The symptoms of genital herpes begin to appear from two to twenty days after the virus is transmitted through sexual contact. The sores become visible on or around the genitals, they are usually painful and itchy, and they may persist for as long as three weeks. And when they're present, herpes is extremely contagious.

Make sure your teenagers know the really bad news about herpes: if they contract the infection, they'll never get rid of the virus. It will become dormant in their body, and in all likelihood it will cause repeated outbreaks of the sores, often during times of stress or illness. Also, a pregnant teenager can transmit the virus to her baby, with serious consequences, including the death of her child.

Even so, the news is not all bleak. The recurrences of herpes outbreaks are usually milder than the initial one, since the body will build up some resistance to try to combat the virus. Also, herpes is not quite as common in teenagers as it is in young adults. Yes, it does occur in adolescents, but it's not as prevalent as other STDs. And unlike AIDS, it's not a life-threatening infection. Even with a pregnant teenager, careful prenatal care can reduce the chances of transmitting herpes to her baby.

Teenagers who think they may have herpes should see their pediatrician. A pregnant girl should tell her obstetrician. Doctors can make the diagnosis only when the sores are present. Although no drug can effectively cure herpes, the doctor may recommend some approaches for symptomatic relief. A drug called acyclovir (Zovirax) can decrease the length of time symptoms are present and lessen the amount of virus that is shed (thus making the youngster less contagious). Depending on the situation, a doctor may prescribe acyclovir as an ointment or a pill; it can even be given intravenously.

Are there still other STDs? Yes, many of them. As we mentioned earlier, there are more than twenty types—some common, others rare. They include pelvic inflammatory disease (see the discussion of it later in this chapter), syphilis (yes, syphilis is still prevalent), hepatitis (see page 302), venereal warts (also called *condylomata acuminata,* which may precede the onset of cervical cancer), trichomoniasis (page 284), chancroid, lymphogranuloma venereum, granuloma inguinale, Reiter's syndrome, Behçet's syndrome, scabies, and pediculosis (lice). Any sexually active teenager is at risk.

Preventing STDs

STDs can be prevented. Obviously the best way for your teenager to avoid them is to refrain from having sexual intercourse. But if your adolescent is sexually active, he can take steps to remain safe. Some of these suggestions have been mentioned earlier. But let's review how he can stay away from STDs:

- Teenagers should know who their sexual partner is. They can't contract an STD unless they're having sex with an infected person. A partner who is not a carrier of the disease can't pass it on to someone else (although partners may not know they have the infection).

- They should limit their sexual contacts. The more partners they have, the greater their chance of exposure to an STD.

- They should use condoms during sex. Condoms can provide protection against AIDS and most other STDs. Although condoms aren't perfect, they can furnish a high degree of safety if utilized properly. And when they are used in combination with spermicidal foam (which can kill some STD microbes), the level of protection is even greater. (Although some teenagers believe that the pill guards them against STDs, there's absolutely no truth to this.)

- Teenagers who believe they may have contracted an STD should see their pediatrician or visit an STD clinic immediately. The earlier a doctor diagnoses and treats the disease, the greater the chances of avoiding complications and spread.

- If they have an STD, they need to be honest about that with their sexual partner, who should also be tested. They should avoid having sex while the active STD infection is present.

PELVIC INFLAMMATORY DISEASE

"Sometimes I think I've ruined my life. All I did was have sex with this boy who I really liked. But I caught gonorrhea from him without knowing that I did. For a long while I didn't feel sick or anything. But then I finally started getting these terrible stomach pains. I went to my doctor, and he told me I had PID. And he said that it was caused by gonorrhea. By that time the disease had spread to my tubes. The doctor doesn't think I'll ever be able to have kids. I'm only sixteen. I don't know what I'm going to do."

We've already briefly mentioned pelvic inflammatory disease (PID). It's a pelvic infection—and one of the most serious complications of sexually transmitted diseases. PID occurs when organisms enter the uterus; if unchecked, they can spread to the fallopian tubes and the ovaries.

We can't overemphasize just how devastating PID can be, particularly for females in their childbearing years. If not treated immediately, PID can lead to the formation of scar tissue in the fallopian tubes, causing ectopic pregnancies (developing outside the uterus) or infertility. On very rare occasions the infectious agent can also enter the bloodstream, resulting in blood poisoning (septicemia).

Gonorrhea and chlamydia are major causes of PID, but as the anecdote above illustrates, many teenage girls never experience any symptoms from a gonorrheal or chlamydial infection. However, once PID itself has developed, some unmistakable symptoms finally occur. These girls may experience serious lower abdominal pain, pelvic tenderness, or irregular bleeding. They may also have a fever, nausea, pain on urination or intercourse, and/or a heavy vaginal discharge.

Contrary to popular belief, if your teenager has lower abdominal pain, acute appendicitis is not necessarily the cause; in fact in many more cases the problem is likely to be PID or even pregnancy. For that reason a sexually active teenage girl complaining of abdominal pain should receive a gynecological examination.

If your teenager is having sexual intercourse, what's her risk of developing PID? Much greater than most parents think. Between the ages of fifteen and nineteen she has a one-in-eight chance of contracting this disease. That's the highest rate for any age category.

To prevent PID's severest complications, a doctor must catch this disease in its earlier stages, when it's still only a cervical infection (cervicitis)—before it spreads to areas of the body where it can do its most serious damage. If it reaches the fallopian tubes, it will become a much more severe—and even a potentially life-threatening—infection. At that time most doctors will recommend that adolescents be hospitalized, largely because compliance with the therapeutic program is essential. The treatment: intravenous antibiotics, a lot of rest, and no sexual intercourse for several weeks.

Once cured, these girls won't necessarily be free of worries. Having already had PID, they'll have an increased risk of getting it again. To make matters worse, their chances of infertility will rise with each new episode of PID—that is, after one PID infection, they have about a 13 percent chance of becoming infertile; that will increase to 36 percent after the second episode and 75 percent after the third. However, bear in mind that these are just statistics—in fact some girls become infertile after just *one* PID infection.

Still other complications are possible as well, including chronic abdominal pain (not helped by antibiotics) and severe menstrual cramps. Unfortunately, millions of women have been affected by this preventable infection in the past generation. Yet most teenage girls and adults have never heard of PID!

VAGINAL DISCHARGE

"Sometimes I just don't understand what's going on with my body. I feel pretty good, but I keep noticing this stuff coming from inside of me. I'm only thirteen, and I've never had sex. So it can't be VD, can it? But if it's not VD, what is it?"

A lot of teenage girls experience a vaginal discharge at one time or another, and it can be the source of confusion and anxiety. Although STDs usually come to mind at the first sign of a discharge, there can be other causes too. In fact most females—whether they're having sexual intercourse or not—have a clear or pearly white discharge every now and then; as mentioned in Chapter 6, it is called *physiologic leukorrhea,* is quite normal, and is nothing to worry about.

However, if the discharge is irritating, has a bad odor, or is any color other than white, a doctor needs to check it. In most cases it will turn out to be relatively insignificant; even so, it can be uncomfortable for the teenager, and thus it needs treatment.

Many organisms can normally live and thrive in the vagina. But agents such as *Candida albicans, Gardnerella vaginalis,* and *Trichomonas vaginalis* are responsible for most vaginal infections. No matter what particular organism is involved, however, the symptoms are often the same—burning, itching, and/or pain during sexual intercourse, in addition to a discharge.

Candidiasis

When your pediatrician tells you that your daughter has a "yeast infection," the *Candida albicans* fungus is to blame. And while candidiasis can be transmitted through sexual intercourse, most teenagers contract these infections through other means.

Some adolescent girls harbor low levels of *Candida* in the vagina, but under certain circumstances conditions within the vagina will change, encouraging the organism to multiply and leading to candidiasis. For instance, teenagers who have been taking certain antibiotics (ampicillin, tetracycline) can develop yeast infections. So can girls taking birth control pills—drugs that alter the hormonal balance in the vagina. These infections also develop more often in diabetics, in pregnant girls, and in teenagers who wear clothing that doesn't permit adequate circulation of air—such as pantyhose (particularly those without cotton crotches) and tight-fitting jeans.

If your daughter develops a yeast infection, what symptoms can she expect? She'll probably experience vaginal itching or burning (often very intense) and a thick, curd-white, odor-free discharge. However, she shouldn't try to diagnose herself. Instead a doctor will have to determine whether she has *Candida* vaginitis or some other type of vaginal infection by performing a pelvic examination.

Your pediatrician can choose from several medications in treating yeast infections, including drugs called *clotrimazole, miconazole,* and *butoconazole.* Some are creams or suppositories, while others are tablets, given intravaginally. In most cases these drugs will work very well, although the infection might recur in some girls. To minimize the chances of a relapse, your doctor may recommend:

- a different kind of antibiotic if one is necessary for treating another condition

- avoiding tight clothing

- wearing cotton underwear (do not wear jeans without underwear)

- reducing her weight (if obesity is a factor)

- if she has diabetes, keeping it under good control

Bacterial Vaginosis

Doctors once believed that bacterial vaginosis was caused by a single organism called *Gardnerella vaginalis.* But recent research seems to indicate that a number of different organisms may be responsible. No matter what causes it, however, adolescent girls (and women) are more likely to contract this infection if they have had a previous sexually transmitted disease, if they have had multiple sexual partners, or if they are using an IUD.

Perhaps the most recognizable symptoms of bacterial vaginosis are a pungent "fishy" odor and a grayish-white discharge. Oral antibiotics are prescribed to treat the infection and usually must be taken for seven days.

Incidentally, in earlier years bacterial vaginosis went by a number of other names, including Gardnerella vaginitis and Hemophilus vaginalis vaginitis.

Trichomoniasis

Trichomoniasis is usually sexually transmitted, caused by the *Trichomonas vaginalis* parasite (a protozoan). The vaginal discharge tends to be greenish, brownish, or cream-colored. Although girls with this infection can be symptom-free, they may experience very intense vaginal burning and itching. These symptoms often surface during or just after a girl's period.

To treat trichomoniasis, your daughter's pediatrician will usually prescribe an oral antibiotic called *metronidazole.* Sexual partners need treatment as well, and intercourse should be avoided until the therapy is finished.

Vaginal Discharge: Final Comments

If your daughter notices a discharge of any kind, she should see her doctor right away. There's no telling when a discharge is something relatively minor such as a *Candida* infection or something far more serious such as gonorrhea. And the longer she waits to treat a serious infection, the bigger the problem it can become—and the more difficult it may be to treat.

Incidentally, if your daughter is pregnant and develops a vaginal infection, her doctor must be made aware of the pregnancy, and he will be careful about which medication to prescribe. Some antibiotics can potentially harm the fetus.

TOXIC SHOCK SYNDROME

Toxic shock syndrome (TSS) is a relatively new illness, first recognized in 1978. Nearly all of these infections have occurred in young women (under age thirty) who had used tampons during their periods.

There's still a lot we don't know about TSS. The exact cause, for instance, has not been pinpointed, although researchers believe *Staphylococcus aureus* bacteria is somehow involved, perhaps producing a toxin that sets the illness in motion.

You may recall that many cases of TSS in 1980 were associated with the use of a high-absorbency tampon called Rely. The manufacturer of that product voluntarily took it off the market, and since then TSS has been on the decrease. So although it is still a problem (about twenty cases each month nationwide), the concern associated with tampon use has declined. Nevertheless, if your daughter uses tampons, make sure she changes them *frequently*. She also should use the lowest-absorbency tampon appropriate for her particular flow. Some doctors recommend that girls wear pads at night.

Although TSS is now relatively uncommon, it's still a serious—and potentially fatal—infection. The initial symptoms of TSS include fever (about 102 degrees Fahrenheit or higher), a feeling of faintness, vomiting, diarrhea, chills, headaches, sore throat, a sunburn-type rash, and even a vaginal discharge. If your daughter should experience any of these symptoms while using tampons, she should immediately remove the tampon and call her doctor. If the physician diagnoses TSS, he or she will prescribe antibiotics as the primary form of treatment, along with the intravenous replacement of lost bodily fluids.

By the way, any girl who has already experienced an episode of TSS should probably stop using tampons for good, since recurrences of the syndrome can occur.

KEEPING COMMUNICATION LINES OPEN

Gynecological problems and sexually transmitted diseases are sometimes hard for parents and their teenagers to discuss. But because these matters are so critical to your adolescent's health, you need to make a special effort to open the lines of communication on these sensitive topics. Let your teenager know that you want her to come to you with her concerns about these issues, even if she might feel some embarrassment in doing so.

Your teenager also needs to be able to communicate with her sexual partner about these matters. And if you've already talked openly with her about them, she'll be better able to discuss them with a peer with whom she may be having sex. Ironically, even when adolescents are willing to sleep with a particular person, they're frequently too shy to ask, "Do you have gonorrhea or any other STD?" or "Do you know if you've ever been exposed to the AIDS virus?" These are important questions that can have *lifesaving* answers. And you need to encourage your teenager to ask them. If the responses are unsatisfactory, sex can wait.

One teenager complained, "I can't ask Bill questions like that. It would just ruin the whole mood."

Maybe so. But your adolescent's health—and life!—is more important than ruining the mood or hurting the feelings of a potential sex partner.

33

COMMON MEDICAL DISORDERS
OF ADOLESCENCE

Although most of us think of teenagers as healthy, strong, and energetic, they are no more immune to illness than any other person, young or old. But when disease strikes during adolescence—already a time when youngsters are preoccupied with the state of their body—teenagers may find themselves dealing with a number of conflicting emotions.

First, because of their excessive "body consciousness," they may overreact to relatively minor physical symptoms. They may interpret an unusual ache as "indisputable" evidence of a heart attack or potentially fatal cancer. On the other hand, they may tend to respond in just the opposite way—denying the potential seriousness of a problem due to the common adolescent feeling of invulnerability. To make matters worse, they might be unfamiliar with health-care facilities and procedures, deterring them from seeking care promptly. Even after a doctor finally makes a proper diagnosis, they may continue to deny the illness, leading to compliance problems with the prescribed treatment. In large part their social and emotional maturity, which evolves throughout adolescence, will govern this response to illness.

What diseases are most common in the teenage years? Actually, many disorders first appear or peak in frequency in this age group. The physical changes of puberty can influence both the development and the progression of several diseases, and in turn, diseases can affect the timing of puberty itself.

There's another fact that many parents find surprising: despite their view that adolescence is a carefree period of life, many of the physical ills that affect teenagers are stress-related. If youngsters are feeling anxiety due to problems at home, at school, or with peers, they may experience chronic fatigue, headaches, or chest or abdominal pain. All these disorders can have a psychological and/or organic basis. Even so, reassure your adolescent that these complaints are real, not imagined, and that they'll respond to medical care as well as counseling and stress-reduction techniques (See Part III).

However, whether your teenager's illnesses have a physical or a psychological basis, or both, it's more important than ever before for him to begin to build an open, trusting relationship with his doctor. After all, as he grows older he may become more reluctant to share his concerns about his body with you (often out of a desire to protect you). That happens with most teenagers; it's a natural and expected turn of events. And that's why he needs a health professional in whom he can confide—someone who can allay his fears about minor concerns and provide excellent care if a serious problem develops. The family should help him choose a doctor who's knowledgeable about the specific health concerns of adolescents, which are often quite different from the problems of early childhood and adulthood.

This is also a good time for teenagers to begin sharpening their own skills as medical consumers. Encourage them to make and keep medical appointments. Help them figure out whom to call, where to go, and what will happen to them when they get there. Tell them that their doctor always owes them a clear explanation of their illness and the recommended treatment, including specific instructions on the use of over-the-counter or prescription medications. And discourage them from "sharing" medications with friends who may have similar symptoms.

On those occasions when your adolescent does talk to you about his health concerns, make an attempt to understand them from a teenager's point of view. When he has a disease that affects physical appearance, for instance, bear in mind that it can have a major impact on his self-image. If your teenager has severe acne, your tendency might be to reassure him that he'll outgrow the condition and that it's not fatal; but although that may be quite true, it's both insensitive and ineffective advice for an adolescent in need of education, effective therapy, and long-term follow-up. As much as—or perhaps even more than—anyone else, a teenager needs compassion regarding his health problems.

Let's spend the remainder of this chapter looking at some of the more common adolescent medical disorders, with an emphasis on when to be concerned and what kind of treatment your teenager can expect.

INFECTIONS IN ADOLESCENCE

Vaccines have changed the face of health care in America and most other parts of the world. They have dramatically reduced the incidence of childhood infections such as polio, rubella, and mumps.

Even so, other infections are far from being obsolete. Varicella (chicken pox), for instance, remains very common. So does measles, which stubbornly persists in high school and college populations.

This should serve as a warning to parents: make sure your teenager has *up-to-date* immunizations (for polio, diphtheria, tetanus, rubella, mumps, and measles). Colleges have only recently begun to mandate the strict vaccination requirements that have been applied to elementary and secondary school students for many years. In particular, adolescent females need protection from rubella, due to the potential for serious birth defects associated with a rubella infection early in pregnancy.

Although the serious diseases mentioned above understandably grab the newspaper headlines when epidemics occur, the everyday infections (such as colds and sore throats) are the ones that really concern most adolescents. After all, they're the illnesses that usually keep teenagers home from school or force them to cancel a date. While childhood infections like croup and middle-ear disease become less common with the anatomical changes of adolescence, conditions like sore throats remain a frequent problem. Your child's tonsils, in fact, usually reach their peak size at the start of puberty, only to shrink to smaller adult dimensions during the teenage years.

What causes sore throats? Most are associated with viral infections such as influenza, but when a sore throat is accompanied by fever, doctors should consider a streptococcal infection (strep throat) and conduct a test to rule it out. A strep infection calls for antibiotic therapy to prevent the development of rheumatic fever (a heart disorder). Your teenager might suspect strep if he has a headache and stomach pains along with his sore throat; by contrast, a viral sore throat is more often associated with a runny nose, coughing, or conjunctivitis ("pink eye" or "red eye"). The only sure way to diagnose strep throat is with a lab test, such as a throat culture.

If your teenager has an eating disorder such as bulimia nervosa—in which frequent vomiting occurs—that can cause sore throats as well (See Chapter 29). And when throat soreness lasts more than a few days in an adolescent, infectious mononucleosis might be present.

Many people think of mononucleosis as one of the classic illnesses of teenagers, even though many children contract this infection during the preschool years, when it may be mistaken for only a simple cold or sore throat. For decades, "mono" has been called the "kissing disease" on the assumption that it's passed from person to person via oral contact. And, in fact, the evidence does point toward the spread of the disease through saliva. "Mono" is a viral illness, just like the common cold or the flu, even though it is somewhat harder to transmit. The specific virus that causes mono is called Epstein-Barr or EBV.

Common "mono" symptoms include fever, sore throat, headache, swollen lymph nodes, and extreme fatigue. However, studies show that one-third of teenagers infected with EBV have no symptoms; two-thirds have classic symptomatic "mono," but half of these are never properly diagnosed.

Even with the right diagnosis there is no specific treatment for mononucleosis, although in the most severe cases, when breathing difficulties arise (due to swelling of tissues in the back of the throat), hospitalization is necessary. Fortunately, however, "mono" is usually self-limiting, and within four to six weeks, 95 percent of patients are completely well. In the meantime, encourage a teenager with "mono" to rest at home, returning to his normal schedule *gradually* as he regains his strength. Since the spleen can sometimes enlarge with this infection, consult your doctor before your youngster resumes vigorous activity such as contact sports; if he returns to sports too early, he could risk rupturing his spleen.

In the past decade physicians have identified groups of adolescents and adults with the so-called "chronic fatigue syndrome," initially thought to be a chronic form of mononucleosis. These patients have prolonged, debilitating fatigue along with a variety of other symptoms, including headache, fever, sore throat, and swollen lymph nodes. Several viruses, including the Epstein-Barr virus, are probably to blame for part of this syndrome. The actual causes and frequency of this complex syndrome remain unclear, and psychological factors may play a role. For example, in the absence of infection, both prolonged fatigue and multiple physical complaints may be important indicators of serious adolescent depression.

SKIN DISORDERS

For many teenagers there is no more agonizing and frustrating condition than acne. It affects 85 percent of all adolescents to some degree. Most cases, fortunately, are mild to moderate (although even one pimple on prom night can "ruin" the entire evening). Approximately 5 percent of acne cases are so severe that scarring may occur.

To better understand acne, we need to dispel some common myths about what causes it. For instance, the presence and severity of your teenager's acne lesions bear no relation to his or her hygiene, diet, or sexual activity. Scrubbing the skin with harsh soaps will not cure acne, and might make it worse. A diet of french fries, pizza, and chocolate won't worsen it. Instead acne is caused by the effects of hormones on the skin's oil-producing glands—hormones that become active during puberty and stimulate the oil glands to produce a substance called *sebum.* This leads to inflammation and the appearance of redness, pustules, and cysts.

Most adolescents are extremely self-conscious about any and every prominent blemish. But since safe, effective acne therapy is readily available, encourage them to seek medical advice for this condition rather than resort to ineffective home remedies.

Most acne can be noticeably improved in four to eight weeks, although adolescents usually require long-term therapy to maintain this positive effect. Some impatient teenagers, however, find it unbearable to wait for progress to occur. As a result they'll often misuse acne medications, subscribing to the theory that if a little works well, a lot will work even better. But they're wrong. Abuse of these drugs usually results in severe side effects such as burning, dryness, or peeling of the skin, forcing doctors to completely stop the therapy.

When teenagers have only a mild form of acne, their doctor may recommend an over-the-counter cream or lotion containing benzoyl peroxide, which will usually manage the problem quite well. However, some forms of acne typically require something more potent—specifically, a prescription medication such as benzoyl peroxide gel, topical retinoic acid, or topical or oral antibiotics (such as tetracycline or erythromycin). In acne's severest form, called *cystic acne,* doctors may prescribe Accutane (13-cis-retinoic acid); this is a highly effective drug but one with potentially significant side effects (including birth defects if the medication is taken during pregnancy).

No matter what the doctor recommends, however, your adolescent can support that treatment by washing daily with a mild soap and by avoiding oil-based cosmetics. He or she should also stay away from oils or greases that might be encountered on the job—in a fast-food restaurant, for instance, or in a gas station or garage.

Although acne is the classic skin condition of adolescence, it is not the only one. Pityriasis rosea is an unusual rash that has a peak incidence during the teenage years. It may begin with a dry, scaling, "herald patch" on the trunk, followed by smaller patches in a "Christmas tree" distribution over the back, chest, and abdomen. The rash may be itchy and persist for up to six to twelve weeks, although it does not pose any dangers.

The cause of pityriasis is unknown. Even though there is no specific treatment, a physician should confirm the diagnosis since pityriasis symptoms can be confused with more serious skin problems, such as fungal infections.

Speaking of fungal infections, many of them—such as "athlete's foot" and "jock itch"—are related to hygiene. To avoid them, your teenager should reduce the moisture in these bodily areas by keeping them clean and dry. He also should avoid tight clothing and wear cotton socks and underwear. To treat these infections, the doctor may recommend topical antifungal creams.

BLOOD AND LYMPH NODE DISEASES

Although adolescents seem addicted to fast foods and frequent dieting, severe nutritional anemias are quite unusual in this age group. Iron deficiency anemia is most frequently seen in adolescent females with excessive menstrual blood loss, and for these girls doctors often advise increased dietary iron intake and ferrous sulfate supplements. Menstruating girls need eighteen milligrams of elemental iron per day, and most multivitamin pills should fulfill this requirement. So-called high-potency vitamin supplements won't provide any added health benefits. Strict vegetarian diets, incidentally, can also lead to anemia because of a vitamin B_{12} or folate deficiency (See Chapter 29).

Some teenagers complain to their doctor about chronic fatigue, commonly attributing it to anemia. As persuasive as the TV ads promoting adult iron supplements to treat fatigue and "tired blood" may be, this weariness is more likely to be a sign of depression or viral infection when it occurs in adolescents.

Other blood and lymph node disorders can play a significant role in the teenage years. For instance, some adolescents have inherited hemoglobin disorders, of which sickle-cell disease is one of the most ominous. An estimated 8 to 10 percent of black Americans carry the sickle-cell trait, which in itself is not associated with any health problems; but when both parents have the sickle-cell trait, the full-blown disease may occur in their children, and these victims will have no normal hemoglobin in their red blood cells.

There is no cure for sickle-cell disease, and in adolescence it can produce a number of serious health problems. These teenagers may have delayed pubertal development. They might also be hospitalized repeatedly due to severe pain in the abdomen and bones. Many of these youngsters, particularly boys with delayed pubertal development, often can be helped by temporary treatment with certain hormones. But as adults they will confront difficult decisions about contraception and pregnancy, since they face the possibility of passing the trait of the disease on to their own children. At that time they should seek genetic counseling.

Adolescents also sometimes have bleeding disorders such as hemophilia. These teenagers have a reduction, or in some cases an abnormality, of specific and essential blood-clotting activity. As a result they need to avoid normal risk-taking behavior (such as contact sports) that could increase the likelihood of bleeding.

Hemophiliacs have faced an additional problem in recent years. As if their bleeding disorder weren't difficult enough to cope with, the clotting factors used to treat their disease had been responsible for transmitting the human immunodeficiency virus (HIV)—the virus responsible for AIDS. Fortunately, however, with the recent availability of blood testing and heat treatment of clotting factors, the risk of hemophiliacs being treated with contaminated blood products has been almost completely eliminated.

Finally, have your teenagers ever detected lumps in the armpit, neck, or groin? If so, they might have become convinced that they had cancer and perhaps rushed off to the doctor for a checkup. In most cases, however, these lumps are only swollen lymph nodes, which have enlarged in response to recent or past infections. They'll slowly return to normal over a period of weeks or months.

CANCER

Unfortunately, cancer does strike teenagers; in fact it is the second leading cause of death among children five to fourteen years of age (six to seven deaths per 100,000). In the fifteen-to-nineteen age group only accidents, homicides, and suicides cause more deaths.

The most common kinds of cancer in teenagers include cancer of the blood (leukemia), lymph nodes (Hodgkin's disease), bone (osteogenic sarcoma, Ewing's sarcoma), and central nervous system (brain tumors). But leukemia is probably the one you've heard a lot about. It is the most common malignancy in teenagers, with symptoms that may include fever, bleeding difficulties, lethargy, poor appetite, weight loss, enlarged lymph nodes, and enlarged organs (such as the liver and spleen).

In young adults Hodgkin's disease is the most common cancer. It also occurs in teenagers, with symptoms such as fever, lethargy, weight loss, night sweats, and/or itchiness, along with enlarged lymph nodes (often in the neck but also in the chest and abdomen).

Bone tumors produce pain and swelling at the tumor site—frequently in the femur and tibia (usually in the knee area), but also sometimes the upper arm bone (the humerus), the ribs, and the pelvis. A bone fracture (or break) can occur in the area of the tumor as well.

When a brain tumor is present, the symptoms can vary, depending on the area of the brain that's involved. Typically, teenagers might develop headaches (often severe, worsening over time), vomiting (frequently without nausea), lethargy, irritability, blurred vision, dizziness, a stiff neck, and/or seizures.

As distressing as this information is, there's also a brighter side to it all. Death rates for cancer in children and teenagers are dropping! And the earlier a teenager seeks medical evaluation and treatment, the better the prognosis in most cases.

Here are some of the numbers: over the past thirty years death rates for those under fifteen years old have dropped dramatically—by 50 percent for leukemia, 80 percent for Hodgkin's disease, 50 percent for bone cancer, and 31 percent for other cancers. About half of all cancers in children and adolescents are treatable, producing long-term survival.

As with cancer in adults, early detection of the disease is extremely important in teenagers. And there are steps your adolescent can take to improve the chances of early discovery. For instance, if boys learn and routinely perform testicular self-examination, they can detect early the presence of cancer of the testes (seen in one to two of every 100,000 fifteen- to nineteen-year-olds and perhaps one in 10,000 young adults) and can usually be cured. Breast cancer is even more unusual in teenagers, but early detection through regular self-exams will significantly improve the chances of a cure (see Chapter 32). Also, these regular breast and testicular self-exams will establish good health habits in your adolescent to help him detect these tumors in adulthood, when they are more common.

Here are some other important guidelines:

- Discourage your teenager from smoking, using snuff, or chewing tobacco. Teenagers who don't smoke significantly reduce their risk of lung cancer in adulthood.

- Regular Pap smear screening of sexually active teenage females can help identify cervical cancer early and improve the chances of curing it. Also, bear in mind that contact with many sexual partners, especially if sexual intercourse has started in early adolescence, exposes a young female to infections like herpes or venereal warts, which have been linked to cervical cancer in adulthood. Thus, if she changes her sexual practices, she'll reduce her risk of developing such cancer. (See Chapter 32.)

- If a doctor prescribed the synthetic estrogen diethylstilbestrol (DES) for a woman when she was pregnant, her offspring (exposed while in the womb) have a small but definite risk of developing genital cancer (and other abnormalities), which can be detected after puberty develops. Many pregnant women used this drug from the late 1940s to the early 1970s to reduce the chances of a miscarriage. Their female teenage children need regular gynecological evaluations (especially if problems, such as vaginal bleeding, occur) to identify cancer if it occurs. As many as 1.5 million female children were exposed to DES; although male offspring can develop difficulties as well, cancer is not one of them (see Chapter 32).

- The addition of bulk (fiber) to your teenager's diet may help prevent colon cancer later in adulthood.

Thus educating your teenager can be lifesaving. Yes, cancer is terrifying, but the news is improving. Education and better medical care are helping. If your teenager has a family history or a personal condition that increases his chances of developing cancer, find out from his physician what he can do to reduce the odds. Children are surviving cancer!

HEAD AND NECK PROBLEMS

Stress-related headaches are perhaps the most common health complaint of adolescence. These tension headaches are usually characterized by steady pain on both sides of the forehead that radiates to the neck. As the name implies, they can be provoked by anxiety, whether related to final exams or a family crisis. In many cases the pain can be alleviated with nonprescription analgesics (acetaminophen, aspirin, and others), stress reduction techniques (including exercise), and/or counseling.

By contrast, migraine headaches involve intense, pounding pain, often concentrated on one side of the forehead and sometimes associated with visual distortions, motor weakness, nausea, and vomiting. (Dizziness, numbness, or tingling in the hands is occasionally a sign of migraines, particularly if they involve one side of the body; but more often such symptoms are present in both sides of the body and are associated with hyperventilation and anxiety.)

If your teenager has migraines, many factors can trigger them, including stress, certain foods (cheese, chocolate, red wine), menstrual periods, and birth control pills. There's probably also a history of these headaches in other family members. Birth control pills probably should be used with caution in patients with migraine headaches and should not be used at all if they appear to cause or worsen migraines.

Although your adolescent may find that simple analgesics such as aspirin or acetaminophen can effectively manage migraine pain, he may require stronger prescription drugs. In some cases a doctor will prescribe these and other prescription medications for intermittent or even daily use as a preventive measure.

Headaches are also sometimes related to temporomandibular joint (TMJ) syndrome. TMJ is usually caused by a misalignment of the jawbone due to an accident or sometimes grinding of the teeth (bruxism). In addition to headaches, teenagers with TMJ may also experience ear pain, neck pain, and/or difficulty chewing. Your adolescent's pediatrician may prescribe mild analgesics, but if they're inadequate, she will usually refer your youngster to an oral surgeon, who may fit him with an appliance to correct the jaw misalignment.

Headaches also can be a warning sign of serious intracranial disease such as brain tumors and vascular malformations. If adolescents complain of headaches that wake them from sleep; occur first thing in the morning; are always located on one side; increase in intensity during coughing, sneezing, or a bowel movement; or are associated with nausea, vomiting, or a stiff neck, a doctor should evaluate them. If other symptoms occur, too—double vision, a change in school performance, personality change, or problems with coordination—a neurological specialist should make the diagnosis.

There's another problem in this region of the body—namely, dental caries or cavities—that's actually *less* of a concern in adolescence than in early childhood. However, even though the incidence of cavities declines with age, the risk of gingival (gum) disease increases. Taken together, caries and gingival disease afflict more than 90 percent of teenagers, making routine dental care an essential health practice. Encouraging proper dental habits (such as regularly brushing and flossing, chewing only sugar-free gum, reducing sugar intake, having regular dental evaluations) during childhood and adolescence will increase the likelihood of having normal teeth in adulthood. Also, if your adolescent's teeth are malpositioned, orthodontic correction (i.e., braces) is best accomplished during puberty, while the facial bones are growing.

Several other conditions in the head and neck area need to be mentioned. Thyroid disorders, for instance, are more common in adolescent females than males. These problems can range from thyroid gland enlargement (goiter) to overactivity (hyperthyroidism) to underactivity (hypothyroidism).

How can your teenager tell if something is wrong with the thyroid? In adolescent females the menstrual cycle is a sensitive indicator of thyroid dysfunction. Hyperthyroidism, for example, is caused by an overproduction of thyroid hormone; it may provoke not only a cessation of menses but also tremors, anxiety, weight loss, flushing, and diarrhea. By contrast, hypothyroidism may result in a prolonged, heavy menstrual flow, plus weight gain, fatigue, coldness, and constipation. Weight gain without these associated symptoms, however, is probably not related to a thyroid problem; in fact nearly all cases of obesity have nothing to do with the thyroid (see Chapter 30). To treat thyroid problems, your teenager's pediatrician may recommend replacement thyroid hormones or suppression of the thyroid, whichever is more appropriate.

Some adolescents have epilepsy (seizure disorders), which may begin or continue during the teenage years. Treatment for epilepsy has improved dramatically in recent years, and drug therapy can completely control most seizures. However, that hasn't completely solved the difficulties associated with epilepsy, since compliance with daily medication schedules has remained quite a problem among teenagers.

If your youngster has epilepsy, and he frequently "forgets" to take his medication, the following motivating strategy may work: remind him that most states require a seizure-free interval of several months (or longer) before an individual with epilepsy can obtain a driver's license. If he really wants his license—and what teenager doesn't?—this may be the incentive he needs to take his anticonvulsant medication conscientiously and regularly. Also, remind him that the use of alcohol may induce seizures, especially if he takes his antiseizure medications erratically. Some studies show that when girls take both oral contraceptives and antiseizure medications, drug interactions could impair the effectiveness of the birth control pills, posing a small but clear risk of pregnancy.

Finally, "cold sores" on the lips—usually due to nongenital herpes virus infections—may appear in teenagers during times of stress, illness, or menstrual periods. After the initial infection the virus will remain dormant in the body, only to resurface periodically with new outbreaks, again in the area of the lips. These cold sores or blisters resolve slowly on their own over several days, but until they do, they can be quite contagious (see Chapter 32).

DIABETES

Diabetes mellitus is the most common endocrine disorder in young people. Diabetes is an autoimmune disease—that is, a disease in which the body "attacks" itself. It often begins between eleven and fourteen years of age, but it can develop at any time.

Diabetes occurs when the pancreas stops producing any or enough of the hormone called insulin. This insulin is necessary for sugar and starches to break down into blood sugar (or glucose), the body's primary fuel. Symptoms include increased thirst, heightened appetite, frequent urination, and severe weight loss. Some girls also develop serious yeast vaginitis (see Chapter 32).

When diabetics initially see their physician for this illness, about 15 percent of them are in a state called *ketoacidosis*—characterized by rapid breathing, extreme lethargy (even coma), severe dehydration, high blood sugar levels, and other difficulties. Emergency treatment (with intravenous insulin and fluids) is necessary to return these individuals to a normal state. Sometimes the diabetes appears to improve and these youngsters require less insulin (the so-called "honeymoon phase"). Eventually, however, they'll regularly need a fixed amount of this hormone (typically thirty to seventy units each day).

Diabetes is not an easy disease to live with, particularly for young people. It's a real challenge for an adolescent to monitor his daily caloric and activity needs to administer the correct dosage of insulin. Too much insulin can cause very low blood sugar (hypoglycemia), which can produce severe fatigue and even fainting. Too little insulin leads to elevated blood sugar.

Diabetes is also a classic example of a chronic illness that can seriously affect a young person's psychological development. (See Chapter 34.) Many teenagers with diabetes have real trouble accepting their disease. No one wants to feel different from his peers—because of an illness or for any other reason. Consequently, adolescents often wish they could just ignore their disease. Some teenagers absolutely refuse to conscientiously take care of themselves. But even those who are careful find it hard to follow the rules (diet, exercise, insulin injections) all the time.

However, we can't overemphasize this point: maintaining proper control of diabetes is extremely important. Without it the risk of diabetic complications— kidney failure, blindness, vascular problems, heart difficulties—increases significantly.

What can you do as the parent of a diabetic? Meet with his physician to discuss the prescribed treatments and be sure you and your adolescent fully understand them. Again, your teenager needs to follow these recommendations carefully. Also, review the principles discussed in the next chapter (Chapter 34), which will help both of you deal with the disease better. You can attend parent groups, too—that is, groups of mothers and fathers of diabetics who meet regularly to discuss their mutual concerns. Find one in your community by contacting the local chapter of the American Diabetes Association or the Juvenile Diabetes Foundation.

If your child is not taking good care of his diabetes, discuss this problem with his pediatrician to explore options such as counseling. Fortunately, teenagers with diabetes now have several positive research developments to look forward to— insulin pumps, pancreas transplants, the artificial pancreas—that may motivate them to manage their disease more conscientiously. If your adolescent keeps his diabetes in good control over many years, he'll be in a better position to take advantage of these and future breakthroughs.

CHEST DISEASES

At the first sign of chest pain most people think the worst: heart attack. With teenagers, however, a heart attack is rarely what's taking place. Heart attacks are extremely uncommon in children and adolescents; when young people experience chest pain, the causes are more likely to be musculoskeletal conditions of the chest wall, hyperventilation, and infections of the lung (pneumonia) or its lining. Let's briefly discuss these conditions as well as some other adolescent concerns involving the chest:

Costochondritis, a localized inflammation of the chest wall, can occur at any age but is actually more common in younger age groups. The cause is unknown, although it commonly provokes pain and tenderness along the border of the breastbone where the ribs attach. The pain may persist for weeks, although heat and anti-inflammatory drugs (aspirin, ibuprofen) may relieve the symptoms.

Hyperventilation—or heavy, deep breathing due to anxiety—is common in adolescent females. It's often accompanied by dizziness, weakness, tingling in the arms, and chest pain. Even though breathing may be labored, no wheezing occurs. Ironically, most people who hyperventilate aren't even aware they're doing it. The treatment: breathing into a paper bag is often helpful in ending the episode.

When breathing difficulties occur in conjunction with a persistent cough, your adolescent may be experiencing a respiratory infection (such as pneumonia) or asthma. The word *pneumonia* sends up all kinds of warning flags for many parents. It's very disturbing to them—even though most of that anxiety is unwarranted. After all, this lung inflammation is generally quite treatable in adolescents.

Infection with a bacteriumlike microbe called *Mycoplasma pneumoniae* is the most common treatable cause of pneumonia in older children and adolescents. It's often accompanied not only by a severe cough but also by fever, chills, headache, and abdominal pain. It's highly contagious too—capable of spreading rapidly through families, schools, and dormitories. However, this *Mycoplasma* infection usually responds to antibiotic therapy with erythromycin or tetracycline. The coughing, though, may persist for weeks, whether the infection is caused by *Mycoplasma* or by a virus. Another common microbial cause, *Streptococcus pneumoniae,* responds readily to penicillin.

Now, what about asthma? It can develop, be outgrown, or continue in adolescence. If your teenager is an asthmatic, you probably are quite familiar with the factors that can trigger his wheezing—such as infections, allergies, and/or stress. Asthma in adolescents may also be associated with childhood eczema (a skin inflammation), as well as "hay fever" symptoms such as sneezing, a runny nose, and itchy eyes. Some adolescents may experience asthma—with its coughing, wheezing, chest tightness, or shortness of breath—during or after exercise.

If your teenager works conscientiously with his pediatrician, he usually can effectively control his asthma. Doctors may recommend reducing exposure to "precipitants" (such as pollen grains), and they might prescribe preventive therapy such as daily inhalation of cromolyn through a special inhaler. They may also recommend oral theophylline drugs or other medication (such as metaproterenol, terbutaline, albuterol, beclomethasone, and others) to help relax the airway. If your teenager's asthma is induced by exercise, he may respond well to inhaled cromolyn sodium or albuterol prior to activity. By carefully using his medication(s) he can lead a full life, including participation in sports. Preventive therapy—and monitoring of your youngster's lung function by his doctor—are very important.

Remind your adolescent that he should not take his asthma lightly. It can be a life-threatening illness. Even so, many adolescents neglect their preventive therapy, only to end up overusing their inhalants when wheezing occurs. Having asthma is an added reason for this teenager to avoid exposure to smoke (as from tobacco or marijuana).

Teenagers also may have other chest problems, including congenital chest deformities, causing the breastbone (sternum) to protrude or become depressed (pectus carinatum or pectus excavatum respectively). Since teenagers are so conscious about their physical appearance, this condition can be devastating. Boys in particular may be reluctant to go shirtless at the beach or disrobe in the locker room, for fear of ridicule from their peers. Doctors will recommend surgical correction only in extreme cases of this chest deformity, partly because of the prominent scar usually left behind.

Similar anxiety often occurs in males with pubertal breast development, called *gynecomastia*. If your son has this condition, reassure him that while this extra breast tissue may be embarrassing, the excess tissue occurs in one-third to one-half of normal boys and will usually disappear on its own within several months. Surgical correction (mastectomy) is possible for unusual cases.

Now, what about adolescent heart problems? As we already pointed out, heart attacks in adolescents are rare, although other cardiac conditions can occur. Mitral valve prolapse, or the "floppy valve syndrome," in which a heart valve is not functioning properly, is one of the most common. The pediatrician can often diagnose this condition during a routine physical exam, using a stethoscope to detect the distinctive "clicking" sound associated with this condition. An echo-cardiogram will probably confirm the diagnosis.

If your teenager has mitral valve prolapse, don't panic. It's usually not a serious condition, and most people are symptom-free. However, chest pain and irregular heart rhythms can occur, and if they do, the doctor may prescribe drugs such as beta-blockers (e.g., propranolol) to control them. Your adolescent also may need to take antibiotics before dental and surgical procedures to reduce the risk of infection of the heart valves (endocarditis).

High blood pressure (hypertension) is another disease generally thought of as an older person's illness. Even so, initial signs of it may surface during adolescence (and even childhood). A school nurse, for example, may be the first to recognize it in a particular teenager. The nurse will obtain blood pressure values in an environment less anxiety-provoking than a doctor's office, where stress may elevate the readings. If repeated measurements confirm an abnormal blood pressure, then your teenager needs further evaluation.

Hypertension is a potentially serious problem, although in adolescents it can usually be well controlled. Your family's pediatrician may recommend weight reduction, aerobic exercise, a cutback in dietary sodium, stress management, and possibly medication. If your adolescent smokes, the doctor will probably insist that he stop.

Finally, many Americans—including adolescents—are becoming more conscientious about their blood cholesterol level and what it means. Cholesterol screening programs are now more widely available for teenagers, in the hope of detecting those few youngsters with marked elevations. When adolescents fall into this high-risk category, they are candidates for aggressive therapy with a low-fat, low-cholesterol diet and perhaps medication. Some doctors also recommend the measurement of blood fats (triglycerides and cholesterol) before prescribing birth control pills, since these contraceptives can adversely affect these readings.

Incidentally, your teenager may be at an even greater risk if an immediate relative—such as a parent—has experienced a heart attack or a stroke before age fifty. Even if your youngster has a blood cholesterol level that his pediatrician considers normal, a sensible diet low in saturated fat and cholesterol still makes good sense as a way to prevent heart and blood vessel disease in the future.

ABDOMINAL DISORDERS

When teenagers complain about sudden, severe abdominal pain, their pediatrician may initially think of a number of possible causes, including an infection in the gastrointestinal tract or liver, food poisoning, appendicitis, kidney stones, gallstones, or an ulcer.

On the other hand, when this abdominal pain is *chronic*—a common phenomenon among adolescents—an accurate diagnosis can be more difficult. The pediatrician will look carefully at a number of factors, including other symptoms that may be present. If the pain is cramplike and spasmodic, without weight loss or vomiting, teenagers could have stress-related "irritable bowel syndrome," characterized by constipation and/or diarrhea. To treat this condition, some nutritional changes are in order, specifically a high-fiber diet. Doctors also may recommend counseling to address specific stresses in a teenager's life. Prescribed medications help some individuals, too.

You've probably heard a lot about fiber in recent years. Research now shows that when constipation occurs, it's often due in part to an adolescent's preference for snacks and fast foods with low-fiber content, eaten on the run. But by adding high-fiber foods—bran, salads, fruits, and vegetables—to the diet, teenagers can begin experiencing normal bowel patterns again. In the process, not only will their abdominal pain disappear, but they also might reduce their risk of heart disease and certain forms of cancer (such as colon cancer) during their adult years.

What if your adolescent's persistent abdominal pain is accompanied by weight loss, delayed pubertal development, or bloody, mucous diarrhea? This may indicate ulcerative colitis or Crohn's disease—both of which are treatable inflammatory bowel disorders. If she experiences cramplike pain and diarrhea following ingestion of milk products, she may have a lactose intolerance—that is, her body may lack the enzyme needed to digest these foods; a milk-free diet can effectively manage this condition, or the doctor may recommend adding the missing enzyme to her nutritional program.

Chronic diarrhea may also be caused by infectious organisms such as *Giardia lamblia,* an intestinal parasite that can enter the body from a contaminated water source. Tests conducted on the stool can usually diagnose this condition. Warn your teenager about the risks of drinking from mountain streams while hiking and camping, since this is a common means of contracting a *Giardia* infection.

Let's review several other possible causes of abdominal pain. Stomach ulcers can sometimes occur in adolescents and are characterized by burning upper abdominal pain that can last for several hours. The symptoms, which can be relieved by food or antacids, tend to worsen at night and may wax and wane over several weeks and months. Drug therapy is highly effective in controlling ulcers, and thus the bland diet usually recommended in the past is considered passé by many doctors.

If your adolescent's pain is in the right upper abdomen—and if he's also experiencing jaundice and loss of appetite—he may have hepatitis, or inflammation of the liver. This condition may be caused by the hepatitis A virus transmitted in food or water or the hepatitis B virus contracted from blood or semen. Other viral infections such as mononucleosis can also cause hepatitis, as can substance abuse (especially when drugs are inhaled or injected).

Fortunately, most forms of acute hepatitis are self-limiting, and symptoms will disappear after several weeks. About 10 percent of hepatitis B patients, however, may develop a chronic, symptom-free form of the disease that will increase their risk of liver cancer. They can also transmit this disease, even when no symptoms are present. Researchers have recently produced a hepatitis B vaccine, now available for individuals at high risk of infection due to their lifestyle or occupational exposure.

There is an additional type of STD that can cause right upper abdominal pain—perihepatitis (or the Fitz-Hugh–Curtis Syndrome). It is caused by gonorrhea or chlamydia (see Chapter 32) and if caught early, is fully curable with antibiotics.

Next, let's briefly mention gallstones. They are a common problem in older women, but adolescent girls can also develop them. If your daughter is obese or is using birth control pills, she may be particularly at risk. Gallstones can also occur in conjunction with certain types of anemia (so-called *hemolytic anemia*), in which a breakdown of blood cells causes stone formation.

Although many people with gallstones have no symptoms, others experience severe pain in the upper abdomen. Your family's pediatrician will confirm the diagnosis of gallstones with an ultrasound examination. If your teenager has severe symptoms, the doctor may recommend surgical removal of the stones and the gallbladder.

BLADDER AND
GENITAL PROBLEMS

Most kids outgrow nighttime bed-wetting (nocturnal enuresis) in early childhood. But it persists in as many as 3 percent of adolescents, usually males. And not surprisingly, it can cause considerable distress, embarrassment, and ridicule.

For most of these teenagers bed-wetting clears up on its own by late adolescence. In the meantime some effective therapies are available. Your doctor may recommend conservative measures such as restricting fluids after supper and going to the bathroom just before bedtime. If that doesn't work, he or she may suggest a bell and pad device, which will awaken your adolescent with an alarm at the first sign of urine touching a sensor placed in his pajamas. With this mechanism he'll gradually learn to awaken on his own when he feels the urge to urinate—before ever passing any urine. Prescription medications such as imipramine (Tofranil) may be useful in controlling this problem too.

The bladder is also the most common site of urinary tract infections in adolescents. These bladder infections (called *cystitis*) are far more common in females than in males, due to a shorter urethra (the tube through which urine flows), making it easier for infectious organisms to make their way into the bladder. A bladder infection can occasionally occur shortly after the initiation of sexual intercourse (so-called "honeymoon cystitis").

Symptoms include burning on urination, an increased need to urinate, and cloudy or foul-smelling urine. A urine culture will confirm a bladder infection as the cause, and your teenager's doctor will prescribe antibiotics. If the infections persist or recur, a more thorough medical evaluation may be warranted to look for other conditions, such as a kidney or bladder infection.

Incidentally, if the same urinary symptoms occur and cystitis is *not* the cause, acute urethral syndrome may be present. This is a sexually transmitted infection in females, often caused by the bacteriumlike *Chlamydia* organism; other organisms have been implicated as well.

Sometimes, in a routine analysis of urine as part of a physical exam, the laboratory may detect protein or blood cells in the urine. This can often be traced back to vigorous physical activity, and in small amounts this is usually an innocuous finding. However, if large quantities are present, this can be a worrisome condition. It may indicate significant kidney problems requiring further evaluation.

Adolescent boys sometimes complain to their doctors about problems involving their testicles, specifically pain or scrotal masses. If the pain begins suddenly, it may be due to trauma or a twisting (or torsion) of one testicle; this will reduce the blood supply to the area, and without quick correction of the condition (typically with surgery) it could result in death of the testicle, sometimes in a matter of hours. Thus, seek medical attention immediately if this testicular torsion is suspected.

Testicular pain frequently occurs in two other circumstances. One is epididymitis, usually a sexually transmitted infection (due to chlamydia or gonorrhea—see Chapter 32) in adolescents that responds to treatment with appropriate antibiotics. The other is testicular congestion, provoked by extended sexual stimulation without ejaculation.

If your son notices a lump or mass in the scrotum, his pediatrician will investigate a number of potential causes. An inguinal hernia is one possibility. It occurs when the abdominal contents slip into the scrotum through a defect in the abdominal wall. When this hernia is present, surgical repair will be required.

A so-called varicocele also can cause a scrotal lump. This is an abnormally distended vein, present in at least 10 percent of males on the left side of the scrotum, which can produce swelling above the testicle. Varicoceles have been associated with infertility in some adult males. If your family pediatrician diagnoses this condition in your teenager, the doctor may recommend surgical repair to remove the vein(s) causing the problem, particularly under the following circumstances: if the varicocele is large, causes discomfort, or if the testicles grow asymmetrically during puberty, with a smaller testis on the side where the problem exists.

A final warning about lumps: be sure your son sees his doctor at the first sign of any testicular mass. Cancer of the testis is the most common malignant tumor in males aged fifteen to thirty-four. Even so, the prognosis is usually good with *early* detection. Have your son ask his doctor to teach him how to regularly self-examine his testicles.

There's another area in which the pediatrician can be helpful. If your son is uncircumcised, he may have concerns about his penile appearance, which will be different from most males since the majority of boys in the U.S. had this surgery as newborns. Your doctor can reassure him that he's quite normal and give him specific information about retracting the foreskin for proper hygiene. In the rare instance that your teenager is unable to fully retract the foreskin (a condition called *phimosis*), elective circumcision is indicated.

BONE AND
JOINT DISORDERS

Before your teenagers' adolescence is over, they will probably have their share of sprains, strains, and possibly bone fractures associated with accidents and sports injuries (see Chapter 31). In addition, they might experience one or more chronic bone conditions that can cause pain and disability.

Scoliosis, or curvature of the spine, affects 10 percent of adolescents to some degree. Although nearly as many males as females have spinal curves, seven times more girls than boys develop curves that require treatment. Most schools conduct scoliosis screening programs in youngsters prior to puberty and before completion of bone growth. Careful screening is especially important during pubertal development, when your child moves from SMR (sex maturity rating) 2 to 4 (see Chapter 5). If the condition is mild, doctors will keep a close eye on the disorder. A moderate, progressive curvature may require wearing a spinal brace for several months or longer. Severe curvature can require surgery in which metal rods are implanted to straighten the spinal column; at the same time, the surgeon will perform a spinal fusion to maintain the correction.

Don't let scoliosis go untreated. It can progress into a major deformity, severely affecting the chest and lungs and causing discomfort and disability.

Back pain, although not common, does occur in teenagers. In this age group simple muscle strain is less often the cause of this pain than in adults. More frequently it may be related to conditions such as infections, stress fractures, or rheumatoid arthritis. The incidence of a slipped disk among teenagers is quite small.

Depending on the cause of the back pain, the pediatrician may prescribe rest, a brief period of limited activity, anti-inflammatory drugs (aspirin or ibuprofen), and heat. He or she should teach your youngster back-strengthening exercises as well as proper techniques for sitting, lifting, and exercising. If the pain persists, if it radiates down the legs, or if the sensation in the legs changes, the doctor may conduct some further evaluation.

Bone and joint pain doesn't occur only in the back. The knees are another common site of discomfort. Osgood-Schlatter disease and patellofemoral syndrome are two examples of "overuse" syndromes resulting in adolescent knee pain. Both of these conditions are due to repeated injury to growing bones (also see Chapter 31).

Despite its imposing name, Osgood-Schlatter disease is a benign condition, most commonly seen during the rapid growth spurt of puberty, usually in very active boys and girls. Your adolescent may complain of a painful, tender lump at the top of the bone below one or both knees. Again, this condition is caused by overuse; your pediatrician will prescribe rest, restriction of vigorous activities when symptoms are present, ice packs, and aspirin or ibuprofen. Casting is rarely required.

Patellofemoral syndrome (chondromalacia patellae) is another painful disorder of the knee and the kneecap, more commonly seen in adolescent females than males. Why females? Doctors believe it's related to the broadening of the female pelvis during puberty, which places a disproportionate stress on the knees. These teenagers will often be unable to sit comfortably for prolonged periods, experiencing pain while driving in a car or sitting in a movie theater. They'll also feel discomfort after movements that stress the knees, such as deep knee bends, walking up stairs, or certain other athletic activities. The treatment: as well as symptomatic care with ice packs and analgesics, your doctor may recommend straight-leg-raising exercises to strengthen the thigh muscles, thus stabilizing the knees. In severe cases orthopedic surgery is necessary.

A rare but serious condition involving the hip is also worth mentioning. Called *slipped capital femoral epiphysis,* it is caused by a displacement of the head of the femur (the long bone that fits in the hip socket). This condition usually first appears around the time of puberty, causing thigh or knee pain and a limp, often followed by hip pain. It's more common in overweight adolescents, it may occur in both hips, and it urgently requires surgical management.

Finally, if your teenagers have a habit of "cracking" their joints (such as the knuckles), don't become overly concerned. Yes, the popping noise may drive you crazy, but it produces no permanent injury. It's one of life's nuisances that you should try to overlook.

34

THE SPECIAL PROBLEMS
OF CHRONICALLY ILL
TEENAGERS

*F*or a parent there is perhaps no worse nightmare. Your child becomes ill, and the symptoms persist for many days and even weeks. Then, after a seemingly endless series of tests, your pediatrician gives you the ominous news: Your youngster has cancer. Or heart disease. Or rheumatoid arthritis. Diabetes. Epilepsy. Cystic fibrosis. Hemophilia.

The number of teenagers with chronic diseases like these isn't clear. Some data suggest that between 10 and 15 percent of children in America have a chronic health problem. Other studies estimate that there are more than two million individuals under age seventeen with physical limitations. For most parents, however, the precise numbers don't really matter. If your teenager is afflicted, the statistics couldn't be any worse.

Of course, even without a serious illness, adolescence is a difficult time of life. Teenagers are experiencing enormous physical changes that transform them from children to adults. They're already quite preoccupied with their body image, and if a serious illness suddenly threatens their physical attractiveness, adolescence can become quite traumatic. To further complicate matters, the normal psychological and emotional adjustments of this stage of life can become aggravated by the stresses and strains that inevitably accompany a chronic disease.

How challenging can a long-term illness be? Think back to your own adolescence and how important it was to be just like everyone else—and then imagine being very different because of a chronic disease. Picture yourself as a diabetic and not being able to eat what your friends do at parties. Or a cancer patient who has lost your hair and feels extremely self-conscious at school. Or a youngster whose heart disease restricts your physical activity, relegating you to the sidelines while your friends are in the heat of the action.

Almost without exception a teenager diagnosed with a serious disease will have to adapt to some major changes in day-to-day life. Fortunately, however, adolescents tend to be resilient, and most will learn to accept the limitations that illness imposes on them. No, it won't be easy, and your youngster may experience some anxiety and anger along the way. But with your support he'll make the adjustments required of him, however unwelcome they may be.

Make sure your teenager is under the care of a doctor who can help in this adaptation process. Unfortunately, recent studies show that over one-third of adolescents with a chronic illness do not have a physician whom they see for even the most general health issues, such as acne, tension headaches, or other problems. Youngsters with chronic illnesses (such as cystic fibrosis, leukemia, congenital heart disease, and others) are living longer than ever before—in fact, more than 80 percent now survive into adulthood; but they need a physician's care to realize this potential for an extended life.

When you first think of all these chronic diseases of adolescence, they seem to have little in common. Cancer, for instance, consists of a group of cells in the wrong place that can be life-threatening by growing at their original site or by spreading to other parts of the body. Diabetes is a disease of abnormal insulin secretion, associated with conditions such as high blood sugar. Juvenile rheumatoid arthritis is an inflammation of the joints and organs, and like these others, believed to be related to a malfunctioning of the body's own immune system. The causes of each are different; the treatments vary considerably (see Chapter 32).

Nevertheless, the adolescents afflicted with these diverse diseases have a lot in common. They share many of the same adjustment problems. They have to cope with similar types of anxieties. They all have periods of apprehension, rage, self-pity, and bitterness.

In this chapter we'll concentrate on those issues that are universal in adolescents with chronic illnesses, no matter what the specific disease. As you'll see, the crises and concerns of an adolescent with cancer are often quite similar to those faced by a teenager with epilepsy, heart disease, diabetes, kidney disease, hemophilia, or another long-term illness.

STRIVING FOR INDEPENDENCE

"I want to do more things for myself. I don't want to have to count on my parents to take care of me. So this disease is really frustrating. It's keeping me in a straitjacket."

As we've emphasized in other parts of this book, adolescence is a time when youngsters want to distance themselves from their parents. Rather than leaning on Mom and Dad, they'll begin forming strong bonds with peers. And at every opportunity they'll strive to assert their independence and begin feeling some of the freedom of adulthood.

But if a chronic disease is part of their life, it can frustrate all those natural yearnings. They may be bedridden much of the time. They may not be able to socialize as freely with their friends as they'd like. They may feel trapped by the wheezing of their asthma or the constant hospital visits associated with their leukemia. To a large extent they may feel they've lost control over their present and their future and that their fate is in someone else's hands.

Yes, as we've already suggested, they'll eventually learn to adapt to the situation at hand. But unfortunately, teenagers often have a more difficult time accepting their fate than younger children. When youngsters have been diagnosed with a chronic disease in infancy or early childhood, they've had to cope with their illness for most or all of their lives. They've learned to accept their diabetes or their cystic fibrosis at a stage of life when even healthy children are dependent on their parents.

Adolescence, however, is different. If your teenager has a chronic illness, he may watch with sadness as his friends start to experience the excitement associated with autonomy and self-reliance—just when he still needs you more than ever. As his peers are withdrawing from their parents, he may be forced to be very dependent on you, day by day, perhaps even hour by hour. This reality can set the stage for outbursts of frustration and conflict between you and your youngster. While you try to care for and shelter him through his illness, he may become increasingly bitter about the disease that keeps him dependent and the parents who—with all the best intentions—seem to be keeping him childlike while he feels a need for increasing independence.

As a parent of a chronically ill teenager, how should you react to this difficult predicament? Within the limitations that his disease imposes he needs to lead as

Sexuality and Dating

"**O**h, come on. You really don't believe my daughter is thinking about sex, do you? She's so ill that I can't imagine anything is on her mind but her disease."

If that's your attitude, you need to change it. Yes, a chronically ill teenager has some major distractions that healthy adolescents don't have to confront. But *every* teenager thinks about sex and dating; ill youngsters have many of the same sexual concerns and anxieties as their disease-free peers.

Remember, this is the time of life when young people come to terms with their emerging sexuality. They're learning about themselves and their bodies and developing self-confidence with the opposite sex. They're forming a sexual identity and beginning to experiment with their sexual feelings and desires in dating situations. (See Chapter 14.)

Even so, parents (and even some doctors) tend to treat chronically ill teenagers as asexual. But they're not. Despite their disease or disability, most can still enjoy a normal sex life as they mature. And as a parent you need to help your adolescent prepare for that.

Of course a chronic illness imposes some complicating factors in all of this. For instance, perhaps the disease has slowed your teenager's physical growth. Or maybe she's confined to a wheelchair or has other physical limitations that create anxiety in her own mind about how she'll be able to function sexually.

If your son has cerebral palsy, for instance, he'll still have the same sexual needs and feelings as a healthy adolescent, although he may wonder if he'll ever be able to date and how he'll be accepted by a potential girlfriend. If your daughter has epilepsy, she may be terribly concerned that she'll have a seizure during an intimate moment with her boyfriend.

These are the kinds of issues you'll have to deal with, and your teenager will need them addressed to her satisfaction. If they're left unresolved, she may respond by isolating herself from members of the opposite sex. Or she might react in just the opposite way—by becoming overly aggressive and promiscuous, desperately seeking acceptance from her peers.

To help your chronically ill teenager adjust in a positive way to this important aspect of her life, talk to her when the right moments appear, as though she were healthy. That means following the same guidelines about sexuality that we described in Chapter 14. Discuss everything from basic physiological functioning (including preparation for menstruation) to protected sexual intercourse. Ask her about her special concerns related to her illness and talk about each of them. Is she worried about being attractive to boys? Is she afraid she'll never be able to have a baby? If you can't answer some of these questions, ask her doctor for help.

normal a life as possible—in school, with friends, in the home environment. Whenever possible, respect his need for autonomy. Let him experience some control over his life, permitting him to make even seemingly insignificant decisions about the management of his disease.

For example, perhaps you've faced the situation of hovering over your diabetic teenager, reminding him, "It's eight o'clock. It's time to take your insulin. Here's your needle. Here's the insulin." As well-meaning as you may be, there's a better way to handle this scenario, particularly if it allows your adolescent to feel some sense of control over the situation. So why not give him the option of taking his injection at seven o'clock or 8:30? He'll benefit from even such small opportunities that make him feel that *he's* making the decisions. And the more control he appears to have, the more likely he is to comply with taking his medication. In the process he's likely to begin feeling better about himself.

THE STRESSES OF CHRONIC ILLNESS

A seventeen-year-old boy with chronic kidney disease endures lifesaving dialysis treatment three times per week.

A thirteen-year-old girl diagnosed with acute myelogenous leukemia faces chemotherapy in the battle to treat her disease.

While other kids are concerned about whom to ask to the junior prom or whether their clothes will meet with their peers' approval, teenagers with a chronic disease have to cope not only with those matters but with much greater anxieties as well. Many of these adolescents have stressors in their lives that most of their friends will never have to confront: Surgery. Chemotherapy. Drug side effects. Body disfigurement. The frightening possibility of a premature death.

Upon learning of their chronic disease, adolescents will have dozens of questions: "How is this illness going to affect the way I look?" "Am I going to have to miss a lot of school?" "Will I be able to play sports anymore?" "How is my boyfriend [or girlfriend] going to react?"

There are no easy answers to questions like these. In the immediate aftermath of being diagnosed with a life-disrupting illness, they may cope the best way they can. Particularly if they have few if any initial symptoms, they may refuse to accept the fact that they're sick and will enter a period of denial. During this time they might rebel and act out in socially unacceptable ways—sometimes even putting their health on the line, behaving as though they had no illness at all.

For example, in the first few weeks after his diagnosis your diabetic teenager might intentionally take an incorrect amount of insulin. Or he might neglect his

---

Your Child and Pain

"**M**om, is it going to hurt?"

Even with a chronic illness pain is not inevitable. Yes, there is an assumption by some parents (and doctors) that teenagers with illnesses such as cancer, arthritis, and sickle cell disease have to learn to live with pain and that nothing can be done to alleviate it. But that's not true. *Most pain is controllable.*

Nevertheless, some physicians aren't aggressive enough in helping teenagers achieve pain relief. If that seems to be the case with your own adolescent, you need to become your child's most vocal advocate, helping her get appropriate care for her discomfort.

Just how important is this pain relief? Not only is pain physically disabling, but it can have a devastating psychological impact as well. Teenagers afflicted with chronic pain often have lower self-esteem than their counterparts with the same disease who are relatively pain-free.

Incidentally, the stress that surrounds your teenager's chronic illness can sometimes make his pain worse. One study, for instance, looked at both children and adolescents with arthritis and found that even when patients had the same severity of joint disease, some had more pain than others. What group experienced the most discomfort? The older patients—that is, the teenagers—reported more pain, perhaps because they were more fixated on what their pain meant. The adolescents concentrated more on their discomfort, they worried about it more—and they had more of it.

---

routine blood sugar tests. This might be his way of saying, "I'm really not sick, and I can do everything that any other kid can do." Or, "I'm in charge of my own body, and I'll do whatever I want."

But, in fact, your adolescent doesn't have the maturity to select appropriate ways of asserting his individuality. And a teenager whose denial leads to risky actions—such as a diabetic who eats a couple of pieces of cake at a party, or a hemophiliac who rides motorcycles—is putting himself at serious risk and asking for trouble.

On the other hand, denial can sometimes serve a useful function. For some teenagers it can actually develop into a positive coping mechanism over the months or years that their illness persists. It will allow them to think of themselves as healthy, except for those specific moments when they *need* to remember that they have an illness in order to care for themselves. It's not necessary for them to focus on their disease other than during those times when they're taking their medication, for example. In general they'll be able to concentrate primarily on the normal aspects of their lives. Studies of cancer survivors have found that this type of denial can help these individuals achieve long-term adjustment to their illness.

Coping with Treatment

Many chronically ill teenagers have difficulty dealing with anxieties about their treatment program. Whether adolescents face lengthy drug therapy or surgery, there's no magical way of helping them cope with these stressors. Even so, here are some suggestions that might be useful.

First, always make yourself available to listen to what's on their mind. Find out precisely what their concerns are, because they might have based some of them on misinformation. They may not fully understand what's going to happen at an upcoming doctor's appointment or what will occur during a particular procedure at the hospital. Be prepared to give them some accurate answers and lots of reassurance. And if they have a question you can't answer, help them get the information from their doctor.

Even with the facts in hand, however, adolescents still might have periods of high anxiety. How can you help them cope if their heart is racing, for instance, or if they're perspiring heavily on the way to the doctor's office? Some teenagers can benefit from deep-breathing and relaxation exercises. Or why not suggest that before or during an unpleasant procedure your youngster consciously guide his thoughts in a more appealing direction?

For example, you might remind him how much he enjoys playing baseball. You might suggest that he play an exciting game in his mind during the treatment. If he wants, you can help him do this as the procedure is being performed.

In much the same way, while undergoing chemotherapy or a spinal tap, he might visualize himself at the beach, enjoying roasted marshmallows with friends. Or during dialysis treatments he might imagine himself participating in another activity he likes to do. This technique works very well for most teenagers—but they have to know that it exists.

Sometimes cancer patients become so anxious about their chemotherapy that they experience side effects such as nausea *before* the treatment ever begins. For instance, adolescents might become nauseated every time they look at a pill or while just thinking about an impending treatment. You can help them cope with this situation—called *classical conditioning*—by distracting them from the medication that awaits them. While in the car on the way to the clinic, play word games together as you drive or see how many different out-of-state license plates you can find.

If you're already at the doctor's office and your teenager is becoming more anxious as he continues to think about the treatment ahead, an approach called *thought stopping* might help. Tell him he has the power to erase those stress-producing thoughts from his mind. Although he may claim, "I just can't get those images out of my mind," he can.

The technique is simple—but it works. Here's what your teenager should do: each time thoughts of that unpleasant medical procedure arise, instruct him to tell his mind: "Okay, stop it. Turn it off. Think about something else." Have your teenager practice this approach, and he'll get better at it with time. Even though he can't control the medical procedure, he *can* control how his mind will deal with it. And he can handle it in a positive, stress-reducing manner.

Incidentally, there are factors other than anxiety or denial that drive a wedge between teenagers and their prescribed drug treatments. Sometimes adolescents waver from their medication schedule as a way of defying their parents. Or if they're living in a college dorm, they may refuse to take their pills or self-administer an injection unless they can do so in total privacy, fearing embarrassment or perhaps ridicule if others observe them. Hopefully your youngster will reveal these kinds of behaviors in your conversations together, and you can help him devise some positive alternatives.

Dealing with Disfigurement

How sensitive are teenagers about their physical appearance? Just think about how they react to a single blemish on their face or to a little too much weight on their body. For some adolescents *anything* that detracts from their attractiveness—including the effects of a chronic illness—can devastate their self-esteem.

In general girls react much more negatively than boys to perceived shortcomings in their appearance. In our culture females are usually judged much more on their physical appearance and consider it a key for social acceptance. Males, however, tend to earn the respect of peers through their physical prowess, athletic ability, and scholastic achievement, and thus an illness that impairs their physical mobility and strength is much more likely to affect them.

Thus, when girls in particular develop cancer or cystic fibrosis, for example, and visible signs of their illness exist, they are likely to withdraw. Some will isolate themselves from even their best friends. Adolescents who have lost their hair in the aftermath of cancer chemotherapy may stop playing sports for fear that their wig might be knocked off in the middle of a game. And although adolescents with epilepsy may have their condition well controlled with medication, the anxiety about having a seizure may be as strong as ever, prompting them to avoid most social situations.

Incidentally, because teenagers are much more attuned to the present than the future, many of them are more likely to express fears over hair loss or a seizure than about death itself. More than just about anything, they want their friends to accept them.

What About Serious Psychiatric Problems?

"Nobody should have to go through the kind of stress my teenager is experiencing," said one parent. "Her physical illness is bad enough, but now I'm worried that with all the anxiety over her disease she's going to have a nervous breakdown too."

As the earlier sections show, chronically ill teenagers have to deal with a lot. Even so, the picture is not quite as gloomy as you might think. Although their coping abilities may seem overloaded at times, adolescents do eventually build up some tolerance to this illness-induced stress.

Take depression, for instance. Few of these teenagers, in fact, actually become chronically depressed because of their illness. Yes, they do experience anxiety over their medical treatments or their acceptance by peers. But as they adjust to these stressors, they're unlikely to develop serious emotional disorders. Except in infrequent cases, your teenager will weather this part of the storm without any major psychiatric problems.

However, if your adolescent seems more withdrawn than usual or shows any other signs of emotional distress or unusual behavior, consult your pediatrician to determine whether you and your youngster should seek help from a mental health professional. If he consistently ignores his treatment regimen (leading to problems such as unnecessary seizures or diabetic-related hospitalizations), counseling may be necessary for him and the entire family.

SCHOOL DISRUPTIONS

School is one of the most important parts of your teenager's life. Not only is it a place for learning and her best opportunity for acquiring the knowledge necessary for a successful adult life, but school is also her greatest socialization vehicle. It's where she can interact with her existing friends, make new ones, and refine her social skills.

No wonder, then, that a chronic illness can be so disruptive. Depending on your teenager's disease, she may miss a lot of school. She might have long hospital stays or be confined to her bed at home. Or she may have frequent outpatient treatments. In any case, her school absenteeism can create real problems—ranging from backsliding in her academic work to loss of contact with her friends. For your teenager this can be a devastating experience.

To make matters worse, this crisis won't automatically resolve itself once she returns to the classroom. Back in school, she may have to deal with still other problems. If she's in a wheelchair or if she has other visible signs of her illness, she may feel painfully different. And she may become convinced that "everyone is looking at me." Depending on her disease, she may also have some other types of anxieties to face. For instance, although most adolescents whose asthma is worsened by exercise can be helped, some may have to sit on the sidelines in their physical education class, feeling ostracized while the other kids are playing basketball or tennis. Adolescents with a chronic illness will tend to have less peer contact outside of school than other teenagers—contact they clearly want and need. Also, if they have an illness or are taking medication that leaves them chronically fatigued, they may have trouble paying attention in class and may fall even farther behind academically.

Even so, the sooner your teenager gets back into the classroom, the better. And you may be able to play an important role in making this a smooth transition. Here's a typical scenario in which a parent can help:

An adolescent has missed a lot of school because of a prolonged hospitalization, and as a result she has developed some real school phobias: "How are my teachers going to react to me?" "Am I going to be able to pick up my friendships where they left off?" "Finals are in two weeks; I'm never going to be ready for them!"

At the same time, there might be some anxiety on the other side too. With diseases such as cancer, AIDS, or heart disease, for instance, the other kids at school may be apprehensive about what to expect and how to react when this teenager returns to class. The mere words *cancer* and *AIDS* are traumatic for some students. And their teachers might feel the same way.

If those kinds of circumstances sound familiar, you can make things easier for all concerned. Just before your child reenters school, set up a meeting that involves you, your teenager, her teacher (or a "representative" teacher if she has several of them), her counselor, and a doctor or someone else from her medical team. Discuss your child's illness, answer all questions, and make sure everyone feels comfortable with your youngster's return.

At the same meeting, find out from the teacher the work your teenager has missed, how much of it she needs to make up, and the best way she can catch up. Also, ask your adolescent if she would like either you or the school nurse to talk to the students in each of her classes, explaining what she's gone through and what these peers can expect.

Why not also do some role playing with your youngster before she returns to school? Ask her questions such as, "If your friends ask you why you were in the hospital, what are you going to say?" or, "What if some students start teasing you because your face is a little full due to the medicine you're taking?" She should prepare for the situations that are likely to arise. Responses that use humor or even sarcasm sometimes are helpful.

Incidentally, teenagers with visible signs of illness—as might occur with cancer, cystic fibrosis, or arthritis—are not the only ones who might need some help fitting back into school. If your youngster has a disease such as epilepsy, for instance, make sure that someone has explained the disorder to her teachers. Also, suggest that your adolescent talk with her classmates to describe what's likely to happen if she has a seizure; she might ask one close friend to help her talk with other peers about her disorder. These students should learn what a seizure looks like and what they should do if one occurs. This kind of preparation will change the nature of their reaction to this disorder. Incidentally, research shows that a chronic illness *not* obvious to others (such as epilepsy or diabetes) can be as disturbing (if not more so) to friends and peers than an illness that's more conspicuous.

DEALING WITH
THE FAMILY'S ANXIETY

A teenager's chronic illness does more than interfere with her own life. The entire family—parents, brothers, sisters, often grandparents—must deal with life disruptions and emotional turmoil, too. As a parent, for instance, your own life may begin to revolve around this disease. How can you make it easier for your youngster? How can you get her the best available medical care? It can become an obsession, intruding on everything else you do.

From the moment your teenager's illness was diagnosed, you may have felt that your life underwent a permanent upheaval. Initially you may have experienced a short period of shock and disbelief. But thereafter, as you've tried adjusting to the reality of a demanding illness, you may have found yourself overwhelmed at times, frequently absorbed with irrational thoughts and unwarranted feelings.

See if any of these emotions hit home:

- Have you felt guilt over your teenager's illness? Do you have an irrational feeling that you somehow caused the condition—perhaps because of a family history of the same disease or because you didn't take her to the doctor immediately when the first symptoms appeared?

- Are you anxious that you're not competent enough to care for your adolescent? Are you communicating these fears to your youngster, perhaps making her feel that her disease is much worse than it really is?

- Do you feel anger that your family has been subjected to this disease that is so disruptive to all family members? Do you feel cheated that you won't be able to raise a healthy child into adulthood? Is some of that bitterness directed at your ill teenager, as though she were at fault for her cancer, arthritis, or heart disease?

- Are you starting to overprotect your teenager, keeping her from living her life to her full capabilities, smothering her with attention? Are you taking such complete responsibility for her care that you're keeping her from becoming as self-sufficient as possible? As a result, is she starting to regress, becoming more dependent on you than is really necessary?

With time a long-term illness ravages some family members. As they watch their son, daughter, or sibling suffer, this takes an increasing emotional toll on them. They may become depressed, irritable, and chronically fatigued. They might isolate themselves from longtime friends. Their finances may become depleted. Some family members become overwhelmed by feelings of hopelessness—convinced that things are never going to change, that the ill teenager is never going to get better. As one stressor piles atop another, marital problems can develop, and divorce sometimes occurs.

Even if the family unit remains strong—and it often does—there are still inevitable and enormous strains and uncertainties. Is the latest treatment going to work? If it does, is your teenager still going to experience relapses? If it doesn't, is there anything left to try? Is she going to reach adulthood? And if so, what kind of an adult life can she realistically expect?

Hopefully your family is one of those that can pull together during this difficult time, grow closer to one another, and become a more sensitive and supportive family unit. These kinds of people share the burdens, they ride out the crises together, and they lead very enriching, high-quality lives.

But what if you feel yourself on the brink of parental burnout? In that case, don't hesitate to get some help. Support groups for parents of chronically ill children can be very useful. They can provide a place to share frustrations, draw encouragement, and exchange ideas about easing the physical and emotional burdens of caring for a sick teenager.

In groups like these you'll also probably learn the importance of giving enough attention to *all* your children and your spouse. As you channel so much of your energy toward caring for your chronically ill youngster, it's an unfortunate reality that you often may overlook siblings. Keep in mind that they deserve parental time, too. They need to know you're accessible and that they can share the joys and anxieties associated with their own childhood and adolescence. Yes, it's understandable that your attention is drawn elsewhere, but if you're not careful, this preoccupation can have serious consequences for your other children. Don't make this mistake.

Younger children in particular sometimes conclude that the reason they're being ignored by Mom and Dad is that they're somehow to blame for their sibling's illness. Older children, on the other hand, may become very resentful and misbehave, perhaps getting involved in drug or alcohol abuse or letting their school grades plummet—all as a way of getting their parents to notice them. Sibling resentment may arise for other reasons too—perhaps because the illness has put a real financial strain on the family, making vacations impossible and keeping spending money for brothers and sisters to a minimum.

You can compound this problem by unfairly burdening your other children with responsibilities related to your ill teenager. If you have a fourteen-year-old with cystic fibrosis, for instance, you might feel tempted to ask your sixteen-year-old daughter to assume an undeserved share of the caretaking and household responsibilities. By doing so, you may push this healthy child into a parenting role, and in response she may react bitterly toward her ill brother or sister. "Sibling rivalry" may be elevated to a new and unfortunate level.

Here's how one teenager reacted to the illness of a brother: "I feel sorry for John. He has cancer, and he has to go through a lot. But look at how much attention he gets from Mom and Dad! I hardly get any at all, and I have to do a lot more work around here now. Sometimes I wish I had cancer so they'd pay attention to me too."

MAINTAINING OPEN COMMUNICATION

Throughout the long weeks, months, and years of a chronic illness, the lines of communication among all family members must remain open. Encourage your children—both the ill adolescent and his siblings—to come to you with their concerns and anxieties.

Bear in mind that you can't talk your ill teenager out of her feelings of sadness and hurt. But you can urge her to keep talking and not to give up on herself. And you can tell her that you'll always be there to support her through this ordeal.

Remain as honest as possible with your sick teenager, even if her illness is terminal. Be prepared for questions about death and don't try to hide any facts from her. But on the other hand, while you should respond with straightforward answers, *emphasize the positive whenever possible.* Thus, if your adolescent has cancer, let her know that many children with the same type of tumor have survived. For instance, you might say something like, "The doctor doesn't know what's going to happen for sure. But many teenagers with the same illness as you live for a long time—and we're going to do everything we can to help you do that."

Some parents still decide to keep their ill children in the dark. Their approach is, "The less bad news she hears, the better." But your teenager might surprise you by how much she instinctively knows about her illness. Many severely ill youngsters sense they are very sick and might be dying. Many don't discuss these feelings out of a desire to protect their parents. Also, they may hear comments about their conditions from other individuals. Thus, rather than trying to perpetuate a conspiracy of silence, it's wise to confront the issue with your teenager. Give her a chance to talk about what she's feeling, including her fears, and correct any misinformation or misunderstandings she may have.

In the process, focus more on *living* than dying. A lot of teenagers considered "terminally ill" may still have months or even years of living to do. There may be a lot of experiences your adolescent wants to share with her family and friends, and you should encourage her to do so. She may not be ready to die yet, and if you support her efforts to remain as active as possible, she just may live longer than any doctor expects, and her life will be filled with happiness.

Particularly during this difficult time, your ill teenager—as well as other members of the family—may need some crisis counseling. Perhaps she's having trouble dealing with a sense of hopelessness about the future, and she's feeling despair about a shortened life span that may deprive her of adulthood, marriage, and a career. Maybe she feels alienated, as though she were the only person in the world undergoing the trying experiences that she's confronting. During periods like this—particularly if you notice major behavioral or mood changes—she might benefit from some private counseling or a support group comprised of other ill adolescents. Ask her doctor for a referral.

Also, encourage your family members to work together during this stressful period. Each of you will have to make some adjustments and compromises. When a problem arises that affects the whole family, everyone should have a voice in resolving it. Remember, when an issue affects one member, it generally affects the entire family.

Finally, allow yourself to get away from the caretaker role from time to time. Go out to dinner or to a movie. Take a vacation now and then. And don't feel guilty when you do. If you schedule some time for yourself (and your spouse as well as the other children), you'll be a better parent and more capable of giving your ill teenager the love and support she needs.

INDEX